Global Gospel

Global Gospel

AN INTRODUCTION to CHRISTIANITY on
FIVE CONTINENTS

DOUGLAS JACOBSEN

Baker Academic
a division of Baker Publishing Group
Grand Rapids, Michigan

Published by Baker Academic
a division of Baker Publishing Group
P.O. Box 6287, Grand Rapids, MI 49516-6287
www.bakeracademic.com

Printed in the United States of America

Library of Congress Cataloging-in-Publication Data
Jacobsen, Douglas G. (Douglas Gordon), 1951–
      Global gospel : an introduction to Christianity on five continents / Douglas Jacobsen.
         pages cm
      Includes bibliographical references and index.
      ISBN 978-0-8010-4993-4 (pbk.)
      1. Christianity. I. Title.
   BR121.3.J328 2015
   270—dc23   2015015871

Scripture quotations are from the Holy Bible, New International Version®. NIV®. Copyright © 1973, 1978, 1984, 2011 by Biblica, Inc.™ Used by permission of Zondervan. All rights reserved worldwide. www.zondervan.com

15   16   17   18   19   20   21   7   6   5   4   3   2   1

In keeping with biblical principles of creation stewardship, Baker Publishing Group advocates the responsible use of our natural resources. As a member of the Green Press Initiative, our company uses recycled paper when possible. The text paper of this book is composed in part of post-consumer waste.

For Mack
and the future he represents

Contents

Preface

THIS IS A BOOK about all the different kinds of Christians who live everywhere in the world. Given that immense scope, it seems only fair to start by asking how anyone can presume to take on such a task. Who has the capacity to describe the full scope of Christian diversity around the world? The simple answer is no one. No single individual is sufficiently equipped to write a book about global Christianity. No one knows enough. No one has lived enough places. No one is so devoid of prejudice that he or she can treat each Christian community in the world with the fairness and sympathy it deserves. All these limitations apply to me.

But the need for some kind of overarching introduction to world Christianity has never been greater. During the last hundred years, Christianity has become global, and the experiences of Christians around the world vary immensely. If all of the world's Christians really are members of one body of Christ, then the realities of this global age require Christians to reach out to one another in new ways, to listen to each as they have never listened before, and to learn from one another what they could never learn by themselves. For that to happen some kind of guidebook is necessary, and this volume seeks to fill that gap. It is a broad introduction to Christianity as it has developed and as it is currently being lived on the five big continents of Africa, Asia, Europe, Latin America, and North America.

Every guidebook is inadequate. Real life is always more complex than any description of it, and this book will undoubtedly get some things wrong. The tone will be off in some places, the emphases may be misplaced elsewhere, and even some "facts" that are included in this volume may eventually be proven wrong. You as a reader may also think I have left out some topics that

I absolutely should have included, or that I have given too much attention to some subjects you consider peripheral. All I can do is ask for your indulgence in advance. This is my best attempt to describe the big story of how Christianity became global, and how the Christian movement is developing around the world today. It is an entry point for the study of global Christianity, not the final word.

Because I write about so many different kinds of Christians in this book, it seems only fair to let readers know something about who I am as a scholar and person of faith. What perspectives or blinders do I bring to this work? What predilections shape how I see and feel the world? What qualifies me to undertake this task?

Like every other Christian in the world, I became a follower of Jesus via one particular community of faith. Mine was a Norwegian immigrant community in Brooklyn, New York. When I was a child, our congregation (the 66th Street Evangelical Free Church) still held services in both Norwegian and English. We Scandinavians were only one of several ethnic groups in our neighborhood, however, and I always knew that I was just one particular kind of human being living among others. Our Christian customs and traditions were enormously important for us, but our neighbors' customs and traditions were equally important to them. Difference was a fact of life, and members of my childhood church never assumed that everyone was supposed to think and act just like us.

My parents were pietists. What mattered to them was personal faith, the individual's unique relationship with God. Doctrine had its place, and Sunday morning worship was dominated by doctrinal sermons that often lasted an hour. But my family's style of faith found fuller expression in the Sunday evening service, a time that was typically devoted to the sharing of testimonies—stories about one's personal journey of faith and experiences of God. My parents made sure I knew that each person's relationship with God is unique and that all of those differing experiences are to be respected. I remember being with my dad in New York City. We had just gotten off the bus in the Port Authority building and were making our way down the escalator to the first floor. A man at the bottom of the escalator was preaching his thirty-second version of the gospel as loudly and quickly as he could to all of us who were exiting the building. I told my father I thought he was crazy. My father's reply was less pejorative, "Don't judge anyone. He might be able to connect with someone you never could." Lesson learned.

While my family and my church emphasized personal faith, they were also surprisingly globally aware. The highest calling was to become a foreign missionary, and dozens of missionaries stopped by our church each year. Almost all of them stayed overnight in our home, which meant I was constantly hearing stories about Christians in places such as China, Japan, the Congo, South Africa, Costa Rica, and Ecuador. My sister and I were mesmerized by the stories we heard, and it was no surprise that my sister became a missionary, spending twenty years in the Democratic Republic of the Congo (then called Zaire).

I was the first person in my immediate family to go to college. An uncle (by marriage) had attended Wheaton College in Illinois, so that is where I went, too. What I learned at Wheaton reinforced much of what I had imbibed in my pietistically Christian Norwegian American home: different people see and experience the world differently. My major was philosophy and my primary mentor was a professor named Arthur Holmes. He called his particular version of philosophy "perspectivalism," stressing the fact that logical reasoning is only one component of human thought. People also bring *perspectives* to their thinking, visions of life that have been shaped and molded by their own experiences and by the categories of understanding they have inherited from cultures and communities in which they have lived. Philosophical study needs to take these human perspectives into account and not focus merely on the abstract logic of ideas. Holmes convinced me that seeing the world through other people's eyes is an enormously important part of any scholarly endeavor.

During my junior year at Wheaton College, I was given the opportunity to spend a semester doing relief work in Bangladesh. Bangladesh had formerly been East Pakistan, and it was birthed as a new nation in 1971 after a contested Pakistani election and a subsequent civil war. About fifteen college students were recruited by a Baptist hospital in the region to help rebuild villages that had been decimated by the war and then hit by a huge typhoon. It was my first foray outside of North America, and it was an eye-opener. At the time, Bangladesh was routinely described as the poorest country on earth, and I expected to find a nation filled with depressed people. I discovered something very different. People seemed happy, and they rarely complained. They welcomed me into their homes and shared their meager rations with me. They were smart, and they tried to educate me about life. As a result I learned that Western learning has its limitations, that poverty is bad but not always debilitating, and that wisdom can be found in many places. Bangladesh is about 90 percent Muslim and 10 percent Hindu, and what I had learned about Islam and Hinduism from religious studies textbooks had not prepared me at all for understanding either the religious dynamics of the region or the gracious hospitality I received.

During my years in college, I was introduced to a broad range of Christian churches and communities. Like many of my peers, I was on a spiritual journey. The Charismatic movement was at its peak, and I found myself deeply attracted to Pentecostalism. For a while I attended a Mennonite Church. I also discovered the writings of the Catholic monk Thomas Merton, and he almost persuaded me to become Catholic. Just as importantly, I stumbled across two books, Aziz Atiya's *History of Eastern Christianity* and David Barrett's *Schism and Renewal in Africa: An Analysis of Six Thousand Contemporary Religious Movements*, and reading these volumes slammed home how utterly Western all of my previous knowledge of Christianity had been.

Intellectual and spiritual curiosity drove me to read everything I could find about Christianity around the globe—which at the time was not much—and I began constructing elaborate timelines, charting contemporaneous Christian developments in different regions of the world. Eventually my curiosity led me to graduate school at the University of Chicago, where I had the privilege of studying with people such as Jerald Brauer, Brian Gerrish, Bernard McGinn, Martin Marty, and David Tracy. Interacting with these scholars, and with my student peers, expanded my vision of the world and Christian faith dramatically. The Divinity School never tried to disabuse me of my evangelical and pietistic sensibilities, but it did make me aware of how many different ways one can faithfully follow Jesus in the contemporary world.

For the last thirty years, I have been part of the faculty at Messiah College in Pennsylvania. My teaching load includes courses on Christianity in all of its varied global forms, and my students—especially those from Africa, Asia, and Latin America—have been invaluable in helping me reflect on that diversity. Without their feedback, writing a book like this would have been impossible. During these past three decades, I have also had the opportunity to visit more than fifty different countries and to observe Christianity firsthand in each of them. These trips have not made me an expert on any of the nations I have visited—it takes years of living in a different culture to become an expert, and my own research and writing is enormously indebted to such experts—but it has been tremendously helpful to visit these locations, seeing Christianity in action, participating in worship, hearing its sounds, and smelling its aromas.

My own local congregation, St. Paul's United Church of Christ in Mechanicsburg, Pennsylvania, has also profoundly influenced me. My wife and I joined St. Paul's back in 1986 because it was one of the healthiest, most community-minded, and least contentious congregations we had ever encountered. It is a church that seeks to be extravagantly welcoming of everyone, and St. Paul's has pushed me again and again to be more embracing of others.

I hope that all of these experiences have predisposed me to be sensitive to and respectful of the many different kinds of Christians who now inhabit the world. Still, I remain painfully aware of how limited my own perceptions can be. Theologically, I remain a Protestant. That is how I instinctively see the world and Christian faith. Thus, even though I have spent decades interacting with Catholic, Orthodox, and Pentecostal Christians, and I find all of these expressions of Christianity to be inspiring, I still know that I am speaking a second language when I discuss Catholic or Orthodox or Pentecostal developments. Perhaps more crucially, I know that I am a white, rich (by global standards), North American, male Christian writing about other Christians around the world, who are for the most part not white, not rich, not North American, and not male. There is a kind of arrogance built into writing a book about people so different from oneself—an arrogance that is part and parcel of being a Western, male scholar. If that kind of hubris appears anywhere in these pages, I apologize in advance. It is not my goal or intention to tell any follower of Jesus around the world who she or he is supposed to be.

The goal of this book is straightforward: to describe the big picture of global Christianity as fairly and accurately as possible. Personal stories play an important role in that task, but so do history and sociology; and in this book history and sociology will predominate. There is a reason for this: the big developments in which we participate as human beings are often almost impossible to see because the immediate experiences of daily life so dominate our consciousness. Ordinary life is like walking through a forest and seeing all the trees, but having no awareness of the shape of the forest as a whole. History and sociology help us discover the broad contours of the forests in which we live. This book focuses on the forest of global Christianity, describing the complex developments and transformation that have made this amazing movement what it is today.

The ultimate purpose of this book is not, however, merely to dispense information. It is to encourage a richer, deeper, and more constructive dialogue among Christians worldwide. The disjointed and segmented character of the Christian movement that prevailed throughout so much of Christian history is no longer viable. The globalization of the planet has linked all of the world's Christians together, and the reputation of the gospel now hinges on how Christians everywhere think and act. More than ever before, Christians around the world need to discover one another, befriend one another, and learn from one another. Otherwise, the Christian movement will likely continue to fragment into ever smaller Christianities (in the plural), with each little group reflecting only part of the full gospel of Jesus Christ.

Christians around the world do not and never will experience the gospel in precisely the same way or speak about God using the same precise terms. God meets human beings where they are, and God speaks in and through many different cultures. Hoping that global Christians will become more interconnected does not mean making Christianity more globally uniform or homogenous. The glory of creation is evident in the wonderful diversity, bordering on cacophony, that is present in the natural world. Similarly, the glory of Christianity is best displayed in its interconnected diversity, with different kinds of Christians praising God and caring for their neighbors in a complex, multihued, interwoven, and mutually enriching choreography of faith, hope, and love. That dance, in its entirety, is the global gospel in action.

Introduction

CHRISTIANITY IS THE LARGEST RELIGION in the world. According to demographers, one out of every three people on the planet is a follower of Jesus. Christianity is also the most geographically dispersed and most culturally diverse religion the world has ever seen. When the twentieth century began, Christianity was still a predominantly European faith. Today, two-thirds of the world's Christians live in Asia, Africa, and Latin America. No other religion has ever experienced so much change in such a short period of time.

Global Christianity today has no easily defined orthodoxy, no geographic center, and no one authoritative leader. Christians everywhere worship the same God, pledge their allegiance to the same Jesus Christ, and are inspired by the same Holy Spirit; but there is immense diversity across contemporary Christianity. The movement has expanded so fast that its growth and diversification have outpaced all attempts to track them. As a consequence, Christians have lost touch with one another, becoming strangers who just happen to confess the same faith.

Contemporary Christians are realizing that the Christian movement as a whole needs to rediscover itself. The inherited language of Christianity, steeped in the Western cultural tradition, is no longer adequate for describing the beliefs, values, practices, and affections of the global Christian community. New voices are waiting to be heard, and fresh formulations of Christian faith and life are ready to be uncovered. The gospel has become global, and Christians all around the world are just beginning to grapple with transformations that have taken everyone by surprise.

Christianity is now incarnated in the beliefs and behaviors of people from all the cultures of the world, and the result is an astonishingly varied palette of Christian experience. For those who are familiar with only a handful of Christian spiritual tints and hues, discovering the full spectrum of Christian expressions can be overwhelming. Encountering difference is often disorienting, at least at first. The Scriptures hint at awkwardness even when Jesus conversed with people from different cultures, individuals such as the Samaritan divorcée (John 4:1–42), the Canaanite woman seeking help for her sick daughter (Matt. 15:21–28), and a Roman soldier (Matt. 8:5–13). In the years following Christ's death, cultural differences, and especially differences between Jews and Gentiles, frequently flared into conflict. This issue was never decisively settled during the early years of the movement, and many pages of the New Testament pay attention to intercultural tensions. Given such precedents, it seems only reasonable to expect that similarly knotty questions related to cultural differences will be part of global Christianity today.

In the past, Christians often settled their intra-religious disputes by geographically segregating themselves from one another. Catholics lived in certain parts of the world, Eastern Orthodox Christians in others, and Protestants of various kinds staked out other pieces of turf to call their own. That kind of segregation is no longer a viable option. Globalization has made everybody more interconnected. No individual or group exists in isolation from the rest of the world, and no local community is entirely independent. What happens in one place impacts what happens everywhere. How Christians act in one region of the globe or in one particular church or denomination shapes perceptions of Christianity elsewhere. When a Baptist preacher in Florida announces that he intends to burn a Qur'an to demonstrate his disdain for Islam, it is Christians in Africa and Asia and the Middle East who pay the price for his reckless rhetoric, not Christians in Florida. If Christians care about their brothers and sisters in faith, they now have to think about how their words and actions may affect the lives of Christians on the other side of the globe. The positive flipside of this situation is that good news also travels quickly around the globe. The image of Christianity in general was bolstered when the College of Cardinals elected Pope Francis—an Argentinian bishop known for his compassion and concern for the poor—as the leader of the Catholic Church. And it was not just Catholics who benefitted. The public image of Protestantism, Pentecostalism, and Eastern Orthodoxy was bolstered alongside Catholicism.

The variety of ideas and practices that exists within the world Christian movement today is enormous, and the gaps between different groups can be huge. What does a charismatic Christian in Africa, who believes wholeheartedly in miracles, share in common with a Lutheran Christian in Sweden, who barely believes in the existence of God? How can a Catholic traditionalist, who thinks the Mass should still be said in Latin, connect with a "spiritual but not religious" Christian, who feels no need to ever attend worship services at all? Is there common ground between progressive Christians who embrace LGBTQ (lesbian-gay-bisexual-transgender-queer) individuals as loved and accepted by God and fundamentalist Christians who believe that God abhors any divergence from heterosexuality? What binds together those Christians who face persecution and death in their current environments and Christians who have no reason to fear for their lives because they control the cultures in which they live?

Contemporary Christians find themselves caught up in what can only be described as a very messy global movement—something akin to a large extended family. *Family* is sometimes defined as the people you must endure even when you do not particularly like them. You are connected to them because they are organically related to you. You can disown them, but their stories remain part of your family history nonetheless. *Family* is a fact. The same basic principle applies to global Christianity. Being a Christian means being part of a huge family of faith that includes many strange people. *Strangeness* is, of course, a relative term. If some non-Western expressions of Christianity look odd to Christians from Europe and North America, be assured that some European and North American varieties of Christianity look equally peculiar to Christians from elsewhere.

However, there is increasing pressure for Christians to reach beyond their communities of comfort and to engage Christians who are different from themselves. This is not easy. For most people, walking into a room full of strangers is stressful. When strangers gather for a meeting, a good host typically breaks the ice with some kind of get-to-know-each-other activity. This book hopes to serve as something like an icebreaker for global Christianity: to introduce readers to the world Christian family so that when they visit other parts of the world, or when Christians from other regions of the globe move in next door, or when they connect online, they no longer seem like strangers.

This volume begins with a very brief history of the Christian movement, explaining how a Jewish breakaway religious sect in the Middle East became the largest and most diverse religion on earth. The second chapter describes the four major traditions of contemporary Christianity: Catholicism, Eastern Orthodoxy, Protestantism, and Pentecostalism. The book then moves on to chapters that describe Christian culture as it has developed and currently exists in Africa, Asia, Europe, Latin America, and North America. These five continents do not cover the entire globe (leaving out places such as Australia and the Pacific), but taken together they account for more than 98 percent of the world's Christians.[1]

In recent years, cultural differences rooted in places of origin have become as crucial for understanding Christianity worldwide as older theological differences (represented by Catholicism, Orthodoxy, Protestantism, and Pentecostalism) were in the past. Learning something about the world's many different kinds of Christians is important for all sorts of intellectual and practical and ecclesiological reasons. Encountering global diversity can also enrich individuals spiritually. The poet T. S. Eliot once said that the end of all life's travels is to return home and see the place as if for the first time. Encountering world Christianity is that kind of journey. Seeing how Christianity has been embodied elsewhere can enlarge a person's capacity to understand and incarnate the gospel at home.

---

1. Australia and the Pacific are discussed in Douglas Jacobsen, *The World's Christians: Who They Are, Where They Are, and How They Got There* (Oxford: Wiley/Blackwell, 2011).

1

Global Christianity

A Very Brief History

CHRISTIANS HAVE HAD GLOBAL ASPIRATIONS from the very beginning of the movement. In what has become known as the "great commission," Jesus told his disciples that they would be his "witnesses in Jerusalem, and in all Judea and Samaria, and to the ends of the earth" (Acts 1:8; see also Matt. 28:18–20). And indeed they became his witnesses. By the end of the first century, the gospel had been preached as far west as Spain and as far east as India. In the next four centuries, Christianity was embraced by millions of people living in the Roman and Persian empires and by many people who lived in other places: Ireland, Armenia, and Ethiopia. After just four centuries, Christianity was well on the way to becoming a global faith.

Then as now, Christians had their differences. The three most important leaders of the early Christian movement—Peter, Paul, and James—never did see fully eye to eye on everything. Rather than choosing among the views of these apostles, however, the early Christian community had the wisdom to embrace them all. Thus, the letters of Peter, Paul, and James were all preserved alongside one another in the New Testament, even though the views expressed (for example, in the books of James and Galatians) sometimes seem almost diametrically opposed. This same multiplicity of vision is evident in the four Gospels, each of which presents its own slightly different portrait of Jesus and his message. Leaders of the early church thought all four books were inspired and needed to be preserved, and they explicitly rejected the idea that

1

the four Gospels should be harmonized together into one merged text. Jesus himself spoke of the need to accept diversity within the movement. When the disciples told Jesus they had ordered a man they did not know to desist from casting out demons in Jesus's name, Jesus replied, "Do not stop him, . . . for whoever is not against you is for you" (Luke 9:49–50).

The most challenging expression of diversity in the early Christian movement concerned the distinction between Gentiles and Jews. The core issue was obedience to Jewish law. Did Gentile followers of Jesus need to obey the law in the same way that Jews did? This question was addressed at the first Christian council that met in Jerusalem around the year 50, less than a generation after Jesus's crucifixion. Gentiles, it was decided, were not required to follow all the regulations of the Jewish Torah, but they were requested to adhere to a handful of Jewish protocols that would make it easier for Jews and Gentiles to work and eat together, most notably to abstain from consuming blood or meat sacrificed to idols. It should be noted that this decision involved compromise. The debate was not framed as a choice between two totally different and mutually exclusive solutions. It was framed in terms of etiquette and mutual respect, and it was assumed that some differences between Jewish and Gentile practices would persist. The account in the book of Acts also says this agreement was reached because "it seemed good to the Holy Spirit and to us" (Acts 15:28). This pairing of the guidance of the Holy Spirit with human reasoning reinforces the commonsensical character of the decision, and for the next two centuries piety and practicality were often blended together as Christianity struggled to accommodate cultural diversity.

The First Globalization of Christianity, Beginnings to 1000

Christianity in the Roman Empire

Christianity spread more quickly in the Roman Empire than anywhere else, due in large part to the ease of travel within the Roman domain. The Roman Empire circled the Mediterranean Sea, and water transportation was much easier than overland travel to Persia or Central Asia. Christian missionaries such as Paul traveled sea routes from city to city, and Christianity was soon present almost everywhere in the empire. Despite this rapid expansion of the movement, the total number of Christians remained relatively small, and, until the early 300s, Christianity remained a persecuted minority religion in the Roman Empire.

The situation changed dramatically when the Roman Empire stopped persecuting Christians and embraced Christianity as its own state religion in the fourth century. Constantine, whose rule began in 306 and lasted until 337, was the first Roman emperor to convert to Christianity. Constantine believed the Christian God had intervened in history to place him on the throne, and he wanted to express his gratitude by supporting the Christian movement. However, there was a problem. Christianity in the Roman Empire was not a single, unified movement. It had fractured into several sub-movements that sometimes viciously disagreed. Constantine believed only one form of Christianity could be correct, and in the year 325, he convened a council of Christian bishops at the city of Nicaea to identify that one true form of Christian faith. When this council decided that the followers of a preacher named Arius were mistaken, Constantine no longer bestowed any favors on that particular Christian group.

Subsequent Roman emperors followed the same policy, showering support on those whose Christianity was deemed to be true and suppressing all others. The definition of "true Christianity" varied from emperor to emperor. Constantine's son Constantius, for example, favored Arian Christianity rather than Christianity as it was formulated at the Council of Nicaea. Almost all the emperors were consistent, however, in upholding the principle that true Christianity must be expressed uniformly—and most bishops agreed. In contrast to the practices of the early Christian community, the official Christianity of the Roman Empire jettisoned the notion of Christian diversity. One was either an orthodox (right thinking and right acting) Christian or one was a heretic. There were no other legal options. With church and state increasingly fused, Roman Christianity's ability to accommodate diversity became a thing of the past.

Early Christianity in Asia

The Christian movement outside the Roman Empire followed a different path of development. This alternative trajectory is illustrated by the history of Christianity in Persia. Christianity was introduced to Persia (centered in contemporary Iraq and Iran) in the late first or early second century, and a substantial Christian community came into existence. The Zoroastrian rulers of the empire were offended by some Christian teachings, and persecution was not uncommon. In the 300s and 400s, thousands of Persian Christians were killed for their faith, far greater than the number who died because of persecution within the Roman Empire. Eventually a truce was negotiated, and Christians were allowed some degree of freedom to practice their faith, but Christianity always remained a minority religion in Persian lands.

Most Persian Christians were members of the Church of the East (sometimes called the Nestorian Church), but there were many Syrian Orthodox

Christians (also known as Jacobites) and Armenian Christians in the region as well. There was never a time when any particular church had a monopoly on Christianity in Persia. Unlike the imperially imposed uniformity of faith that prevailed in the Christian Roman Empire, Christianity in Persia (and in the rest of Asia) was always pluralistic.

The diversity of teachings and practices within Asian Christianity expanded as Persian missionaries moved eastward, preaching the gospel along the Silk Road, an ancient trade route that ran from the Middle East through Central Asia all the way to China. Communities along the Silk Road were religiously pluralistic, as are many modern cities, and people of different faiths crossed paths every day. In this cosmopolitan setting, Asian Christians enlarged their accommodation of diversity as they learned how to share the gospel winsomely in a pluralistic setting. One of the most widely traveled missionaries of the time was a monk named Alopen, who made it all the way to China in the year 635. Using a communication style borrowed from Buddhist monks he met along the Silk Road, Alopen composed *sutras* (didactic poems) explaining how the Cool Wind (the Holy Spirit) came upon Mo Yan (Mary), who gave birth to Ye Su (Jesus), who taught humanity how to live. It is not surprising that in China Christianity became known as "the religion of light," a faith that every good-hearted person could embrace.

Early Christianity in Africa

Christianity was introduced to Africans on the day of Pentecost, and by the second century, Christians could be found all across the northern coast of the continent. This territory was part of the Roman Empire, but soon Christianity began to spread southward, and Africans who had nothing to do with the Roman Empire embraced the gospel. Christianity was introduced to Axum (northern Ethiopia) in the mid-300s, and it soon became the official religion of the state. Ethiopian Christianity was strengthened in the 500s by the arrival of the "Nine Saints," monks from Syria who erected church buildings and encouraged the creation of a network of monasteries that would later become the backbone of the Ethiopian church.

Nearby Nubia (modern Sudan) was Christianized during the mid-500s, but the dynamics there were more complex than in Ethiopia. Nubia comprised three cooperating kingdoms, and two competing groups of missionaries entered the region about the same time, one of them Chalcedonian (Eastern Orthodox) and the other Miaphysite (Coptic Orthodox). As a result, Nubians developed a more flexible and tolerant disposition toward Christian diversity than was typical in Ethiopia, and Nubia later granted freedom of worship to Muslims as well.

Early Christianity in Europe

European Christianity is as old as Christianity in Africa. The apostle Paul preached the gospel in Greece within two decades of Christ's death, and a Christian congregation was founded in Rome just a few years later. Up until the fifth century, however, European Christianity had no distinctive sense of identity. It was merely part of Christianity in the Roman Empire. The break point came in the 400s when the western half of the Roman Empire collapsed because Germanic tribes were flooding into the region. The European Christianity of today descends from the faith that was eventually embraced by those barbarian tribes.

From the time Saint Patrick (d. 460) first attempted to convert the Irish until the end of the first Christian millennium, the evangelization of Europe followed basically the same pattern. A charismatic monk or nun would come into a region preaching the gospel and performing miraculous acts that challenged pagan deities and demonstrated the power of the Christian God. The turning point usually came when the local king or queen embraced the gospel and forthwith required everyone else in his or her realm to do the same. The conversion process involved some degree of personal choice, but conversion was generally a group phenomenon, not individual. Bit by bit, tribe by tribe, the European continent slowly became Christian, with the gospel generally spreading from south to north. Scandinavia was the last region in Western Europe to convert, around the year 1000. Similar changes took place in Eastern Europe. Southern Russia was Christianized in the late 900s and the northern Baltic region followed shortly thereafter.

The years between 500 and 1000 were a time of widespread social unrest in Europe, and this context shaped European Christianity as it was being formed. Because there was no overarching government in the region, local decisions mattered. Christianity became a localized faith. The practices of European Christianity were very diverse during the initial era when evangelism was underway, but the old Roman ideal of uniformity soon reasserted itself. As Christianity became more fully established in the region, and as the continent became more politically stable, the pressures of uniformity increased. This was especially evident during periods such as the rule of Charlemagne (774–828) when the central government was strong and when church and state were closely aligned.

By the year 1000, Christianity had become the most geographically wide-spread religion on earth. It had millions of followers spread across Asia, Europe, and northern Africa. No one in this region knew that the Americas existed, so from their perspective Christianity had been introduced to almost all the known world. During most of this era, the center of gravity of the Christian movement was located in the East. Until 900, there were more Christians living in Asia than in Europe, and most of the movement's spiritual and intellectual centers were similarly located in Asia. Four major church traditions (Eastern Orthodox, Miaphysite, Church of the East, and Catholic) vied for followers, trying to prove that their own understandings of God, the gospel, and humankind were better than others. Vast cultural and theological differences shaped how Christians lived their faith around the world: different ways of envisioning Jesus, different understandings of salvation, different styles of worship, different rules about family and marriage, different uses of music and the arts, different attitudes about those who had died, and different practices of personal piety. Between the years 700 and 1000, Christianity was almost as diverse as it is today. But that was about to change.

The Great Contraction and a New European Focus: 1000–1900

The geographic and theological diversity that characterized Christianity in the year 1000 narrowed dramatically over the next five centuries as Christianity contracted in Asia and blossomed in Europe. One of the major causes of Christianity's contraction in the East was the rise of Islam, which exploded into existence during the early seventh century and then spread rapidly across the Middle East and North Africa. Much like the Roman Empire, Islam merged religion and the state. Accordingly, Islamic military conquests in North Africa and the Middle East had religious ramifications. At first, Christians residing in conquered territory were allowed to follow their religious faith without restrictions. Later, more limitations were placed on Christians and pressures to convert to Islam were increased.

A tipping point occurred when Western Christian armies, in a series of military ventures called "crusades," attempted to reconquer the Middle East in the years lasting roughly from 1100 to 1250. One major consequence was that many Muslims came to view Christians as religious enemies rather than seeing them as part of a shared religious tradition going back to Abraham. Persecution intensified in general, spiking under a ruler named Timur Leng who controlled most of Central Asia and the Middle East during the years 1370–1405. Christians suffered tremendously, and the Christian population plummeted. Churches, and even entire Christian towns, were destroyed. By 1405, it was hard to find a viable Christian community anywhere in the region. The Christian movement has never suffered a more devastating blow than the one delivered by Timur Leng. For all practical purposes, Asia was rendered a Christian wasteland.

Christians fared slightly better in Africa. Christianity had faded into oblivion in much of Islamic North Africa before the Crusades began, but it remained strong in Egypt, even in the face of sometimes serious persecution. Christianity also remained the dominant faith in Ethiopia, unlike neighboring Nubia, where Christianity had declined sharply and eventually disappeared around the year 1400. The fact that Christianity survived in Egypt and Ethiopia did not mean that Christianity was flourishing in these places. Churches in Egypt struggled just to retain their current members, so there was little enthusiasm for spreading the gospel elsewhere. Christianity was not eradicated in Africa as it was in Asia, but it became far less robust.

While Christianity in Asia and Africa was experiencing decline, the opposite was happening in Europe. European Christianity, and especially western European Christianity, was booming. The political order, which had been chaotic before 1000, stabilized, and the economy began to flourish. The European population, almost all of which was Christian, exploded. Although the Black Death ravaged Europe in the mid-1300s, causing a significant decline in the population, the region later rebounded and the European percentage of the world Christian population continued to rise. By 1500, the great majority of the world's Christians—more than 80 percent—were living in Europe, and Christianity itself was now perceived as a European rather than global religion.

European Christianity was growing not only in size but also in its sense of confidence and self-assurance. During the years between 1100 and 1350, the great Gothic cathedrals were built, the first genuinely systematic Christian theologies were written, and the first Christian universities were founded. Confidence taken to an extreme can become aggressive, and in the medieval period, European Christianity flexed its muscles, both figuratively and literally. This new European religious belligerence was expressed to outsiders via the Crusades to recapture the Holy Land, and it was expressed to insiders via the violent suppression of all heretics and religious dissenters.

The subsequent history of Christianity in Europe is complicated, but the longing for homogeneity remained strong. The Protestant Reformation of the sixteenth century added new levels of tension to the region, but it did little to quench Europe's fixation on religious uniformity. Eventually, Europe split into three separate and distinct ecclesiastical subregions—Catholic, Eastern

Orthodox, and Protestant—and each region allowed only one form of Christian practice to exist. Christians following other paths were tolerated at best and were often actively persecuted. The idea of religious freedom took root in Europe very slowly, and it did not really flourish until the twentieth century. As a result, many localities in contemporary Europe are still largely homogeneous in religious composition.

The size, wealth, and confidence of European Christianity deeply influenced the modern missionary movement. European Catholic missions had begun in the thirteenth century, but they dramatically expanded in the 1500s. European Protestant missions began later, around 1800, but grew quickly in size and soon rivaled the Catholic movement. Whether they were Catholic or Protestant, missionaries from Europe shared a common conviction that their own particular version of Christianity was the one and only true expression of Christian faith on earth. Most early European missionaries were blind to the cultural dimensions of their faith. They thought their faith had not been shaped by any particular culture at all; it was just pure Christianity. As a result—because they saw no daylight between the gospel and their own Christianized cultures—most European missionaries promoted the gospel and their own culture as if they were one and the same. It should come as no surprise that people elsewhere often believed them. By the late 1800s, people around the world had come to see Christianity as a Western religion that was trying to make everyone else simultaneously both Christian and Western. The proposition that Christianity could become a global, multicultural faith was almost unimaginable.

The New Globalization: 1900 to the Present

In 1900, two-thirds of the world's Christians lived in Europe, and many of the Christians living in North America and Latin America were of European descent. Europeans and their new world descendants thus accounted for more than 90 percent of all the Christians in the world. Then the demographics of global Christianity began to change, and they changed with almost unbelievable rapidity. Over the last hundred years, Europe's share of the world's Christian population has collapsed from about 65 percent to 25 percent, and it is still falling. Meanwhile, the number of Christians in Africa, Asia, and Latin America has exploded. Today, roughly a quarter of the world's Christians are African, another quarter live in Latin America, and about 15 percent reside in Asia. North America, often seen religiously as an extension of Europe, accounts for only 10 percent of the world's Christians (see fig. 1.1).

Figure 1.1
Changing Christian Population by Continent

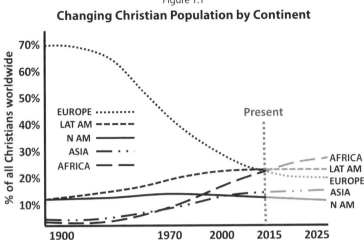

The message is clear: Christianity is no longer European. It has become the most thoroughly diverse, multicultural religion of all time. It is also the most globally dispersed. Islam, which is the world's second-largest religion, flourishes only in Asia and Africa, while Hinduism (the world's third-largest religion) and Buddhism (fourth largest) are almost entirely Asian (see fig. 1.2). Christianity, by contrast, is found everywhere.

Describing Christianity Today

The speed with which Christianity spread around the world took everyone by surprise, including the world's Christians themselves. A hundred years ago it was common for Christians to describe the globe as divided into two regions: Christendom (Europe and the West in general) and various "foreign mission fields" where Christianity was just being introduced. This view aligned nicely with Europe's nineteenth-century colonization of the world. European Christianity was seen as the ideal to which the rest of the world should aspire. "Mission churches" were set up in the colonies to guide progress toward this goal.

When the era of European colonization came to an end in the mid-twentieth century, a new vocabulary had to be devised. Terminology adopted by many Western Christians now described the world Christian movement in terms of "older" versus "younger" churches. "Older churches" in this rhetorical framework referred to the old established churches of the West, while the phrase "younger churches" referred to the more recently formed Christian communities in Africa and Asia. On one level, this new way of describing Christianity

Figure 1.2
Global Distribution of Four World Religions

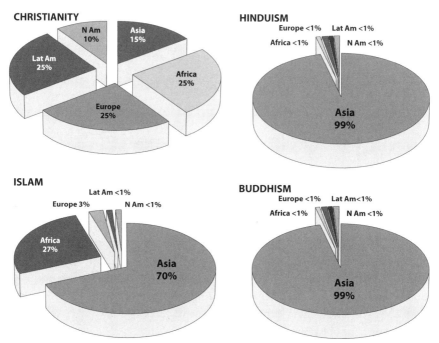

worldwide seemed simply factual. Europe's churches were old, and the churches in Africa and Asia were not. But not all taint of Western Christian superiority had been removed. The term *older* could be heard as a synonym for *wiser*, and the adjective *younger* could imply that churches in Asia and Africa were still in need of instruction from their more mature fellow believers in the West.

In recent years, a new pairing of terms has emerged. The world Christian movement is now frequently described as consisting of a global Christian North and a global Christian South. North and South in this usage do not correspond to the equator but instead to a slanted line that runs from Central America to Siberia and separates Europe and North America from Africa, Asia, and Latin America (see fig.1.3). This new terminology is clearly an improvement over the past because it does not imply any superiority of the North. In fact, the opposite is sometimes the case with the vocabulary of Christian North versus South employed to suggest that churches in the global Christian South are vibrant, devout, and alive while churches in the Christian North are soft, flabby, and spiritually stagnant or dying.

All generalizations have strengths and weaknesses. The great strength of the North versus South model is that it underscores the dramatic shift that has taken place during the last hundred years. In 1900, 80 percent of all Christians still lived in the global Christian North, and only 20 percent lived in the South. Today those numbers are nearly inverted. Now the South is home to almost two-thirds of the world's Christians while only 35 percent live in the global North (see fig. 1.4). This kind of demographic shift is unprecedented in both size and rapidity, and the implications have not yet sunk in for many Christians. Many northern Christians still think that northern-style Christianity is the global norm, but that is no longer the case. If numbers matter, then Christians from the global South can make a strong case that their religious practices should be the global standard.

Figure 1.3
The Global Christian North and South

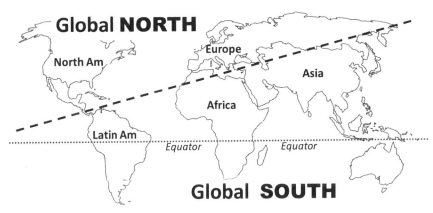

Figure 1.4
**Percentage of Global Christian Population Living
in the North and South: 1900 and 2015 Compared**

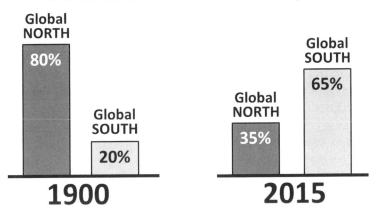

A striking disadvantage of the North-South model is that it perpetuates the idea that all of the diversity that exists within the global Christian movement can somehow be shoehorned into just two big categories. Even when the names of those two categories, North and South, are no longer offensive, the mere act of dividing the Christian world in two, and only two, big regions preserves the old European dualism of "us" and "them." A better description of world Christianity might employ the word *flat*, using that term in the same way as the award-winning journalist Thomas Friedman in the title of his book *The World Is Flat*. When Friedman says the world is "flat" he means that, because of the internet, everyone everywhere competes economically on level ground.[1] Christianity has entered a similarly flat era in its own history. Today, no single region of the Christian world can claim to be the dominant center. Christianity is globally dispersed, and Christians everywhere now have equal potential to shape and influence the movement as a whole (see fig. 1.5).

Figure 1.5
The "Flat" World of Contemporary Christianity
The Percentage of the World's Christians Living in Each Region Today

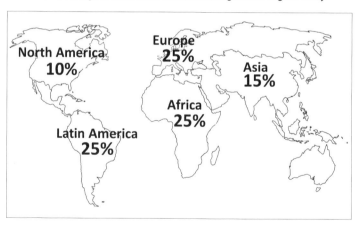

The worldwide Christian community has become multicentered, with each regional expression of Christianity having its own distinctive (and often internally contested) understanding of the gospel and its appropriate embodiment on earth. Christians in Africa accordingly have important insights to share with fellow Christians in Europe in much the same way that European Christians have insights to share with Africans. And the same observation

1. Thomas L. Friedman, *The World Is Flat: A Brief History of the Twenty-First Century* (New York: Farrar, Straus and Giroux, 2005).

can be made about every other region of the world. Christianity has entered a new era and mutual edification has become the rule, a time when Christians from all the world's cultures and regions have much to learn from one another. Differences of wealth, power, social class, and education continue to shape this global conversation because richer Christians (mostly from Europe and North America) typically have more resources available for making their views heard. However, the global Christian movement is becoming irreversibly more egalitarian.

The Christian world is getting flatter, and Christians everywhere are facing a situation that parallels the early church. In its first years, Christianity had no ready lists of preferred beliefs and practices, and it had not yet devised any formulas for quickly assessing who was in and who was out of the movement. People who were trying to follow Jesus faithfully were likely to encounter significantly divergent perspectives among their fellow believers. In ancient times, the setting for this complex conversation was limited largely to the Middle East and the Mediterranean region. Today it encompasses the whole world.

2

Four Christian Traditions

THERE ARE CURRENTLY ABOUT 2.5 billion Christians in the world. They belong to more than 35,000 different church groups or denominations, and they gather for worship in more than 5 million local congregations. All these groups have their own distinctive religious practices, and every Christian has his or her own unique relationship with God. Christians worldwide, however, tend to cluster into several large groups or traditions that embody different broadly defined ways of being Christian. The four largest of these groups, which together account for about 98 percent of all the Christians in the world, are Eastern Orthodoxy, Catholicism, Protestantism, and Pentecostalism. Understanding of global Christianity requires at least some knowledge of these four ecclesiastical traditions.

Catholicism is by far the largest of these traditions and includes half the world's Christians. Eastern Orthodoxy is the smallest, with roughly 10 percent. Protestantism and Pentecostalism, which are significantly younger than the other two traditions, each account for about 20 percent of the global Christian population (see fig. 2.1). In terms of geography, Christians from all the traditions can now be found almost everywhere, but Orthodoxy's heartland is Eastern Europe and the Middle East; the Catholic tradition is strongest in Southern Europe and Latin America; Protestantism is especially prominent in North America and Northern Europe; and Pentecostalism is growing steadily throughout the global South.

There are several Christian groups that do not belong to any of these four big traditions. Perhaps the most well known of these alternative traditions is the Church of Jesus Christ of Latter-Day Saints (LDS), more popularly known as the Mormons. The LDS movement began in upstate New York in the early 1800s, and it has grown rapidly since then. There are now roughly 15 million Mormons worldwide, about half of whom live in the United States. The doctrines and practices of Mormonism rely on the *Book of Mormon*, and other Christians have frequently condemned Mormonism as a cult or sect. Attitudes have moderated in the last twenty years or so, and theological dialogue between Mormons and other Christians has become more common. Nonetheless, Mormonism represents a unique understanding of Christian faith and practice that differs significantly from the four major traditions of Orthodoxy, Catholicism, Protestantism, and Pentecostalism. The same could be said about groups such as the Jehovah's Witnesses, the New Church (Swedenborgian), and *La Luz del Mundo* (located mostly in Mexico).

Figure 2.1
Four Major Christian Traditions
Approximate Percentage of Christians Worldwide

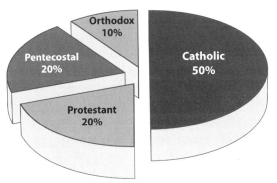

The four major Christian traditions have much in common. More than half a century ago, the British writer C. S. Lewis coined the term "mere Christianity" to describe this common thread of faith. Mere Christianity, as described by Lewis, includes a common understanding of God as the Creator of all that exists, of Jesus as the Savior of the world, and of the Holy Spirit as the Presence of God within the community of believers, empowering Christians with special gifts and nudging them to love and serve others. Lewis also thought that mere Christianity included a core Christian ethic that simultaneously emphasizes personal moral purity, concern for others, and the enjoyment of God's good creation. It is crucial to remain aware of the common threads of Christian faith and practice in an age when Christianity has become so fragmented and diverse. As varied as the four traditions may be, they all acknowledge the same Lord Jesus Christ, and they are all united at some level around a basic or "mere" Christianity, despite their very real differences.

It is also important to remember, however, that mere Christianity does not equal Christianity in all its fullness. Mere Christianity is too *mere* to produce full-bodied faith. It is an abstraction, not the real thing. Saying all Christians embrace mere Christianity is like saying everyone eats food. This is obviously true, but it is also an inadequate description of the human diet. People do not eat food; they eat tomatoes and rice and ice cream and oranges. People like some foods and dislike others, and even if they are nearly starving, there are some foods, such as broccoli, that some people simply will not eat. Real Christianity, as opposed to mere Christianity, is like this. Real Christianity has taste and flavor and particularity. A different analogy likens mere Christianity to the musical score for a song, while real Christianity is actually singing that song. The notes on the page are the same for everyone, but a song can be sung in many different styles and tempos and still be recognizably the same song. In global Christianity today, most followers of Jesus are singing the same "mere" gospel song; but the variety of renditions is immense, and people often have strong preferences for one style over another. Following this musical analogy, the four big Christian traditions can be seen as four different broad styles of singing the Christian faith, and they are as different as opera, bluegrass, jazz, and rock and roll.

Historical Developments and Broad Comparisons

The four big traditions of Christianity that exist today are all part of one family tree (see fig. 2.2). Eastern Orthodoxy and Roman Catholicism share common roots in the imperial church of the old Christian Roman Empire. Protestantism later branched off from Catholicism, and Pentecostalism, in turn, sprang off from Protestantism. As evident in figure 2.2, the four traditions have not always been the main Christian alternatives. During the first thousand years of Christian history, several Asian- and African-based traditions also vied for prominence. These alternative traditions have dwindled over time, however, and no longer have the large numbers of followers they once claimed. All four of today's big Christian traditions have demonstrated an ability to change with time and to accommodate diversity. Traditions are never static. Traditions grow and evolve, branching upward and outward, adjusting to their changing environments. The roots of a tradition matter, but so do all the limbs and branches that grow over the years.

Figure 2.2
Family Tree of Four Christian Traditions

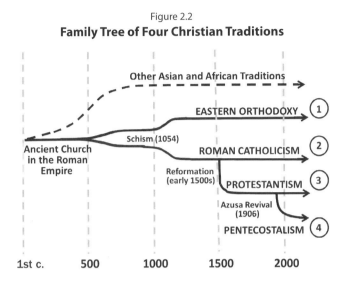

Orthodoxy and Catholicism have long histories that were intertwined for hundreds of years. Both traditions trace their roots back to Jesus and the disciples, and both traditions affirm the principle of apostolic succession: that Jesus appointed the earliest leaders of the church (the apostles), who then appointed their own successors (bishops), who, in turn, appointed their successors producing a chain of unbroken leadership that continues all the way to the present. Even though these two traditions share much in common, their histories began to diverge in the 300s. The process of separation was slow (see fig. 2.3), and it was instigated in large part by language. Catholicism evolved from the Latin-speaking church in the western Roman Empire, while Orthodoxy arose from the Greek-speaking church in the eastern Roman Empire. These different linguistic and cultural perspectives eventually led to more substantial arguments about theology and ecclesiology. The mutual excommunications of the pope and the patriarch of Constantinople in 1054 are often cited as the breaking point between these two ancient churches, but the Catholic crusader attack on Constantinople in 1204 sealed the deal. By the time Constantinople fell to the expanding Islamic Ottoman Empire in 1453, most Catholic and Eastern Orthodox Christians were thoroughly estranged.

In contrast to the slow drifting apart of Orthodoxy and Catholicism, the split between Catholicism and Protestantism was both sharper and more dramatic, disrupting the religious landscape of Europe like a massive spiritual

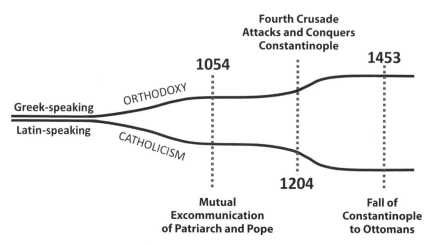

Figure 2.3
Gradual Division between Catholic and Orthodox Traditions

earthquake. There had been some earlier tremors—such as the Waldensian movement in thirteenth-century Italy, the Lollard movement in fourteenth-century England, and the Hussite movement in fifteenth-century Bohemia—but the Protestant Reformation of the sixteenth century caused a colossal rupture. Protestantism was a "protest" against what reformers saw as the Catholic perversion of the gospel, and the lines of divergence were clear from the start.

The much more recent emergence of the Pentecostal movement in the early twentieth century has been no less dramatic but is significantly less well defined. The drama comes from the spiritual vigor of Pentecostalism itself, with its attentiveness to the miraculous power of the Holy Spirit as evidenced in gifts of healing, prophecy, visions, and speaking in tongues. The lack of clarity results from the fact that Pentecostalism continues to have many similarities with Protestantism. One of the chief differences between the two traditions concerns the emphasis placed on *word* versus *spirit*. Protestants tend to be word oriented, emphasizing the cognitive content of the biblical revelation and its logic-based interpretation. Pentecostals, by contrast, tend to emphasize spirit, the experienced reality of God in one's life and in the world. Rather than simply talking about God and seeking to follow the instructions of Scripture, Pentecostals seek to feel God in their lives and to see God's miraculous power unleashed in the world today. Besides differing in theology and practice, the four big Christian traditions also differ significantly in their social organization or ecclesiology (see fig. 2.4). The Catholic tradition is housed entirely in one specific church, the Roman Catholic Church, which is headed by the pope, who is viewed as the successor of Peter and the rightful leader of all Christians worldwide. For Catholics, there is no difference between saying one is a Christian and saying one is a member of the Church (meaning the Catholic Church). It is all one and the same. Orthodox Christians have a similarly church-centered point of view, but they believe the church universal is embodied in a limited number of mutually respectful, ethnically distinct, and spiritually equal Orthodox churches in the plural. Orthodoxy is not a church; it is a closely connected network of churches.

Figure 2.4
Social Organization of the Four Major Christian Traditions Compared

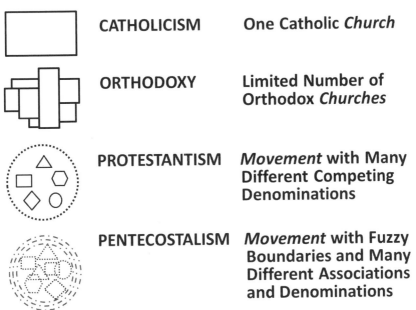

CATHOLICISM   **One Catholic *Church***

ORTHODOXY   **Limited Number of Orthodox *Churches***

PROTESTANTISM   ***Movement* with Many Different Competing Denominations**

PENTECOSTALISM   ***Movement* with Fuzzy Boundaries and Many Different Associations and Denominations**

In contrast to Catholicism and Orthodoxy, which are *churches*, Protestantism and Pentecostalism are best understood as Christian *movements*. These two movements comprise many different churches and para-church organizations, but neither of them is institutionally united in the way that the Catholic and Orthodox traditions are ecclesiastically structured. The Protestant movement, for example, is held together by just a handful of theological convictions. Three assertions launched the movement: the priesthood of all believers (meaning every individual has direct access to God), the singular authority of the Bible (in contrast to tradition or church hierarchy), and salvation based on grace alone through faith alone apart from any human effort. Aside from these few core tenets, Protestantism allows a wide variety of different expressions of faith to flourish alongside one another. In fact, Protestantism has become so diverse that it is almost impossible to describe Protestantism in a way that all Protestants will find agreeable. Pentecostalism is, if anything, even more decentralized and disorganized than Protestantism. The boundaries of Pentecostalism are fuzzier than those of Protestantism, and member groups are more diverse in organizational structure. As movements, in contrast to being churches, Protestantism and Pentecostalism have greater flexibility than either Catholicism or Orthodoxy, but they also have less sense of common identity.

Another point of difference between Catholic and Orthodox traditions, on the one hand, and Protestantism and Pentecostalism, on the other, has to do with history. Catholic and Orthodox Christians place great value on historical precedent; actions today are expected to be consistent, or at least compatible, with patterns of behavior in the past. Worship in the contemporary Catholic and Orthodox traditions is not identical to worship from centuries ago, but there is a close resemblance. Protestants and Pentecostals, by contrast, emphasize newness and change. Many Protestants describe themselves and their churches as "reformed, but ever reforming," and some scholars locate the essence of Pentecostalism in its capacity to "begin something new."[1] As individuals, Protestant and Pentecostal Christians can be just as fixed in their ways and resistant to change as Catholic and Orthodox believers. The difference being described here has to do with the orientations of these traditions as a whole. The Catholic and Orthodox traditions are for the most part historically minded and committed to maintaining continuity with the Church of the past. Protestant and Pentecostal groups, by contrast, tend to be more future-oriented, always open to seeking novel ways of expressing their faith.

Orthodox Christians and Catholic Christians share many beliefs and practices. In both traditions, the Virgin Mary ("Mother of God," or *theotokos*, as she is called by Orthodox Christians) plays a significant role in the story of salvation. Both traditions honor saints and encourage prayers for the dead. Both traditions follow similar annual liturgical calendars, even though Catholic and Orthodox Christians calculate the date of Easter differently. Both traditions support monasticism. Orthodox and Catholic Christians also agree that their church buildings are in some sense sacred, and because of this many Catholic and Orthodox churches are open around the clock so that Christians can pray or meditate in these holy places whenever they want. Historically, most Protestant and Pentecostal Christians have rejected all of these ideas. They do

---

1. Nimi Wariboko, *The Pentecostal Principle: Ethical Methodology in New Spirit* (Grand Rapids: Eerdmans, 2012), viii.

not give Mary any special respect, and sometimes they hardly mention Mary at all; they do not give any special attention to the saints; they do not pray for the dead; they largely ignore the liturgical calendar; they do not support monasticism; and they do not treat their buildings as sacred spaces. In fact, most Protestant churches are closed and locked between services, a practice that was originally adopted during the Reformation of the sixteenth century specifically to dissuade converts to Protestantism from thinking that churches were somehow more holy than other buildings or locations. In recent years, a few Protestant and Pentecostal Christian leaders have begun to change their opinions and have expressed modest appreciation for Mary, the saints, the liturgical calendar, and monasticism, but overall the differences remain stark.

Because the four traditions tend to cluster so frequently into these two sets of two—Orthodox and Catholic together versus Protestants and Pentecostals—the Orthodox and Catholic traditions will be discussed in one section of this chapter, while Protestants and Pentecostals will be discussed in another. What follows is not an exhaustive description of these traditions, but simply an introduction to their most significant characteristics.

Orthodox and Catholic Traditions

The Orthodox Tradition

In the Orthodox tradition, the Divine Liturgy, a two- to three-hour service of worship and sacrament, is a special moment in time when Christians on earth briefly enter into the worship of God that is eternally taking place in heaven. The *oculus*, or domed ceiling, that is part of the traditional architecture of Orthodox churches is considered to be a window into heaven. The painting in the dome typically portrays Christ as the Pantocrator, the ruler of the world (see fig. 2.5), surrounded by angels and apostles who look down from heaven on the gathered congregation. The act of worship is a time of entering into the presence of God in communion with all the saints and followers of Jesus from all times and places. It is intended to be a foretaste of heaven.

The Orthodox tradition considers every newborn baby to be a child of God. At birth, every person is already marked with the image of God. That image is embryonic, but it is there, ready to be nurtured into a much fuller and more complete reflection of God's divine goodness. Each sin that someone commits blurs that reflection, but the image of God can never be totally eradicated from any human life. The goal of human existence is for each person's character to be so smoothed and polished by the Holy Spirit that the image of God is reflected perfectly without blemish or distortion in his or her life. Salvation for

Figure 2.5. Panto-
crator image from
domed ceiling
of an Orthodox
church (Chora
Church, Istanbul,
Turkey)

Orthodox Christians refers to this lifelong trajectory of becoming holy. It is a process, not an event, and Orthodox Christians call that process *theōsis* or deification. The metaphor used by the eighth-century Orthodox theologian Manşūr ibn Sarjūn (also known as John of Damascus) is that a fully saved person is like a piece of iron glowing red from being heated in a fire; what is visible is not the blackness of the steel but only the orange-redness of the hot metal. In the same way, a fully saved or deified human being is alight with the glow of God's own divine presence and love.

The pathway to salvation in the Orthodox tradition is paved by the sacraments and especially by the Eucharist, which is also called Holy Communion, the "medicine of immortality," and the "antidote for death." The last two terms are metaphors taken from the realm of health, and this says a great deal about how Orthodox Christians view salvation. Salvation in the Orthodox perspective is a restoration of the spiritual health and wholeness that God intends for all people, a long and slow process of spiritual growth and convalescence that prepares people for eternal life. The term "Holy Communion" underscores a different facet of salvation in the Orthodox tradition: it is inherently communal. Orthodox Christians are fond of saying that no one is saved alone; God saves people in the plural, not individuals in isolation. Because people

Figure 2.6. Orthodox icons (left: on a shelf in a home; below: painted on the walls and ceiling of a church)

are saved in community, natural groupings of people in families, villages, and even whole nations are seen as constituting something like complex spiritual organisms in which all the members flounder or flourish together. This is why the Orthodox tradition is housed in a variety of national or ethnic churches; God saves people corporately in the human communities where God has placed them. Within the Orthodox tradition, the notion of communion extends far beyond the merely human, however. The goal of salvation is to enter ever deeper into communion with God, to be enveloped by the same divine love that binds together the three persons of the Holy Trinity.

The notion of salvation as deification, as a journey toward ever more intense fellowship with God, is the foundational theological assumption of the Orthodox tradition, and it is the incarnation—God present on earth in human flesh—that undergirds this view of salvation. The incarnation is also the reason why icons (see fig. 2.6) play such an important role in Orthodoxy. Icons are not just paintings; they are created objects that participate in God's holiness and that communicate God's holiness to those who venerate them. Icons are miniature incarnations of God on earth, pieces of wood and paint that somehow participate in the holiness of the pictured person who, in turn, reflects the glory of God into the world. Icons declare that salvation really is possible, that people can be spiritually united with God. To deny the power and holiness of icons is to deny the possibility that God is capable of and willing to be united with the creation. But if God can somehow be united with wood and paint, God can surely inhabit human lives and transform them.

The Catholic Tradition

Worship in the Catholic tradition, in contrast to the Orthodox, focuses not on the liturgy as a whole but on one specific part: the celebration of the Eucharist, ingesting the bread and wine that has through the service of the Mass been transubstantiated into the literal body and blood of Jesus. The architecture of Catholic churches reinforces the centrality of the Eucharist by making the altar at the front of the sanctuary the focal point of the entire build-ing (see fig. 2.7). The word *Mass* comes from the Latin term *missa* (meaning "dismissal"), which refers to the benediction and call to service that is given to the congregation at the conclusion of the liturgy. Fed both literally and spiritually by the body and blood of Christ, Catholics are challenged to go forth in mission to love God and serve others. Expectations about how often to attend Mass have varied over time. In the medieval period, going to Mass once a year was the norm and communing more frequently was discouraged. Today, devout Catholics often participate in Mass daily.

The Catholic view of salvation assumes a bleaker starting point than Or-thodoxy. Catholics believe human beings are born with something called "original sin," a form of corporate guilt inherited from Adam and Eve that separates individuals from God and renders them spiritually dead. Original sin prevents people from experiencing God's grace, which means the first step toward salvation is dealing with this congenital spiritual defect. According to

Figure 2.7. Catholic chapel showing centrality of altar (covered in white cloth) (Franciscan monastery, Toledo, Spain)

Catholic teaching, the remedy for original sin is baptism, which washes the soul clean. The rest of life then becomes, in a manner similar to Orthodoxy, a lifelong journey toward purity and holiness and away from the temptation to fall back into sin. *Salvation* refers to this whole process, and the ultimate goal is to become sufficiently holy that one can stand in God's presence without embarrassment.

Catholics believe the process of salvation is based on God's grace but also requires human effort. The Church provides help in the form of the seven sacraments. Baptism, the Eucharist, confirmation, marriage, holy orders, and anointing of the sick are sources of spiritual sustenance and strength, and the sacrament of reconciliation (or penance) is the remedy for individuals when they fall into sin. Among these seven sacraments, the Eucharist and reconciliation (which is part of one's preparation for the Eucharist) are central. These are repeatable sacraments that nurture faith and promote spiritual growth. The Eucharist also reminds Catholics of the passion, death, and resurrection of Jesus, and it makes Jesus physically present within the community of believers today.

Even with the aid of the sacraments, Catholics assume that only a handful of individuals will complete the journey to full holiness before they die. These few special individuals are honored as saints. For the rest of humankind, God provides a postmortem remedy for their lack of spiritual perfection in the form of *purgatory*, a place or experience that purges the remaining sin from one's soul and completes one's preparation to stand in God's presence. Catholics used to believe that purgatory was a literal place with real flames and real pain and where the duration of the purging process could be calculated in days, weeks, and years. Today, most Catholics view purgatory more symbolically, as a way of saying that death is not the end of the journey to God and that even obvious sinners, if they are repentant, can eventually be purified and make their way to heaven.

This Catholic understanding of salvation is predicated on God's boundless love for humankind. The image of God as the "hound of heaven," a phrase coined by the Catholic poet Francis Thompson in the early 1900s, captures this sentiment. Because God loves people so dearly, God is loath to give up on anyone, and God hounds them relentlessly until they finally respond to that love. This vision of God as the persistent lover of humankind pervades Catholic imagination. At the same time, Catholic preachers and theologians have also placed great emphasis on guilt as a core barrier to salvation, and on Christ's death as the only means of dealing with that guilt. Christ takes each person's sin on himself and then submits himself to the divine punishment that every human deserves. Christ dies in our place on the cross so that we can live. This is why the crucifix, Christ on the cross, has become the worldwide symbol of Catholic faith (see fig. 2.8). It reminds Catholics of their guiltiness before God and of the pain Christ suffered on their behalf. Relatedly, many Catholics see human suffering as a gift from God, a way of participating in the pain of Christ that makes their own salvation possible. Both visions of God—God as the loving hound of heaven and God as the one who declares people guilty and worthy of death—exist side by side in the Catholic tradition, and Catholic spirituality often oscillates between the two.

Catholicism and Orthodoxy Compared

The Nicene Creed is the foundational document for both Catholic and Orthodox Christians (and for some older Protestant churches as well). This creed has also elicited controversy between the two traditions ever since the Catholic Church inserted the word *filioque* into the text during the medieval period. *Filioque* means "and the Son." This word was added to the creed so Catholics now say, "We believe in the Holy Spirit, the Lord, the Giver of

Figure 2.8. Crucifix decorated with flowers (Catholic church, Belize City, Belize)

life, who proceeds from the Father *and the Son*." At issue here was not just the addition of one Latin word, but the unilateral decision by the Western Church to change the wording of the creed without consulting the churches of the East. It is this lack of ecclesiastical etiquette that eventually led to the mutual excommunications of 1054. But the change of wording is also significant, and it points toward a theological difference between Catholic and Orthodox views of God. Orthodox Christians generally view God the Father as supreme, and they envision Christ and the Holy Spirit as siblings of a sort who derive their existence from the Father. In technical theological language, Christ is "begotten" by the Father alone, and the Holy Spirit "proceeds" from the Father alone. Catholics view the Trinity differently. For them, the Father and Son are closely related, and it is the Holy Spirit who has a different status. The Catholic idea that the Spirit proceeds from the Father *and from the Son* reinforces this perspective (see fig. 2.9). For many Christian laypeople, these differences will seem like mere quibbles, but Christian history is replete with instances where small differences in theology have produced heated debate and even bloodshed.

Figure 2.9
Catholic and Orthodox Understandings of Trinity

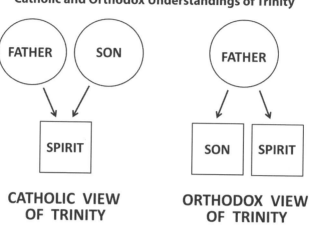

CATHOLIC VIEW
OF TRINITY

ORTHODOX VIEW
OF TRINITY

Perhaps the most obvious difference between Catholicism and Orthodoxy is that Catholics have a pope and Orthodox Christians do not. In Christianity's early centuries, the pope, the bishop of Rome, was one of five "patriarchs" who had oversight of the Christian community in a specific geographic territory or patriarchate. Four of these patriarchs were located in the eastern, Greek-speaking half of the Roman Empire (Alexandria, Antioch, Constantinople, and Jerusalem), and one patriarch was located in the Latin-speaking West (Rome). Together they formed the *Pentarchy*, or "rule by five." The bishop of Rome always had a place of honor within this Pentarchy, because the church at Rome was founded and led by the apostle Peter, who had been given a special leadership role within the Christian movement by Jesus himself, but all five patriarchs were considered to be spiritually equal.

In the mid-400s, Rome was conquered by the so-called barbarians and ceased to be part of the Roman Empire. During the following centuries, the Latin West became ever more separated from the Christian communities in the eastern half of the Roman Empire (frequently called the Byzantine Empire). Cut off from the East and functioning as the sole head of the Church in the West, the bishops of Rome became increasingly vocal about their claims of leadership over the Christian movement as a whole. This was not a new theology. Christians in the western half of the Roman Empire had always believed that Jesus had given Peter the supreme leadership role in the early church, and they were convinced that this role had been passed down to subsequent bishops of Rome, who also served as pope (or "father") of the Church as a whole. During the medieval period, however, this conviction was asserted with new vehemence. In 1302, for example, Pope Boniface VIII declared in *Unam sanctam* that "it is absolutely necessary for salvation that every human creature be subject to the Roman Pontiff." The rhetoric of the Catholic Church and its popes today is much less strident. The Second Vatican Council, meeting in the 1960s, essentially nullified Boniface's claims, and Pope John Paul II publicly repented on behalf of the papacy for the sometimes overblown claims that had been made by his predecessors.[2] Still, the Catholic tradition considers the pope to be the leader of all of God's people on earth, divinely appointed to be "servant of the servants of God" with responsibility for preserving the unity, holiness, apostolicity, and universality of the one true Church.

The Orthodox tradition continues to affirm the older model of leadership associated with the Pentarchy, which is why the Orthodox tradition is housed in a cluster of independent but deeply connected churches rather than in one institutionally unified Orthodox Church. The number of independent Orthodox churches has increased over the years from four to about fifty, but these churches remain fraternally connected by their shared theology and liturgical practices and through ongoing efforts to consult with and care for one another.

Another point of similarity between the Catholic and Orthodox traditions is their practice of encouraging some members of the Christian community to take special vows of commitment to God that set them apart as distinctively "religious" in contrast to ordinary laypeople. This religious calling or vocation can take two different forms. Some individuals follow a contemplative path, and they become monks or nuns who live in separate monastic communities where they dedicate themselves to study and prayer. Others adopt a more active religious life, preaching the gospel and serving the needs of others in the world instead of in a monastery. Becoming one of the "religious" typically includes taking lifelong vows of celibacy, obedience, and poverty. Some monks or male religious become priests, but most do not.

Compared to Catholic monastic life, Orthodox monasticism is generally integrated more directly into the life of local parishes. Orthodoxy also tends to blur the lines between the contemplative religious life and the active religious life. Most Orthodox monks and nuns live in monasteries, but Orthodox monasteries are often located in a town, and monks frequently serve as spiritual

2. See Pope John Paul II, *Ut unum sint* (1995). Article 88 of this encyclical reads in part: "I acknowledged on the important occasion of a visit to the World Council of Churches in Geneva on 12 June 1984, the Catholic Church's conviction that in the ministry of the Bishop of Rome she has preserved, in fidelity to the Apostolic Tradition and the faith of the Fathers, the visible sign and guarantor of unity, constitutes a difficulty for most other Christians, whose memory is marked by certain painful recollections. To the extent that we are responsible for these, I join my Predecessor Paul VI in asking forgiveness."

advisors for laypeople. Monasticism is also the typical Orthodox pathway to becoming a bishop. Bishops in the Orthodox tradition are expected to be celibate, but priests are not. In fact, the Orthodox tradition assumes it is good for priests to be married so they can more easily understand and minister to the needs of married parishioners. The Catholic tradition, by contrast, requires priests to be unmarried (with only a few rare exceptions to this rule), and the typical route to becoming a Catholic bishop is through the priesthood, not the monastery.

Protestant and Pentecostal Traditions

Just as Orthodoxy and Catholicism are linked together, Protestantism and Pentecostalism are separate but interconnected traditions. Unlike Orthodoxy and Catholicism, Protestantism and Pentecostalism do not have continuous histories that go all the way back to Jesus. They are more recently founded traditions, but most Protestant and Pentecostal Christians do not see this as a problem. Instead, they reject the notion that apostolic succession somehow guarantees fidelity to the life and teachings of Jesus. What matters for Protestants and Pentecostals is not the institutional succession of leadership, but lived faithfulness to Christ and Christ's teachings in the present. Some Protestant and Pentecostal Christians would go even further, arguing that too much emphasis on the past can be an impediment to faith. Repetition causes fervor to cool, and faith can lose its power. Protestants and Pentecostals continually go back to what they see as the source of the Christian movement—the Bible for Protestants and the Bible and the Holy Spirit for Pentecostals—seeking to be inspired afresh by the life and words of Jesus.

The Protestant Tradition

The core tenet of Protestantism is that Christian beliefs and practices should be based on the Bible *alone* and that salvation is a relationship between God and the individual *alone* based on grace and faith *alone*—and Protestants never seem to tire of stressing the singularity of these affirmations. Protestant belief in the Bible as the sole religious authority for Christians was formulated in opposition to the Catholic claim that the proper foundation of faith was not the Bible alone, but the Bible as interpreted in the Catholic tradition. Martin Luther, the German monk who helped to launch the Protestant Reformation in the early 1500s, wanted to free the Word of God from ecclesiastical control so it could be heard afresh in changing times and places. Because of this emphasis on the Word, the sermon became the most important part of Protestant worship.

Figure 2.10. Protestant church illustrating the prominence of the pulpit (Hungarian Reformed church, Sibiu, Romania)

The architecture of many Protestant churches reinforces this conviction with the pulpit serving as the central focus of attention (see fig. 2.10).

The Protestant notion that salvation is obtained by grace alone through faith alone diverges significantly from Catholicism and Orthodoxy, which both teach that salvation requires some degree of human effort or cooperation in addition to faith and grace. Protestants also reject the idea of salvation as a lifelong process and instead view salvation as an action or event that occurs at a particular moment and that results in an instantaneous change of status with God. Protestants generally affirm Catholicism's legal understanding of how Christ's death effects salvation—Christ's death pays the penalty owed to God for each individual's sin—but Protestants push this legal metaphor much further than Catholics. For Protestants, what matters for salvation is the fact that God, like a judge in a courtroom, declares sinners to be righteous on the basis of Christ's death. It is that declaration combined with the legal imputation of Christ's own holiness onto the life of the believer that makes one ready to face God. It is not necessary to be empirically holy; what matters is being made legally holy by God's grace. Most Protestants believe Christians should strive for holiness, struggling to overcome any sin that remains in their lives, but changes in behavior have nothing to do with salvation itself. In fact, Protestants use a different word, *sanctification*, to name this process of becoming holy. For Protestants, sanctification follows salvation and is motivated by gratitude for salvation already received.

When the Protestant movement began in the 1500s, most Protestants assumed that God alone determined who would and would not be saved. According to this view—sometimes called Calvinism in honor of John Calvin (1509–1564), the Swiss theologian who articulated the doctrine most clearly—God is totally in charge of selecting or *electing* (the more common theological term) who goes to heaven and hell, and people can do nothing to change their assigned status. Before the end of that century, however, some Protestants were arguing that humans must have at least some small role to play in accepting or rejecting salvation. This second position—sometimes called Arminianism in honor of Jacob Arminius, the Dutch theologian who championed it—has gained strength over the years, and it is now the majority view within Protestantism worldwide.

Much of the appeal of Protestantism, both in the past and today, centers on the notion of the "priesthood of all believers." Medieval Catholicism viewed priests as intermediaries between individuals and God. By contrast, Protestantism stresses the individual's direct access to God. Protestants also assume that it is everyone's job, both pastors and parishioners, to further the work of God in the world. Thus the Protestant reformers asserted that every follower of Jesus—every man, woman, and child—had a religious vocation or *calling* that was commensurate with their God-given talents, their personalities, and their social locations. These ideas about vocation and the priesthood of all believers made Protestantism a more egalitarian tradition than Catholicism and resulted in much higher levels of lay activism.

Protestantism's understanding of vocation is also rooted in the belief that Christians are simultaneously saints and sinners. This understanding of the Christian life suggests that no human action is ever entirely pure. Even the best of human behaviors include some element of sin, some hint of pride, some self-interest, some envy, or some debased pleasure. Rather than being debilitating or giving rise to cynicism, Martin Luther, the theologian who first developed the doctrine, saw this insight as liberating. Christians did not need to be perfect to serve others, they needed only to be willing to serve and to admit mistakes when they made them. Living a Christian vocation thus became an exercise in trying to do God's will, asking others to assess the spiritual quality and effectiveness of one's actions, acknowledging mistakes and errors, and then trying to do better next time. The goal was not personal sainthood, but wiser, more effective service.

During the last five hundred years, Protestantism has taken on two very different organizational forms, one primarily European and the other North American. Historically, European Protestantism has been housed in a variety of government-supported state churches. These churches were originally organized from the top down and had monopoly control over religion in the nations where they existed. They were meant to serve the religious needs of all the people, and they also had various civic functions that included keeping records of births, marriages, and deaths. Protestant state churches continue to exist in Great Britain and in much of Scandinavia today, though they no longer control religious life.

In North America, Protestantism became much more egalitarian. Christianity was organized from the ground up, and the result was a stunning array of new church groups that saw themselves simultaneously as partners in promoting the gospel and as competitors in faith. This odd mix of cooperation and competition prompted North America's Protestant churches to come up with an entirely new word to describe themselves: *denominations*, different expressions of one shared Protestant faith. As Protestantism has spread around the world, the more freewheeling American-style Protestantism has become the global norm, not the state church model of Europe.

The diversity within the Protestant movement is immense. In the 1500s, Protestantism comprised five main subgroups—Lutheran, Anglican, Reformed, Unitarian, and Anabaptist—but within a century these original traditions had spawned a host of new offshoots such as Baptists, Methodists, and Presbyterians. Today there are thousands of different Protestant churches and denominations around the world, each championing its own slightly different version of Christian faith. While these churches have much in common, Protestant denominations are generally more well known for the few distinctive doctrines or practices that set them apart. Baptists are known for baptizing adults, Mennonites emphasize pacifism, the Churches of Christ do not use musical instruments, and Nazarenes champion total sanctification as a second work of grace. This emphasis on distinctive beliefs and practices explains why so few Protestants use the word *Protestant* to describe themselves. Instead of saying they are "Protestant," many Protestants identify themselves by the distinctive practices of their differing denominations. At least that is how most Protestants would have described themselves in the past. Many Protestants today feel that the historical distinctives of their denominations are overblown. Rather than emphasizing competitive differences, they are more comfortable talking about cooperative similarities. This attitude has produced a new movement within Protestantism known as *nondenominationalism*, and in some parts of the world (especially North America) it is now the fastest growing sector of the movement.

In terms of general orientation of faith (versus formal denominational differences), the most significant division within the contemporary Protestant movement is the difference between those who think of themselves as liberal or progressive and those who say they are conservative or evangelical. Many Protestants do not fit neatly into either category, but these two alternatives are often used to describe Protestantism worldwide. Liberal or progressive Protestants tend to support causes such as the ordination of women and full rights for members of the LGBTQ community; they view the Bible as an authoritative text but do not consider it to be free of all errors; they willingly acknowledge that they have doubts about some traditional Christian doctrines such as the existence of a literal hell; and they are respectful of other religions as pathways to God. Conservative Christians or evangelicals, by contrast, typically support "traditional values" (including traditional gender roles and sexual orientations); they believe the Bible is the literal and authoritative word of God; they express certainty about their own theological convictions; and they go out of their way to share the gospel with others because they believe that non-Christian religions offer no hope of salvation.

Despite these differences, evangelical and progressive Protestants agree on many things: the life and teachings of Jesus are central; the Bible is the core text to be consulted; and the vocabulary of faith includes grace, confession, and forgiveness. Evangelical and progressive Christians also worship in similar ways. They sing many of the same songs, they read the same biblical passages, they pray the same prayers, and they use the same little plastic cups when serving communion. They also affirm in common that Christians have an obligation to care for those in need. That said, Protestant evangelicals and progressives rarely interact; they live in two different ecclesiastical worlds. Institutionally, most progressive Protestant churches belong to the World Council of Churches, an organization that describes itself as "a worldwide fellowship of churches seeking unity, a common witness, and Christian service."[3] The largest global evangelical affiliation is the Lausanne Movement, launched by Billy Graham and his associates in 1974, a loosely structured organization seeking "to further the total biblical mission of the Church, recognizing that in this mission of sacrificial service, evangelism is primary, and that our particular concern must be the unreached people of the world."[4]

The Pentecostal Tradition

Pentecostalism, like Protestantism, is a movement and not a church, but it is more fluid and less organized than Protestantism. This fluidity is intentional. The Pentecostal movement seeks to follow the Holy Spirit wherever the

3. See the World Council of Churches website, http://www.oikoumene.org/en.
4. See the Lausanne Movement website, http://www.lausanne.org/about-the-lausanne -movement.

Spirit leads, even when the direction is unexpected. Too much organization and sophistication can get in the way of spiritual responsiveness, and many Pentecostal groups do their best to minimize the institutional dimensions of church life. Some Pentecostal groups even reject the notion of being called churches or denominations. For example, the Assemblies of God (one of the largest Pentecostal organizations in the world) insists that it is not a denomination at all but simply a "fellowship" of congregations seeking to follow God's will. Anti-organizational and anti-hierarchical rhetoric does not always align neatly with the realities of Pentecostal church life. Some Pentecostal organizations are very tightly controlled by their leaders, who are apt to ignore any innovation that is not initiated at the top. Still, most Pentecostals seek to remain open to the movement of the Spirit and want their churches to be flexible in responding to God's call.

Part of what makes Pentecostalism distinct is its expansive view of salvation. Salvation in the Pentecostal tradition is forward-looking; it is about constantly moving into deeper and richer fellowship with God. In many ways, the Pentecostal view of salvation is closer to Orthodoxy than it is to either Protestantism or Catholicism. For Catholics and for Protestants, salvation is largely construed as cleansing from the guilt of past sins. Orthodox Christians instead emphasize the future, progressing toward deification and having the image of God fully restored in one's life. Both Orthodoxy and Pentecostalism view salvation as following a pathway toward ever greater communion with God. Many Pentecostals also affirm the Protestant view of salvation as a once-and-done event, but that event is construed as the beginning and not the end of salvation in all its splendor. For Pentecostals, salvation is a lifelong (and some would say an eternal and never-ending) journey into ever deeper fellowship with God.

While this book describes Pentecostalism as one of the four major traditions that make up contemporary Christianity, some Christians (including some Pentecostals) would be surprised by that description because they see Pentecostalism as simply one more variety of Protestantism. There is warrant for this perspective. Pentecostalism initially emerged out of Protestantism, and the two movements still share many characteristics. For example, most Pentecostals, along with most Protestants, believe in the priesthood of all believers, they believe salvation is provided by grace alone through faith alone, and they see the Bible as the only written source of authority for Christians.

However, Protestantism and Pentecostalism have very different centers of gravity. Protestantism centers on the word: on doctrine and scriptural teaching. Pentecostalism centers on experience: the felt presence of God in a person's life. When asked about his creed, one early Pentecostal leader said simply,

"My experience is my creed."[5] Another said that becoming Pentecostal was like swallowing "God liquidized."[6] Pentecostals believe the words of the Bible, and they embrace its message, but they read the Bible in order to live like the people whose stories are told in the Bible rather than to theologize about the Bible's ideas. Pentecostals want to experience God's power to heal those who are sick and to cast out demons. They want to dance, cry, laugh, sing, shout, and perhaps even faint as they feel the Spirit moving within them.

A quick look at the historic roots of Pentecostalism underscores its differences from standard Protestantism. The Azusa Street Revival that took place in Los Angeles in 1906 is often cited as the beginning of the movement. The African American preacher William J. Seymour, who led the revival, highlighted the differences between thinking about God (Protestantism) and actually experiencing God in one's life (Pentecostalism). He frequently told seekers that they could not "get the filling" if they were caught up in "thinking thought." They had to become like "little babes" to get the blessing, and they had to set their adult minds aside.[7] Early Pentecostalism was, like Protestantism, rooted and grounded in the Bible, but it was also based on experience. Pentecostals have produced systematic theology from the earliest days of their movement,[8] but experience plays a far greater role in Pentecostal theology than most Protestants would find appropriate.

Part of what makes Pentecostalism unique—different not only from Protestantism but also from Catholicism and Eastern Orthodoxy—is that the movement is defined by a handful of shared *emphases* rather than by a list of distinctive affirmations. Many of the beliefs that Pentecostals emphasize are also emphasized by other Christians. Pentecostals emphasize the guidance of the Holy Spirit. They emphasize miracles. They emphasize that God can and will heal the sick. They emphasize all the spiritual gifts listed in the New Testament. And they emphasize the physical dimensions of faith; they expect to feel God's presence in their bodies. Many other Christians would agree with these emphases to some degree. They believe that the Holy Spirit can guide believers, that miracles are possible, that the sick are sometimes healed, that all the gifts of the Spirit may occasionally be experienced today, and that some people do indeed feel God physically in their lives. What is different is the degree of expectation. Pentecostals expect these kinds of things

5. Joseph H. King, quoted in Douglas Jacobsen, *Thinking in the Spirit: Theologies of the Early Pentecostal Movement* (Bloomington: Indiana University Press, 2003), 169.

6. David W. Myland, ibid., 122.

7. These phrases are all taken from the Azusa Street Mission's paper, *The Apostolic Faith*, quoted in Jacobsen, *Thinking in the Spirit*, 66.

8. See Jacobsen, *Thinking in the Spirit*.

to be part of normal, everyday Christian life; most other Christians see them as extraordinary, exceptional occurrences. This relatively modest difference of expectation, however, produces huge differences in spirituality.

Because the Pentecostal tradition is based on emphases, rather than on affirmations that conflict with the views of other Christians, it has a unique relationship with the other three traditions. Typically, the different Christian traditions are presented as either-or options. For example, a person is either Protestant or Catholic. (Anglo-Catholics, who are "high church" members of the Church of England, claim to be simultaneously both Protestant and Catholic, but they are the exception that proves the rule.) This is why Catholics do not allow Protestants to participate in the Mass, because being part of one tradition means that one is not a member of the other. Christians, in their view, must make a choice.

But this kind of either-or logic does not apply to Pentecostalism. Because Pentecostalism is defined by its spiritual emphases rather than by its unique theological affirmations, it is possible to be Protestant or Catholic or Orthodox and simultaneously to be Pentecostal. Institutionally, there are some ecclesiastical organizations that are distinctively Pentecostal in the sense that they have named some explicitly Pentecostal spiritual emphases as the norms for their group. Many other Christians around the world have adopted Pentecostalism's spiritual emphases on their own without joining any distinctively Pentecostal church. These individuals are often called Charismatic Christians. They embrace elements of Pentecostalism, but ecclesiastically they remain Catholics or Orthodox Christians or Protestants of some kind. All of this means that the boundaries of the Pentecostal movement are much fuzzier than those of the Catholic, Eastern Orthodox, and Protestant traditions, and the number of Pentecostal Christians in the world is accordingly much harder to count.

While the Azusa Street Revival is often cited as the beginning of the Pentecostal movement, Pentecostalism's beginnings were diffuse. Similar movements of the Spirit arose in Asia and Latin America about the same time as the Los Angeles revival, and something akin to Pentecostalism emerged in Africa several decades before the Azusa Street meetings. This first wave of Pentecostalism, beginning around 1900, produced new churches or denominations with an explicitly Pentecostal orientation. In the United States, these denominations are often called "classical" Pentecostal churches. In Africa and elsewhere around the world, they are often called simply "independent." In both cases, these churches openly profess Pentecostal emphases, and they assume that all of their members should embrace the same Pentecostal approach to Christian faith and practice. In the United States and across the globe, these formally Pentecostal churches have grown enormously during the twentieth century.

In 1900, they were nonexistent; today, an estimated 200 million people may belong to these first-wave, classical and independent Pentecostal churches.

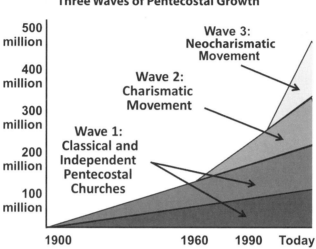

Figure 2.11
Three Waves of Pentecostal Growth

A second wave of Pentecostal Christianity began in the 1960s in the form of the Charismatic Movement. Charismatic Christians, as described above, embrace a Pentecostal understanding of Christianity, but maintain formal membership in a non-Pentecostal church or denomination. The largest Charismatic movement in the world is the Catholic Charismatic Renewal, which is especially strong in Latin America. It is very difficult to estimate the number of Charismatic Christians around the world, but there may be close to 100 million in Latin America alone.

A third wave of Pentecostal development known as the neocharismatic movement began in the early 1980s. This movement has produced a wide range of new organizations that tend to be more doctrinally and experientially flexible than first-wave "classical" Pentecostal denominations but simultaneously more churchly minded than most Charismatic Christians. Neocharismatic congregations often employ the rhetoric of "spiritual warfare," saying everyone is required to choose one side or the other in the great battle between God and the forces of Satan. Neocharismatic Pentecostals also typically teach that God will materially bless those who have sufficient faith to claim those blessings. Their "word of faith" teaching is rooted in biblical sources such as the book of Proverbs, but in some settings it is refashioned into a crass promise of "health and wealth." Neocharismatic Pentecostalism has become tremendously popular in Africa and Asia, and it has many adherents in Latin America and North America as well.

One characteristic that distinguishes Pentecostalism from the other three traditions is its emphasis on the emotion of joy. Pentecostal Christians enjoy God's presence in their lives and they worship God with fervor, spontaneity, and pleasure. In traditional Catholicism, Orthodoxy, and Protestantism, religious duty often nudges joy to the side. Catholic, Orthodox, and Protestant Christians sometimes attend worship services on Sundays because they feel like they *ought* to; it is their religious duty to attend. They may enjoy being part of those services while they are there, but joy is not the first word associated with these non-Pentecostal churches. For Pentecostals, however, joy is central. Worship is fun; it is celebratory; it is sometimes positively raucous. For the past century, Pentecostalism has been the fastest growing religious movement on earth. The movement's focus on joy is surely one reason for this growth.

A basic understanding of the four major Christian traditions is a prerequisite for understanding Christianity globally because communities of Orthodox, Catholic, Protestant, and Pentecostal Christians are now found all around the world. Christians who are associated with the same major tradition will have much in common, irrespective of the particular continent on which they live. However, cultural and regional differences also deeply influence Christian faith and practice. Christians living together in a particular culture or region of the world may accordingly have as much (or more) in common with other local Christians—regardless of whether those local Christians are Orthodox, Catholic, Protestant, or Pentecostal—than they have in common with members of their own tradition who live elsewhere around the globe. The next five chapters of this book focus on these regional differences, examining Christianity as it has developed and is currently lived in Africa, Latin America, Europe, Asia, and North America. Each chapter ends with a discussion of the distinctive cultural theology that is now emerging in each of these very different regions of the world.

3

Africa

In December 1999, the Eighth General Assembly of the World Council of
Churches (WCC) convened in Harare, Zimbabwe. It was truly a gathering of the nations, and the massive worship tent was visually alive with a
stunning diversity of colorful fabrics and regional fashions. One of the most
meaningful worship services focused on the "healing of the nations" and was
based on the text of Revelation 22:1–2: "Then the angel showed me the river
of the water of life. . . . On each side of the river stood the tree of life. . . .
And the leaves of the tree are for the healing of the nations." Worship leaders
distributed leaves from a local vegetable, which worshipers then exchanged
with others nearby, repeating the words, "Take and eat for the healing of your
country." All of the participants then took the leaves and ate them.

There were good reasons for highlighting peace and reconciliation because
the years leading up to the WCC assembly had been violent ones in many
parts of the host continent. The genocide in Rwanda had occurred a few years
earlier, and South Africa had only recently transitioned to majority rule after
years of bloody struggle against apartheid. At the time the Harare Assembly was in session, Liberia was ruled by Charles Taylor and was embroiled
in a vicious civil war; the child soldiers of the Lord's Resistance Army, led
by Joseph Kony, were terrorizing Uganda; and fighting between factions in
northern and southern Sudan was at its peak.

The WCC had gathered in Africa only one time before, in 1975 in Nairobi,
Kenya. That earlier assembly was a celebration of Africa's transition—both

in general and in Christian terms—from colonial rule to postcolonial independence. When the Nairobi assembly had gathered in 1975, about 11 percent of the world's Christians were residents of Africa. At the time of the Harare gathering in 1999, just twenty-four years later, the number of Christians in Africa had skyrocketed, leaping to 19 percent of the world's Christian population. By 2030, more Christians will live in Africa than in any other continent.

Harare had been selected as the conference site both to underscore Christianity's fantastic growth in Africa and to draw attention to the region's challenges. President Nelson Mandela of South Africa made a special appearance at the assembly and so did Robert Mugabe, the president of Zimbabwe. Mugabe arrived with a large entourage intended to demonstrate his power and importance. Mandela, by contrast, came alone. He thanked those in attendance for their support and said it was the prayers of the churches that had kept him alive during his long years in prison. He spoke poignantly of Western missionaries who taught him in their schools and cared for him at their hospitals. Rather than rehearsing the crimes of colonialism, which he knew all too well from personal experience, Mandela chose instead to express gratitude to the WCC for its strong advocacy of his leadership and for its unequivocal stand against apartheid. No one doubts that Christianity has had an enormous impact on the continent for both good and ill, but Mandela emphasized the positive. Africa is now beginning to exert enormous influence on Christianity all around the world. If Mandela's vision prevails, that influence will be one of humility, justice, reconciliation, and hope.

The History of African Christianity

There are two historical layers of Christianity in Africa: one ancient, the other more recent in origin. Africa's ancient Christianity dates back to the very beginning of the Christian movement, and it is preserved in today's Orthodox Christian churches of Egypt and Ethiopia. Africa's more recently formulated version of Christianity was planted in the late 1400s but did not fully blossom until the twentieth century. The following narrative tells the story of these two African expressions of faith in Jesus. The first section provides a brief overview of older African Christianity from the time of the apostles to the fifteenth century. This is followed by three sections discussing Africa's more recent encounter with European Christianity: starting with the precolonial period (1400s to 1880), moving through European colonial rule (1880–1960), and ending with the postcolonial era (since 1960). Christianity would not exist in Africa if the missionaries that Mandela praised in his speech at the WCC had never arrived, but African Christianity is what it is today because Africans took that message, reinterpreted it through the lens of their own African experience, and made it their own.

Ancient African Christianity from the First Century to the Late 1400s

Christianity has deep roots in Africa. Africans from Egypt and Libya were present on the day of Pentecost when the apostle Peter preached to a crowd gathered in Jerusalem, and they spread the message of Jesus when they returned to their native lands. By the late second century, there were Christians living all along the North African coast. By the fourth century, Christianity was present in Aksum (Ethiopia), and from there it soon spread to Nubia (Sudan). African church leaders and theologians played a major role in shaping early Christian history. Origen (185–254), who lived in the city of Alexandria in Egypt, is often identified as the first systematic Christian theologian. Athanasius (296–373), who also lived in Egypt, championed the full divinity of Christ at the Council of Nicaea. Augustine (354–430), who lived in what is now northeastern Algeria, is often cited as the most influential thinker in all of Christian history.

African Christianity began to decline in the mid-600s when Islam took over much of the region. The Prophet Muhammad died in 632, and his followers began spreading the message of Islam to areas far beyond the Arabian Peninsula. By the year 700, all of North Africa was under the control of the Islamic Caliphate. (The caliph is the successor of Muhammad and head of the Islamic community, a position that is both religious and political in nature.)

At first, Christians in the conquered territory were not encouraged to convert. The Muslim rulers imposed a special tax (*jizra*) on non-Muslims, and conversions diminished this source of revenue. After 750, a new dynasty (the Abbasids) took control of the Caliphate—one that placed greater emphasis on religious uniformity—and pressure to convert increased. The Christian population declined significantly, and by the year 1000 Christianity had been eliminated from much of North Africa. Two exceptions to this general pattern were the Coptic church in Egypt and the Ethiopian church further south that both remained strong. Over the next several centuries, Islam expanded southward down the eastern coast of Africa and southwest across the Sahara to West Africa. By 1400, Africa was a religiously divided continent, with Islam dominant in the north and traditional African religions continuing to flourish in the south (see fig. 3.1).

Figure 3.1
Religious Map of Africa, c. 1400

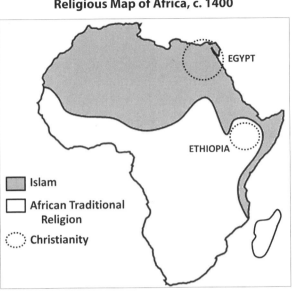

Early Modern Encounters with European Christianity (Late 1400s to 1800s)

In the late 1400s, Portugal began sending ships down the Atlantic coast of Africa, exploring possibilities for trade, looking for allies who might help them combat Islam, and seeking to convert local people to the Catholic faith.[1] In 1491, Portuguese missionaries arrived in the central African region known as the Congo (now Angola). Within a few years they had baptized the king. That king soon recanted his conversion, but his son remained a faithful Christian and soon ascended to the throne. Ruling as King Afonso I (1506–1543), Mvemba Nzinga reorganized the local calendar around Christian holy days, collected and destroyed the ritual objects of traditional African religion, and built churches across his domain. Sometimes he took the pulpit after Sunday Mass to instruct the people about how to live as followers of Jesus. Eventually, Afonso sent his son, Henrique, to Portugal to be trained and ordained as a priest. The son returned not only as a priest but as a full-fledged bishop, and Congo seemed poised to become a thoroughly Catholic state.

But the tide soon changed. Henrique died shortly after returning to the region, and no one was willing or able to take over his place as bishop. Celibacy

1. See Adrian Hastings, *The Church in Africa: 1450–1950* (Oxford: Oxford University Press, 1994), 71–129.

was a major stumbling block. African Christians valued large families, and they could not comprehend why a man would voluntarily deny himself a family in order to become a priest. The Congolese asked Rome to allow their priests to marry, but the request was denied and the Christian movement faltered. The local monarchy also began to unravel, and when it did the Portuguese stepped in to take direct control of the kingdom. By this time, slavery had become one of the main economic activities in the region, and slave trade increased dramatically under Portuguese rule. The church's main function devolved into baptizing slaves before they were shipped off to the Americas. Slave traders considered baptism to be an act of Christian mercy because it guaranteed slaves a place in heaven if they did not survive the journey across the Atlantic, and about a quarter did not. Most Africans probably saw baptism as nothing more than another part of the terrible process of being captured, put on boats, and sent off into oblivion.

Despite Christianity's association with the evils of slavery, a brief revival of Congolese Christianity took place in the early 1700s. The revival was led by a charismatic prophet named Beatrice Vita Kimpa, who declared that Jesus was an African, born in the kingdom of the Congo. She criticized the prominence of images, such as statues of saints and even the crucifix itself, and proposed reforming Christianity based on moral principles. Vita Kimpa was arrested and executed by the Portuguese authorities. Her movement disintegrated, and by the time Western missionaries reentered the region in the late 1800s, only a very faint memory of Jesus remained.[2]

There were many other European Christian forays into the continent. Until 1800 all of these expeditions were led by Catholics, but in the early nineteenth century Protestants began joining the ranks of European missionaries serving in Africa. Protestant timing was fortuitous since their efforts began just as the African slave trade was finally ending. England banned slave trading in 1807 and outlawed slavery entirely in 1833, and the British navy was instructed to stop any boats transporting slaves across the Atlantic and to return recaptured slaves to Africa. These abolitionist efforts boosted the reputation of Christianity, and especially Protestantism, among Africans.

A number of early Protestant missionaries also stressed the importance of African leadership within the African church. This was especially true of Henry Venn, head of the Anglican Church Missionary Society (CMS). Venn endorsed what he termed "three self" Christianity: every church, wherever it was located in the world, ought to be self-governing, self-supporting,

---

2. See John K. Thornton, *The Kongolese Saint Anthony: Dona Beatriz Kimpa Vita and the Antonian Movement, 1684–1706* (Cambridge: Cambridge University Press, 1998).

and self-propagating. In an attempt to promote this vision of Christianity in Africa, Venn formed a partnership with a recaptured slave named Samuel Ajayi Crowther (see fig. 3.2). Crowther was from the Yoruba tribe in what is now Nigeria. He had been seized and sold into slavery at the age of twelve, but was recaptured by the British navy and resettled in the British colony of Sierra Leone. Educated by Protestant missionaries at the famous Fourah Bay College, Crowther became a Christian and later traveled to London to complete his ministerial studies. He was ordained an Anglican priest in 1843. A few years later, in the mid-1850s, Venn asked Crowther to start an African-led three-self church in the Niger River basin. Crowther funded the Niger Mission by mixing river trade with evangelism, and an independent and

Figure 3.2. Samuel Ajayi Crowther (1809–1891)

thoroughly African Christian community was soon flourishing in the region. The project was so successful that Crowther was consecrated bishop in 1864.

Attitudes were changing in Europe, however, and Venn's vision for a genuinely African form of Christianity was increasingly seen as unrealistic. A new generation of British missionaries felt they needed to establish European control over the mission to ensure that West African Anglicanism remained sufficiently "orthodox," which meant sufficiently similar to Anglicanism as it was practiced in Great Britain. Arriving in West Africa in the 1880s, they took over the mission and, because of their inexperience with local culture, quickly ran it into the ground. It would be sixty years before another African was appointed bishop, and the hope that Crowther and Venn had shared for an independent African church languished.

Missionaries were not the only Europeans settling in Africa during these years. Others came seeking business opportunities, especially in the southern region of the continent. The first European settlers to arrive were employees of the Dutch East India Company who were there to resupply company ships transiting between England and the Spice Islands (now part of Indonesia) in Southeast Asia. Begun as a company outpost in 1652, the Cape Colony soon attracted many other Dutch settlers because of its pleasant climate and fertile land. By 1795, the colony covered roughly a quarter of present-day South Africa.

The colonization of southern Africa caused racial tensions. European settlers pushed some local people off their ancestral lands so Europeans could move onto them; they forced others into slavery and still others were incorporated into the colony by marriage or cohabitation, giving rise to a mixed-race population that white South Africans called "Coloureds." When England took control of the Cape Colony in the early 1800s, the Dutch Afrikaners fled inland (in a journey that is now called the "Great Trek"), where they encountered the Zulu nation that was also expanding the scope of its domain. Overwhelmed by social change from this combined Zulu and Afrikaner influx, the various tribes that had traditionally inhabited this inland territory were thrown into a state of crisis. Trying to put their lives back together again, some embraced the gospel. When word of these conversions reached Europe, scores of missionaries flooded into the region to take part in what they hoped would be a great "harvest of souls." By the late 1800s, there were more missionaries per person in South Africa than anywhere else on earth.[3]

Many new "mission churches" were created by missionaries working in the area, but some Africans resisted Western efforts to control the gospel message and hoped that more authentically African ways of being Christian would emerge. One person who played a key role in developing a more thoroughly African version of Christianity was a man named Ntsikana, a member of the Xhosa tribe. Ntsikana was a traditional African who had never been particularly attracted to Christianity. One day, he was surprised by an unexpected vision of light and a sensation that "something"—he was not sure how to describe it—of great spiritual or divine power had entered his body. He later identified this something as Christ. Ntsikana became a lifelong worshiper of the Christian God, even though he never joined any existing church or created his own. Calling himself a candle sent from God to bring light to the world, Ntsikana expressed his faith mainly by writing hymns, many of them still sung by South Africans today. The most famous is called simply the "Great Hymn," and it describes God as a shield, a fortress, a refuge, a hunter of souls, and perhaps most memorably as "the Great Blanket with which we are clothed."[4] God, as envisioned by Ntsikana, loved and cared for all people. Ntsikana's experience convinced many Africans they could approach God directly without adopting the European understanding of Christianity that missionaries had brought to the region.

These stories from the Congo, the Niger River, and South Africa only scratch the surface of Christianity's history in Africa before European colonization began in earnest, but they give a sense of its diversity. They also reflect the very limited impact that European Christianity had on Africa prior to the twentieth century. In the late 1800s, the religious map of Africa remained almost identical to the map of 1400 (see fig. 3.3). While the gospel had been newly introduced to many parts of Africa, it had taken root in only a few limited locations. Perhaps 5 percent of the continent's population was now Christian, but most of these Christians were clustered in Egypt, Ethiopia, and South Africa. In the rest of Africa, Christianity was hardly known at all.

Figure 3.3
Religious Map of Africa, c. 1880

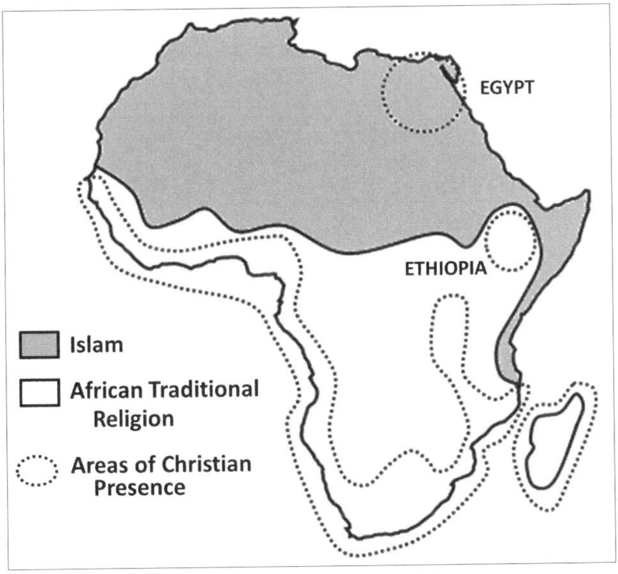

The Colonial Era (1885 to 1960)

A new era in the history of African Christianity began in the late nineteenth century when the nations of Europe unilaterally decided to take control of the continent. The motivation was largely economic. The industrial age was dawning, and European nations were searching for cheap natural resources. Between 1885 and 1915, Belgium, France, Germany, Great Britain,

Italy, Portugal, and Spain engaged in a great "scramble for Africa." When the frenzy of colonial conquest was over, almost every inch of the continent had been claimed by some European nation, with Ethiopia and Liberia being the sole exceptions. Great Britain and France were the most aggressive coloniz-ers. France controlled most of West Africa and parts of central Africa, and England claimed much of eastern and southern Africa along with Ghana, Nigeria, and Sierra Leone in the west (see fig. 3.4).

Figure 3.4
Colonial Africa, c. 1915

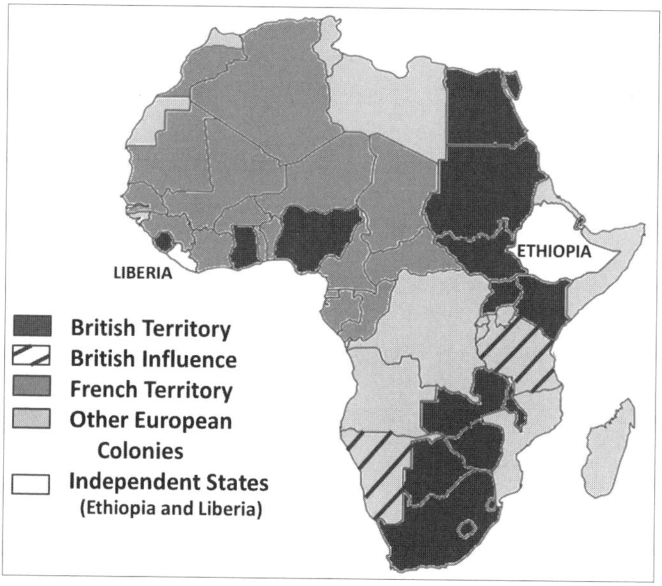

While colonization was clearly intended to benefit Europe, many Euro-peans also felt it was their responsibility to help Africa join the modern world. They assumed that Western European civilization represented the pin-nacle of human history, and they felt obligated to help other, less-modernized cultures become more like Europeans. In the parlance of the day, this was the colonial "white man's burden." But rather than being exposed to the best of European culture, Africans working for colonists often experienced the worst. Under the personal rule of King Leopold of Belgium, for example, thousands of Africans in the Congo were worked to death on rubber planta-tions and gold mines. Conditions became so horrific that the Belgian govern-ment finally intervened, taking control away from the king and trying to make amends.

Christianity and colonization were closely connected during this era. Many missionaries, like many colonial political rulers, believed that part of their role was to bring modern civilization to Africa. European Protestants considered literacy, hard work, time consciousness, democracy, and self-discipline—all hallmarks of modern, Western culture—to be necessary components of Christian living. Catholics held similar views. Pope Pius XI explained in his encyclical *Rerum ecclesiae* (1926) that the Catholic Church existed in order to "spread the light of the Gospel and the benefits of Christian culture and civilization to the peoples who [sit] in darkness and in the shadow of death."[5] Missionaries and colonial governments often worked closely together, especially in the area of education. Missionaries started schools as a way to win converts for Christ, and European governments benefitted from an educated native workforce that could help them run their colonies. Because most missionaries provided these services at no cost to the state, governments frequently gave missionaries near-monopoly control over education in colonial Africa.[6]

Relationships between missionaries and colonial governments were not, however, always congenial. Missionaries were often the most vocal critics of the colonial enterprise because they witnessed the effects of harmful colonial policies and reprehensible behavior by some colonial officials. Colonial governments, in turn, supported missionary efforts only when they advanced the colonial cause. In predominantly Muslim territories, the presence of Christian missionaries who were aggressively seeking converts inevitably produced religious tension and made governing more difficult. Thus the French government often barred Christian missionaries from the predominantly Muslim parts of Africa that they controlled, and Great Britain did the same, even to the point of favoring Muslims over local Coptic Orthodox Christians in Egypt.

The thousands of missionaries who worked in Africa during the colonial era were far from identical.[7] Some were pompous, and others were humble. Some were joyful, while others were cranky. Some were well educated, and others not. They also held widely divergent theological opinions. What they shared in common was tremendous religious fervency. These were not ordinary Christians but zealots, eager to pass their own spiritual energy on to their African converts. This intensity of faith became even more pronounced in the 1930s when American missionaries began to outnumber those from Europe.

5. *Rerum ecclesiae*, paragraph 1, http://w2.vatican.va/content/pius-xi/en/encyclicals/docu ments/hf_p-xi_enc_28021926_rerum-ecclesiae.html.
6. Elizabeth Isichei, *A History of Christianity in Africa: From Antiquity to the Present* (Grand Rapids: Eerdmans, 1995), 229.
7. See John Baur, *2000 Years of Christianity in Africa: An African Church History*, 2nd rev. ed. (Nairobi: Pauline Publications, 1998).

American missionaries in Africa were disproportionately drawn from the fundamentalist and evangelical churches, and many of them were associated with "faith missions" that required missionaries to raise their own support from friends and family members rather than receive a fixed salary from a denomination. After being introduced to Christianity by such intensely devoted missionaries, many African Christians came to assume that zeal and fervency were part of the normal Christian experience.

While Christianity flourished in Africa, partly because of the work and dedication of all these Western missionaries, Christianity would never have succeeded as it has if Africans themselves had not taken up the work of spreading the gospel. The names of most of the thousands of African evangelists who crisscrossed the continent during these years have been forgotten because they were not included in written records, but their impact was tremendous.

One of the most remarkable of these individuals, and one of the few known by name, was William Wade Harris. Harris was born and reared in Liberia and converted to Christianity as a young adult. Drawn toward politics, he was arrested and imprisoned by the colonial government. He said that while he was in jail he was visited by the angel Gabriel, who summoned him to be a prophet. Released from prison in 1910, Harris began preaching the gospel up and down the African coast between Ghana and Sierra Leone. A powerful preacher and phenomenal healer, all he carried on his journeys was a Bible, a cross, a rattle (to signal his presence), and a bowl (for baptisms). He was adamantly opposed to African traditional religion, and he required converts to burn their fetishes and to become monogamous. Harris is credited with converting one hundred thousand Africans to Christianity. He could easily have started his own new church, but he insisted that his only calling was to preach the gospel. Harris told his converts that other Christian leaders would soon arrive, and they would organize churches. When Methodist missionaries came to the region a few years later, they found thousands of African Christians waiting to welcome them.

As the nineteenth century drew to a close, there were countless African preachers, prophets, teachers, and evangelists traversing the continent. Unlike Harris, many of them were eager to found their own new churches that were entirely African in origin and organization. These new African Independent or African Initiated Churches (AICs) first began to appear in South Africa in the late 1800s, and their numbers grew exponentially following the First World War. Members of these churches proclaimed a gospel of "good news" for Africans in contrast to what they viewed as the anti-African message of Christianity being spread around the continent by many Western missionaries. Missionary Christianity said that ancestors were irrelevant, that miracles

Figure 3.5. African Independent Churches: A baptism service of the Celestial Church of Christ (Benin)

rarely happened, and that dreams and visions did not matter. Many Africans discovered a very different message when they read the Bible for themselves, finding support for the acceptability of polygamy (except for bishops), the importance of saints and ancestors, the expectation that miracles were common, and the significance of dreams and visions as ways for God to communicate with individuals. After concluding that missionary Christianity was not biblical, they left the missionary churches and launched their own new, independent congregations and denominations (see fig. 3.5). By the 1960s, more than six thousand AICs had been established across the continent.[8]

The colonial era left a mixed legacy. Colonization clearly contributed to the destruction of traditional African ways of life, but Western missionaries and their African associates also built schools and hospitals, helped moderate the harshness of colonial rule, and shared the gospel with many individuals who otherwise would never have heard about Jesus. In terms of sheer numbers, the growth of Christianity was impressive. At the beginning of the colonial era, roughly 5 percent of the African population was Christian. By the time colonialism ended, almost a third of Africa's population was Christian, including 45 million Catholics, 35 million Protestants, 20 million members of the new African Independent Churches, and 20 million members of the old Orthodox churches of Egypt and Ethiopia.

Christianity in Postcolonial Africa (1960 to the Present)

The colonial era of African history ended almost as quickly as it began. World War II disrupted colonial arrangements and gave local leaders a new

8. David B. Barrett, *Schism and Renewal in Africa: An Analysis of Six Thousand Contemporary Religious Movements* (Nairobi: Oxford University Press, 1968), 265–70.

taste of freedom. When the war was over, there was no going back to the old ways of colonial rule. Though most of the colonial powers initially resisted the idea of independence, they quickly relented because the direct and indirect costs of trying to reimpose colonial rule were simply too high. In the year 1960 alone, sixteen African countries claimed their independence, and by 1970 the African map was beginning to look largely the same as it does today.

Political independence was accompanied by a new blossoming of spiritual independence as well. African Christianity as a whole, and not only the AIC movement, was quickly becoming thoroughly African in leadership, content, and style. Most American and European missionaries fled Africa during World War II, and this gave local African Christians a chance to step into vacant leadership positions. When missionaries returned after the war, many discovered that "their" churches were no longer the same. Under African leadership, they had grown substantially and many had shifted their emphasis away from Western-style reason and orderliness toward a more free-wheeling focus on the Spirit. Missionaries were divided about how to respond. Some tried to regain control, but others welcomed the changes and partnered with African leaders as equals.

A new dynamic was created in 1971, when John Gatu, general secretary of the Presbyterian Church in East Africa, called for an immediate moratorium on all missionary activity in Africa. Gatu said a full stoppage of all missionary activity was needed in order to end the "structures of . . . spiritual exploitation" that were inherent in the missionary venture.[9] Only a few Western churches and mission organizations agreed to suspend operations, and the majority of African Christians also rejected the idea of a complete halt to missionary activity. Nonetheless, Gatu's call for a moratorium was a turning point in the history of African Christianity, signaling that the rules of the game had changed. African Christians were no longer content to be tutored by the West. They would decide for themselves what the future of African Christianity would be.

Ecclesiastical independence was also redefined during these years. In the nineteenth century, Henry Venn had framed independence in terms of three "selfs": self-governing, self-supporting, and self-propagating. Now a fourth self was added to the mix: self-theologizing. African Christians were developing their own fresh articulations of Christianity in the context of African life and culture. The Jesuit Nigerian theologian Agbonkhianmeghe E. Orabator says, "Doing

---

9. Bengt Sundkler and Christopher Steed, *A History of Christianity in Africa* (Cambridge: Cambridge University Press, 2000), 1027–28.

theology is not an exercise in conceptual weightlessness."[10] Every theology comes from somewhere, and a new kind of Christianity was emerging within Africa. Religious scholars such as Lamin Sanneh, a prominent Roman Catholic theologian from Gambia, have noted that Christianity has succeeded best in places where "indigenous religions were strongest, not weakest, suggesting a degree of indigenous compatibility with the gospel."[11] Most African Christians now assume that God has continually been speaking to Africans, first through the ancestors, then through the Bible, and always through the Holy Spirit. Even relatively conservative evangelical theologians such as the late Kwame Bediako, a Presbyterian from Ghana, agreed that "space has to be made for a positive pre-Christian religious heritage in the African Christian consciousness."[12]

Pentecostalism has flourished in postcolonial Africa.[13] In 1970, perhaps 15 percent of the Christian population in Africa was Pentecostal or Spirit-centered. Today, about 35 percent of African Christians are Pentecostal, though that number may be too low given that more than 80 percent of Africa's Christians believe in miracles, a key marker of Pentecostal faith. As Pentecostalism has grown in popularity, its emphases have changed. Fifty years ago, Pentecostal preaching focused on the gifts of the Spirit, including speaking in tongues, healing, and prophecy. Today, it is much more common to hear messages about prosperity and about deliverance from demonic oppression so people can succeed at claiming all the blessings God has promised.

This "word of faith" style of Pentecostalism can be attributed in part to non-African preachers such as the German evangelist Reinhardt Bonnke (Christ for All Nations) and the American preacher Kenneth Hagin (Rhema Church), but its success is also due to influential African Christian leaders such as Mensa Otabil, Nicholas Duncan-Williams, and Benson Idahosa, who are as Afrocentric as they are Pentecostal. Some of Africa's Pentecostal-style churches have developed wide-ranging international ministries. Two groups, the Nigerian-based Redeemed Christian Church of God and the Living Faith Church (also known as the Winners' Chapel), for example, have established congregations all over Africa and also in the United States and the United Kingdom.

The twentieth century has been a success story for Christianity in Africa (see fig. 3.6). In the early twentieth century, about 10 percent of the African

---

10. Agbonkhianmeghe E. Orabator, *Theology Brewed in an African Pot* (Maryknoll, NY: Orbis, 2008), 153.

11. Lamin Sanneh, *Whose Religion Is Christianity? The Gospel beyond the West* (Grand Rapids: Eerdmans, 2003), 18, 32.

12. Kwame Bediako, *Christianity in Africa: The Renewal of a Non-Western Religion* (Maryknoll, NY: Orbis, 1995), 260.

13. See Ogbu Kalu, *African Pentecostalism: An Introduction* (New York: Oxford University Press, 2008).

population was Christian, 30 percent was Muslim, and 60 percent still followed traditional African religion. Today, 50 percent of the African population is Christian, 42 percent is Muslim, and only 8 percent would identify themselves as followers of African traditional religion (though this number does not reflect the large percentage of the Christian and Muslim populations who still engage in traditional religious practices from time to time). Today, Christianity is leveling off as a percentage of the continent's population (around 50 percent), but the number of Christians in Africa is still growing rapidly because of high birth rates (the highest in the world).

Figure 3.6
Religions as Percentage of Total African Population, 1900 to Present

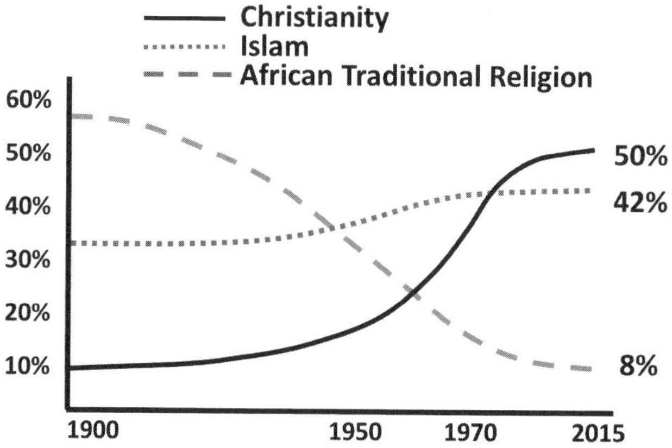

Contemporary African Christianity

Contemporary Africa is a huge continent with immense internal diversity. This section begins with a high-altitude overview of the current status of religions across the region, including relationships between Christians and Muslims. This is followed by a discussion of religious violence, including Christian-versus-Christian violence. Finally, the spectrum of individual religious beliefs and practices in African Christianity today is summarized.

Africa's Religious Geography

Religion divides contemporary Africa into two distinct geographic regions. The northern half of the continent is predominantly Muslim, as it has been for centuries, and the south is now solidly Christian. Christian-Muslim tensions often run high along the tenth parallel where these two faiths meet (see fig. 3.7).[14] The experience of Christians living south of the tenth parallel is very different from those living in the Muslim-dominated north.

Figure 3.7
Map of Christianity in Contemporary Africa

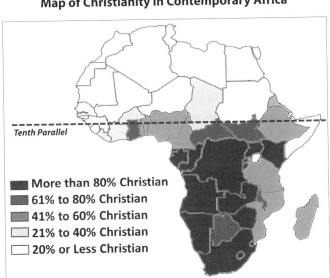

In most of sub-Saharan Africa, Christians and Muslims usually get along quite well. Most Christians in the southern half of Africa think Muslims are generally honest, devout, moral, tolerant, and generous, and a majority of Muslims in this region have similarly favorable attitudes about Christians. About half of Christians in sub-Saharan Africa say they trust Muslims, and half of Muslims say they trust Christians. When asked if they think the influence of Christianity is growing in their country, about half the Muslim population and three-quarters of the Christian population agree, and similar proportions of Muslims and Christians say this is a good development. If the question is reversed, inquiring about the increasing prominence of Islam in their countries, Christians and Muslims generally agree that Islam is also becoming more influential and most believe this is good as well. About half of the members of each community agree that Christianity and Islam have

14. See Eliza Griswold, *The Tenth Parallel: Dispatches from the Fault Line between Christianity and Islam* (New York: Farrar, Straus and Giroux, 2010).

a lot in common, but the other half believe that the two religions are very different.[15]

In sub-Saharan Africa, both Christians and Muslims would like their own religious values to be more influential in the laws and public policies of the nations in which they live. Roughly half of African Christians think the Bible should dictate the law of the land, and about the same percentage of Muslims think *Sharia* law should govern public life. Christians and Muslims think differently about punishments for crime. Half of Muslims think corporal punishment, such as whippings and hand amputations, are reasonable punishments for theft, but only 20 percent of Christians agree. Forty percent of Muslims consider stoning to be an appropriate penalty for adultery, compared to only 10 percent of Christians. One-third of sub-Saharan Muslims believe the death penalty should be imposed on anyone who leaves the Muslim religion, while almost all Christians are opposed to coercion of any kind in matters of faith. Despite these differences, most Christians and most Muslims say they are treated fairly by their governments and that they are "very free" to practice their own religion as they please. Most also say they are worried about the influence of extremist religious groups, and both Christians and Muslims express more concern about Muslim extremists than Christian extremists. A majority of Christians and Muslims agree that violence is never acceptable, even when members of religious groups are attacked or their religion is mocked.

Muslim-Christian relationships in sub-Saharan Africa raise hope that Christians and Muslims can live peaceably together, but the situation along the northern coast of the continent provides less room for optimism. Over the last hundred years, the Christian population in North Africa has dwindled from very small to almost nonexistent. Christians now make up less than half of one percent of the populations of Algeria, Libya, Mauritania, Morocco, Niger, and Tunisia. The only significant exception is Egypt, where the Coptic Christian community still accounts for approximately 10 percent of the population.

Persecution of Christians in North Africa has become routine. The Arab spring that began in December 2010 raised hopes that more democracy in the region would result in more religious freedom for Christians, but this has generally not been the case. Reports about Christian persecution have instead increased. Although there have been some positive accounts of Christian-Muslim

---

15. Data in this paragraph and the next two are drawn from *Tolerance and Tension: Islam and Christianity in Sub-Saharan Africa* (Washington, DC: Pew Forum on Religion and Public Life, 2010).

friendship—especially in Egypt, where Muslims have gone out of their way to protect their Christian neighbors—the simple fact that Christians need protection is evidence of how tenuous their lives are.

Religious Violence

The history of Africa is filled with stories of suffering and oppression. The violence of slavery gave way to the violence of the colonial system, and conflict has continued in independent Africa. Some blame this continuing violence on the weak institutional infrastructure of many African countries. The Ugandan theologian Emmanuel Katongole suggests instead that the many conflicts that have affected the continent stem from the destructive stories Africans embraced about themselves during the years of European colonial rule.[16] Whatever the explanation, millions of people have lost their lives in recent years, and millions more have been dislodged from their homes and communities, far more than on any other continent. The number of nations involved in violent conflict sometime during the last twenty-five years is stunning (see fig. 3.8). In Africa today, more than three million refugees have fled across international borders seeking safety, and at least ten million internally displaced persons have been forced to relocate involuntarily within their own countries.[17]

Figure 3.8
African Nations Experiencing Significant Conflict and Violence 1990–2015 Shown in Gray

Christians have participated in almost all these conflicts, as both aggressors and victims. The genocide in Rwanda represents the extreme case. Between April 7 and July 4, 1994, Hutu Christian Rwandans engaged in a massive coordinated slaughter of Tutsi Christian Rwandans. During those one hundred days, eight hundred thousand people were killed. This was not an impersonal genocide carried out by strangers using advanced weaponry. Neighbors hacked neighbors to death with machetes. People who had lived together for decades,

16. Emmanuel Katongole, *The Sacrifice of Africa: A Political Theology for Africa* (Grand Rapids: Eerdmans, 2010).

17. See the UNHCR (United Nations High Commissioner for Refugees) website and *Global Overview 2012: People by Conflict and Violence* (Geneva: Internal Displacement Monitoring Center, Norwegian Refugee Council, 2012), 10, 15–33.

who had done business with one another, and who had watched one another's children grow up suddenly became their neighbors' executioners, wielding their blades as Christians, killing other followers of Jesus.

The causes of the Rwandan genocide were rooted in the colonial era, when the Germans and later the Belgians joined hands with the Tutsi royal court to subjugate the country. The Tutsis were a minority in the country, but their alliance with the colonial powers allowed them to enjoy greater wealth and higher social standing than their Hutu neighbors. Mutara III, who ruled 1931–1959, was the first Tutsi king formally to convert to Catholicism, and in 1954 he dedicated the nation to Christ the King. As Catholic missionaries introduced new ideas about social justice to Rwanda, King Mutara redistributed some lands and cattle to Hutus, but these actions were not sufficient to squelch concerns about social justice. A Hutu emancipation movement coalesced in the late 1950s, and Hutus took control of the government in the early 1960s, when the country gained independence and became a democracy.

By 1990, 90 percent of Rwandans were Christian, and Christian ideas and values permeated public discourse. But Hutu-Tutsi tensions continued to simmer even as the Christian population of Rwanda grew. When the Hutu president of Rwanda was killed in a plane crash in 1994, no one knew who to blame, but Hutus held Tutsis liable. Soon the word went out to kill the "cockroaches," a term Hutus used derogatorily to refer to Tutsis. Some pastors, priests, and nuns aided the assassins, and more than 10 percent of the victims were murdered inside a church (see fig. 3.9).[18] (By contrast, the Muslim community was the safest place to be, and no one was killed in a mosque. Partly because of this, Islam has been growing significantly in Rwanda ever since the genocide.) The killing did not end until the Rwandan Patriotic Front, under the leadership of Tutsi commander Paul Kagame, finally captured the capital city of Kigali in July. In 2000, Kagame was elected president of the country, and he still holds that office today.

In May 1994, while the genocide was still underway, Pope John Paul II spoke bluntly about the travesty, "This is an out-and-out genocide for which unfortunately even Catholics are responsible. . . . They are bringing the country to the brink of the abyss. Everyone must answer for their crimes to history, and, indeed, to God. Enough bloodshed! God expects a moral renewal from all Rwandans . . . and the courage of forgiveness and brotherhood."[19] In the intervening years, Rwanda has slowly recovered. Memories of the genocide

18. Carol Rittner, John K. Roth, and Wendy Whitworth, eds., *Genocide in Rwanda: Complicity of the Churches?* (St. Paul: Paragon, 2004), 181.

19. Quoted in ibid., 80.

Figure 3.9. Ntrama Church (Bugesera District, Rwanda), one of many Rwandan churches where killings occurred

are gradually fading, and life looks relatively normal on the surface. The churches are flourishing. Rwandan Anglicans have assumed a leadership role within the global Anglican Communion, and the Marian shrine at Kibeho, the site of several apparitions of Mary in the early 1980s, attracts visitors from all around the world. But beneath the surface, plenty of pain, prejudice, and disillusionment linger. Many Rwandans struggle to comprehend how something so horrible could have happened inside their almost entirely Christian country.

The violence of the genocide in Rwanda soon spread to neighboring countries. Zaire, which was becoming increasingly unstable, was invaded by Rwanda in 1996. Zaire's dictator president Mobutu Sésé Seko was driven from office and replaced by the rebel leader Laurent-Désiré Kabila, who changed the country's name to the Democratic Republic of the Congo (DRC). Kabila initially had difficulty consolidating power, and other regional forces became involved in the Second Congo War, which lasted from 1998 to 2003. Kabila was assassinated by a bodyguard in 2001, and his son, Joseph, assumed leadership. Today the eastern region of the DRC is still unstable, and more than five million people have died so far. All of this is taking place in a country that is even more solidly Christian (close to 95 percent of the population) than Rwanda.

Christianity obviously does not prevent social violence. Europe, which is just as heavily Christian as the DRC, instigated two world wars during the last century. Still, it is disheartening that so much blood is being shed in a country that is supposedly Christian. It is also troubling that Christian leaders have often been specially targeted for killing because they have tried to stand above the fray. In the DRC, trying to be neutral is dangerous, and it is even more hazardous to attempt peacemaking. All of this has made the DRC one of the most dangerous places in the world to be a Christian, especially for those who are concerned about issues of peace and justice. This is not a situation where Christians are being persecuted by others; it is Christians who are killing other Christians.[20]

Christian Beliefs and Practices

Africa as a whole is an incredibly religious place. Almost everyone (99 percent) believes in God, and about a third of all Africans (not just Christians) say they have received a direct revelation from God. Half also say they have received a definite answer to prayer. More than 50 percent of all Africans say they have witnessed divine healing, and about two-thirds say they believe God will grant health and wealth to those who have enough faith to claim them. A staggering 84 percent of Africans say that religion is *very important* in their lives. This stands in sharp contrast to Europe, where only 21 percent say that religion is very important, and it is significantly higher than both North America (57 percent) and Latin America (66 percent).[21]

About 80 percent of African Christians attend worship at least once a week, and many attend more frequently. This is double the reported attendance of North American Christians, which itself is high compared to the rates in the rest of the world. More than half of African Christians say they have been born again, and most believe the Bible should be interpreted "literally word for word." African Christianity is known worldwide for its fervency in worship and for its devotion to Christ. Given these characteristics, many Christians in the West have concluded that African Christianity is basically evangelical. But attaching this label to African Christianity does not make sense. The views of African Christians do not fit neatly into Western Christian religious categories, and calling African Christians evangelicals gets as much wrong as it gets right. Many African Christians would say it is better

---

20. See John L. Allen Jr., *The Global War on Christians: Dispatches from the Front Lines of Anti-Christian Persecution* (New York: Image, 2013), 50–53.

21. The percentages here and in the following paragraphs are all drawn from *Tolerance and Tension*.

to view the continent as a kind of spiritual laboratory where Christianity is slowly being stripped of its Western biases and renewed as a non-Western religion. This theological experiment is still underway, and it is premature to make predictions about how it will end.

The wide range of African Christian beliefs as they exist today was documented by the Pew Forum on Religion and Public Life in a large 2010 survey. Pew researchers found that the overwhelming majority of African Christians believe in God, but they also discovered that 20–30 percent of African Christians think of God as an impersonal force rather than as a personal being. Responses to this question varied significantly from country to country. In Liberia, more than half of Christians think God is impersonal; in Zambia, this is true of only 12 percent of Christians. Other questions elicited similarly unexpected and regionally diverse perspectives. The vast majority of African Christians believe that both abortion and homosexuality are wrong, and about three-quarters believe polygamy is wrong as well. But 15–20 percent of African Christians think polygamy quite acceptable, including 45 percent of the Christians in Chad. More than half of African Christians approve of women becoming pastors or priests, but nearly half disagree. About half say that "many religions can lead to eternal life." About one-third of the Christians in Mozambique and Uganda have traditional African sacred objects in their homes, and fully half of the Christians in South Africa have participated in traditional African religious ceremonies and believe sacrifices to the spirits or ancestors can protect them. Most Christians in Africa do not believe in witches, but 94 percent of Tanzanian Christians do. About half of the Christians in Africa believe people can be cursed by an "evil eye," and 40 percent believe in reincarnation.

This distinctively African blend of Christian faith and practice cannot be called conservative or evangelical or orthodox or liberal. African Christianity has its own unique profile—or, more accurately, profiles—that cannot be shoehorned into Western categories. Theology itself is construed differently. Generally speaking, African Christians view the Western theological goal of formulating abstract definitions of Christian truth for all people in all times and places to be both unachievable and spiritually wrongheaded. In Africa, the point of theology is not to talk about God or Christian truth in the abstract, as if God could be subject to human scrutiny or as if the theology had nothing to do with the lived experience of human beings. Theology in Africa is practical. It is undertaken for the purpose of helping Christians to reflect on who they are called to be as followers of Jesus in the unique cultural contexts where God has placed them.

African Theology and the Concept of *Ubuntu*

If there is one term that captures the distinctively African, and yet universally Christian, cultural theology that has emerged in Africa, it is the word *ubuntu*. *Ubuntu* refers to the interconnectedness of all people, and it serves simultaneously as a statement of fact and as a moral ideal. *Ubuntu* describes all human beings as dependent on and responsible for one another. In the words of the well-known South African theologian and Anglican archbishop Desmond Tutu, *ubuntu* is part of "the very essence of being human." It underscores the fact that "my humanity is caught up, is inextricably bound up, in yours."[22]

The word *ubuntu* is not used everywhere in Africa, but the concept is pervasive, and the meaning is always the same: people were created to live in community with one another. This African notion of being rooted in community is foreign to many of those who can be described by the acronym WEIRD: Western, Educated, Industrialized, Rich, and Democratic. "WEIRD" people tend to see themselves as self-sufficient and independent. To most Africans, such "WEIRD" thinking is simply incomprehensible. How could anyone fail to see that all living things, not just humans, are interconnected? How could anyone understand themselves apart from their relations with others?

In the West, books about Christian spirituality often have cover images that depict a single individual in prayer or a peaceful landscape devoid of any human presence at all—a mountain, a forest, or a meadow of tall grass—and these books generally offer advice about an individual's relationship with God in isolation from all others. Such books do not appeal to most Africans. In Africa, Christianity is about the community, not the individual. To be an African Christian is to be enveloped in relations with others, and spirituality happens in the midst of that communal experience of life. What happens to one person happens to all. Joys and sorrows, hopes and fears, are experienced by everyone together. Worship is the joyful, exuberant, full-bodied celebration of God and God's presence within the community of believers on Earth.

The strength of this distinctively African sense of human connectedness is accompanied by the limitation that a robust communal identity can sometimes blind individuals to their shared humanity with members of other groups or tribes. The Rwandan genocide is the most horrific example of this, but there are many other places in Africa where tribal identities and tribal animosities continue to undercut any broader sense of connection with others, even other Christians. Unquestionably, *ubuntu* is dangerous when it is applied to only

22. Desmond Tutu, *No Future without Forgiveness* (New York: Doubleday, 1999), 31.

one social group or community and all others are demonized as outsiders. But when *ubuntu* is universalized to include all of humanity—which is the more typically African way of understanding the term—then it has enormous potential to positively shape Christian life and thought. Three specific theological expressions of *ubuntu* will be discussed in the following pages: *reconciliation, communion with the ancestors,* and the *African vision of God* as the Maker and Guardian of everyone and all creation.

Reconciliation

Concerns about reconciliation resonate across the African continent, but the ideal of reconciliation is especially important in South Africa because of its long history of racism. Racism is deeply rooted in the South African past, but it was not codified into formal public policy until 1948 when apartheid became the law of the land. The word *apartheid* means "separation" or "apartness," and it applied the principle of separateness to every dimension of life, including housing, governance, public spaces, and even religion. What made apartheid a distinctively Christian concern was not simply the injustice of the system but that supporters of apartheid declared the policy to be biblical. Church leaders said that God had created different races for a reason, so it was the responsibility of Christians to maintain those differences. One statement from the Reformed Church in the Transvaal, issued in 1951, states bluntly, "According to the Word of God the idea that Christianity ought to diminish differences in race, nation, and status is most certainly wrong."[23]

The struggle to end apartheid was protracted and bloody, involving both political and religious battles. The religious issue was largely settled in 1982 when the World Alliance of Reformed Churches (WARC) declared it was a heresy to say apartheid was God's will for the world. Apartheid itself ended in 1990 when Nelson Mandela, the leader of the African National Congress (the main anti-apartheid organization), was released from jail after twenty-seven years behind bars. Four years later, Mandela was elected president of the new multiracial Republic of South Africa.

While the end result was successful, the process of abolishing apartheid involved decades of violence. Mandela knew the country needed to heal, and he knew that political reform alone would not be sufficiently restorative. Mandela asked his friend Desmond Tutu, the Anglican archbishop of South Africa (see fig. 3.10), to help with the healing process. Together, they created a Truth and

23. Klaus Koschorke, Frieder Ludwig, and Mariano Delgado, eds., *A History of Christianity in Asia, Africa, and Latin America, 1450–1990: A Documentary Sourcebook* (Grand Rapids: Eerdmans, 2007), 262.

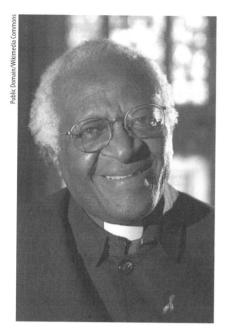

Public Domain/Wikimedia Commons

Figure 3.10. Desmond Tutu, head of the South African Truth and Reconciliation Commission

Reconciliation Commission (TRC) in 1996. Led by Tutu, the TRC examined the violations of human rights that had occurred during apartheid, with the aim of restoring the dignity of victims and providing a pathway to amnesty for those who confessed their crimes before the Commission.

The foundational assumption of the TRC was *ubuntu*, that every human life has value and that all human beings are interconnected. Tutu repeatedly reminded other members of the Commission that even the worst offenders were people, not monsters or demons, and that all people are "children of God with the capacity to repent . . . [and] change." The first step toward change was confession, being honest with oneself and others about what had occurred. Truth was the key—reconciliation is impossible apart from the truth—and sometimes Tutu literally begged individuals who came before the Commission to be honest about their actions, however awful they may have been. Once the truth was heard, it became the burden of victims to try to forgive. This was much more difficult than confessing faults, but Tutu repeatedly argued that there was no other way forward. In his words, there is "no future without forgiveness" (see textbox, African Theology: Desmond Tutu).

The ground rules of the TRC—truthful confession, sorrowful repentance, and gracious forgiveness—will sound familiar to most Christians. They parallel New Testament admonitions about how people ought to behave when relationships go awry. But applying those principles to national reconciliation—even in a country where more than 80 percent of the population is Christian—is audacious. It is difficult to quantify how well the TRC's bold experiment succeeded in its mission, because reconciliation is hard to observe and even harder to measure. But there is no reason to doubt that the TRC opened new space for reconciliation and that the nation as a whole benefitted greatly from its work.

Reconciliation in other African nations has taken different forms. One of the most interesting examples comes from the West African country of Liberia, where the work of reconciliation began as a grassroots movement.

African Theology: Desmond Tutu

Truth and Reconciliation: Making the Future Possible

Desmond Tutu is a bishop in the South African Anglican Church. He served as the first black archbishop of Cape Town and as general secretary of the South African Council of Churches during the years when the fight to end apartheid was at its most heated. Tutu received the Nobel Peace Prize in 1984 in recognition of his peacemaking skills and his work against apartheid. In this excerpt, Tutu reflects on his experience as chair of the Truth and Reconciliation Commission (TRC) in the years following the end of apartheid.

> As I listened in the TRC to the stories of perpetrators of human rights violations, I realized how each of us has this capacity for the most awful evil—every one of us. None of us could predict that if we had been subjected to the same influences, the same conditioning, we would not have turned out like these perpetrators. This is not to condone or excuse what they did. It is to be filled more and more with the compassion of God, looking on and weeping that one of His beloved had come to such a sad pass. . . .
>
> And, mercifully and wonderfully, as I listened to the stories of the victims I marveled at their magnanimity, that after so much suffering, instead of lusting for revenge, they had this extraordinary willingness to forgive. . . .
>
> There is a movement, not easily discernible, at the heart of things to reverse the awful centrifugal forces of alienation, brokenness, division, hostility, and disharmony. God has set in motion a centripetal process, a moving toward the center, toward unity, harmony, goodness, peace, and justice. . . . [Ultimately] there are no aliens, all belong in the one family, God's family, the human family. . . .
>
> Forgiving and being reconciled are not about pretending that things are other than they are. It is not patting one another on the back and turning a blind eye to the wrong. True reconciliation exposes the awfulness, the abuse, the pain, the degradation, the truth. . . . True forgiveness deals with the past, all of the past, to make the future possible.*

* Desmond Tutu, *No Future without Forgiveness* (New York: Doubleday, 1999), 85–86, 265, 270, 279.

The key activists were Christian and Muslim women working together to end a war and to reestablish a national sense of community and mutual care. Liberia had been involved in a civil war for more than a decade when Charles Taylor, a former warlord, came to power and set himself up as president of the country. His rivals were incensed and continued fighting. Warfare in Liberia was vicious and often unfocused, with contending "armies" comprised largely of children who had been abducted from their families and forced to become soldiers. Kept high on drugs and alcohol, boys with guns were looting, killing, and raping across the nation.

The women of Liberia eventually decided this violence and lawlessness had to stop. A Christian laywoman named Leymah Gbowee emerged as the leader. She was motivated to action by a dream in which God told her to "gather the women and pray for peace."[24] It is significant but not surprising that this movement was led and developed by women. Christianity in Africa is largely a female enterprise. In most churches on Sunday morning, women outnumber men by two or three or sometimes ten or twenty to one. The Christianity of African women is not usually concerned with fine points of theology. They do not care if the word *filioque* is included in the Nicaean Creed or not, and they don't have strong feelings about whether Calvinism or Arminianism is right. What does grab their attention is the nitty-gritty concerns of life: caring for children and parents, making sure everyone is fed, tending the sick, and calming community disputes. Reflecting on these concerns—trying to figure out how to act effectively as followers of Jesus—requires just as much insight and intelligence as writing a PhD dissertation on systematic theology, but it has a very different focus. It was this kind of strategic theological thinking that drove Gbowee and her colleagues to organize against the war in Liberia.

Christians make up more than half of Liberia's population, and the reform movement was initially organized through churches. Muslim women soon joined their Christian sisters because, as they said, bullets do not care about a person's religion. The women of Liberia knew the violence was senseless, and it was destroying every shred of decency in the country. Their work was not easy, but the women of Liberia persisted and eventually forced the men of Liberia to the bargaining table. The fighting stopped, Charles Taylor was deposed, and a woman, Ellen Johnson Sirleaf, was elected president in his place.

For the Christian and Muslim women of Liberia, peace meant not merely the absence of war but also reconciliation: the restoration of healthy relationships between people—between members of warring groups, between perpetrators and victims, between Christians and Muslims, and between men and women. Gbowee originally developed her perspective working with child soldiers, when she observed that war wounds and lost limbs were only part of the challenge. The deeper issue focused on *ubuntu*, on helping these young men to regain their souls and reintegrating them into the larger community. Justice—in the sense of punishing the perpetrators for the crimes they had committed, which would have been the inclination in the West—was set aside as socially dysfunctional. It would only have perpetuated conflict and violence rather than healing and rebuilding respectful relationships with others.

24. See Leymah Gbowee, *Mighty Be Our Powers: How Sisterhood, Prayer, and Sex Changed a Nation at War* (New York: Beast Books, 2011).

The Ancestors

Most Africans assume that life does not end with death. Death is seen as a transition from the world of the living to the realm of the ancestors. These two realms intersect in ways that allow the ancestors to continue to play a role in the world of the living. They remain part of the network of human interrelations that defines *ubuntu*. Africans often say "the dead are not dead," and recently deceased relatives are sometimes referred to as "living-dead." The living dead can be sources of comfort or fear. People who were evil in life remain evil in death, and they can do great harm to the living, making people sick, ruining crops, causing miscarriages, and more. Even people who lived relatively good lives while physically present on earth need to be honored appropriately in death so that they will not wreak havoc on the living.

Fortunately, most of the dead do not remain connected to this world forever. Eventually they lose interest and migrate away. But some of the living dead stay on to become ancestors. The deceased who receive the privilege of becoming ancestors are people who lived their lives well during their days on earth, who were morally upright, and who strengthened their families and communities. These ancestors are not beings who must be placated until they find rest in the afterlife and stop bothering the living. Instead, they are seen as family members who continue to guide and protect their descendants in the present. For the most part, one's ancestors are limited to people with whom one is related by blood, but some individuals attain such a remarkable level of good character and positive influence while they are alive that they become universal ancestors for everyone after they die. This is the case, for example, with Nelson Mandela, whom many Africans now consider an ancestor, a person who was powerful but compassionate in life and who remains a source of wisdom and inspiration in death. Many Africans, including Christians, venerate their human ancestors and look to them for guidance, which they receive through dreams or divination. Even when they have been steeped in Western ways of Christian thought and life, African Christians often continue to feel the presence of the ancestors. Gabriel Setiloane, a Methodist theologian from Botswana, explains,

> Ah, . . . yes . . . it is true.
> They are very present with us
> The dead are not dead; they are ever near us;
> Approving and disapproving all our actions,
> They chide us when we go wrong,
> Bless us and sustain us for good deeds done,

For kindness shown, and strangers made to feel at home.
They increase our store, and punish our pride.[25]

Setiloane's description of experiencing the ancestors points toward another role of the ancestors, that of helping Africans negotiate the moral complexities of life. Western Christians think of morality in terms of abstract rules and principles of conduct that apply similarly to all people in all situations, such as the imperatives not to lie and not to steal. While recognizing the importance of such guidelines, Africans believe that human relations are too complicated to be captured by any simple list of rules. Living properly and well requires insight, nuance, wisdom, patience, caution, and even cleverness. There are times when not telling the truth is necessary for maintaining the health of a given community. There are times when taking something from another is necessary for some greater good. Morality is something that must be learned by experience, not by rote formula. The ancestors are people who lived through social quandaries and negotiated them well. People who are still on this side of death can draw on the wisdom and guidance of the ancestors as they navigate the moral and relational complexities of life.

African churches have responded in different ways to the continuing role of the ancestors in Christian faith and life. In general, the African Initiated Churches and the Catholic Church have been willing to engage the issue. They typically acknowledge the reality of ancestors, and they have developed guidelines regarding what is allowable for Christians and what is not. Many Catholics, in particular, blend the notion of the ancestors into church teaching about the communion of the saints: that all Christians living and dead are part of one body in Christ and are able to offer aid and assistance to each other (see textbox, African Theology: Agbonkhianmeghe E. Orobator). Protestant and Pentecostal churches have generally been less accommodating of the ancestors. They either remain silent on the topic, or they claim that the so-called ancestors are in reality evil spirits sent to woo Christians away from reliance on God alone. But regardless of church policies and teachings, many Christians continue to honor the ancestors.

Some African theologians are now seeking to incorporate the ancestors more fully into their thinking. The New Testament book of Hebrews is frequently quoted: "In the past God spoke to our ancestors through the prophets at many times and in various ways" (1:1). African Christians believe God did

25. Gabriel M. Setiloane, "How the Traditional World-View Persists in the Christianity of the Sotho-Tswana," in *Christianity in Independent Africa*, ed. Edward Fashole-Luke (Bloomington: Indiana University Press, 1978), 407.

African Theology: Agbonkhianmeghe E. Orobator

Living with the Ancestors: The Power of the Resurrection

Agbonkhianmeghe E. Orobator is a Nigerian Catholic priest and the provincial superior of the Eastern Africa Province of the Society of Jesus (Jesuits). He also serves on the faculty of the Hekima College Jesuit School of Theology in Nairobi, Kenya, on the board of the Zaidi Centre for Lay Spirituality, and on the editorial board of the *Journal of Religion in Africa*. In this reading, he explains how the ancestors are understood in African traditional religion and in his own Catholic faith.

> As an African Christian, when I profess faith in the communion of saints and the resurrection of the dead, my creed finds deep resonance in my traditional beliefs and understandings of the meaning of life and death. . . .
>
> For many African people, life in the hereafter as an ancestor is not an easy matter. Oftentimes there is a trial, or an ordeal that the departed person has to undergo in order to join the community of ancestors. . . . [As Christians], we have learned that life hereafter could also be quite trying. In fact, we commonly believe that it involves some form of judgment that will decide the ultimate fate of the dead. . . .
>
> Underneath all these practices, whether Christian or traditional African, lies an important expression of faith in the power of the resurrection. In other words, these practices embody our deep belief in the truth that death does not end it all; death does not have the final word on life. . . . Perhaps even deeper lies the belief that Christianity and African religion share: that the care is mutual. We care for our departed ancestors by keeping them warm, clothed, and fed—with libations and ritual offerings. In return, our ancestors watch over us—with intercessions and protection. The prayers that we offer for the living dead warm their resting place and give them a hand in the journey to eternal life. Their ongoing care for us keeps us united with them in one communion of the living and the dead, raised to life by the life-giving resurrection of Jesus Christ.*

---

* Agbonkhianmeghe E. Orobator, *Theology Brewed in an African Pot* (Maryknoll, NY: Orbis, 2008), 111, 115–16.

indeed speak to their ancestors, and they believe their ancestors knew God to some degree even before any Christian missionaries arrived. Bénèzet Bujo, a Congolese Catholic theologian, has suggested that Christ should be seen as savior of all humankind, both the living and the dead. He explains, "Africans who live in close communion with their ancestors should not think that becoming a Christian means abandoning the ancestors. Christ died for the virtuous ancestors too, and they live in communion with him."[26] Christians in the West

---

26. Bénèzet Bujo, *African Theology in Its Social Context* (Nairobi: Pauline, 1992), 129.

rarely worry about the salvation of their dead ancestors, but Christians in Africa and Asia do, and their ruminations on the topic may help Christians in the West gain a new sense of how deep, rich, and intergenerational the Christian communion of saints may be. For Africans, the notion of *ubuntu* applies to both the living and the dead.

The God of Everyone and All Creation

Most Africans are thoroughly monotheistic, believing in one Creator God who is the God of everyone and everything. Every living entity on the planet has its source of life in God. This means that *ubuntu* is not merely a human concern; it includes all of creation. How people treat one other and treat the planet shapes and mirrors the relationship of humans with God. Many indigenous groups around the world echo this same sentiment, but their voices have been muted in Asia and the Americas because most of these groups have been conquered and culturally marginalized. In Africa, this ancient understanding of God's universality and omnipresence remains strong (see textbox, African Theology: Mercy Amba Oduyoye).

God, as perceived by Africans, cannot be corralled into any one creed or controlled by any one community, not even the Christian community. Most African Christians, therefore, assume that Christians and Muslims worship the same God. Different individuals and groups worship God in different ways, but there is only one high God who rules over all. To African Christians, the use of a possessive pronoun when talking about God is incomprehensible. To refer to God as *my* God or *our* God is nonsense because God cannot be owned. God is the God of everyone.

In traditional African religion, God is the source and creator of all that exists. In many cultures, God is considered to be so elevated above the world that God cannot be approached directly by humans. A person can interact with God only through intermediary spirits and lesser deities. Christians in Africa have moderated this sense of distance. For them, God is the almighty creator and also the "greatest of friends," the "Father of laughter," the "mantle which covers us," and the "great nursing mother." Africans glory in giving God many different names, and each name reveals something special and wonderful about God. God is called an "unbreakable stone," "consoler and comforter," "watcher of everything who is not surprised by anything," "drummer of life," "the one who sees both the inside and the outside," and "the one we meet everywhere."[27]

---

27. Agbonkhianmeghe E. Orobator, *Theology Brewed in an African Pot* (Maryknoll, NY: Orbis, 2008), 23–25.

African Theology: Mercy Amba Oduyoye

God Is Everywhere and Over Everyone

Mercy Amba Oduyoye is a Ghanaian Methodist theologian. She served as deputy general secretary of the World Council of Churches from 1987 to 1994 and founded the Circle of Concerned African Women Theologians in 1989. She is currently director of the Institute of African Women in Religion and Culture at Trinity Theological Seminary in Ghana. In this reading, she discusses the broad understanding of God that is shared by almost all Africans, whether they are Christian, Muslim, or traditional in their personal religious faith and practice.

> The fool says in his heart "There is no God." In traditional Africa there are no such fools. . . . God is experienced as an all-pervading reality. God is a constant participant in the affairs of human beings, judging by the everyday language of West Africans of my experience. A Muslim never projects into the future nor talks about the past without the qualifying phrase *insha Allah*, "by the will of Allah." Yoruba Christians will say "DV" ("God willing"), though few can tell you its Latin equivalent, and the Akan will convince you that all is "by the grace of God." . . . Th[is] belief in the all-pervading power and presence of God endows the universe with a sacramental nature. . . . As God is the foundation of life, so nothing happens without God. . . .
>
> [In Africa,] all human relations are affected by the belief that we all belong together in God. *Onyame nti* (because of God, or for the sake of God), we act or refrain from acting. God is experienced as the sole creator and sustainer of all things, who expects human beings to be to God as children and to each other as siblings, and to respect the earth and other natural phenomena. . . .
>
> God is experienced as the good parent, the grandparent Nana, a source of loving-kindness and protection. Some say Nana is father while others say Nana is mother, but the sentiment is the same: human beings experience a closeness to God which they describe in terms of motherhood and fatherhood. There was never any need to debate the existence of God. The challenge was always to discern God at work. Does God take sides? If so, whose side is God on, and why?*

* Mercy Amba Oduyoye, "The African Experience of God through the Eyes of an Akan Woman," *Cross Currents* 47, no. 4 (1997–1998), www.aril.org/african.htm.

These names for God include a striking mix of the majestic and mysterious as well as the casual and accessible. The Kenyan theologian John Mbiti prefaced his book about concepts of God in Africa by asking God to "forgive me for attempting to describe him." He explained that anything written about God is necessarily "limited, inadequate, and ridiculously anthropocentric," and it is impossible for any mere creature to comprehend the mind or being of its own creator. Even the best theologians can do nothing more than cry out to God with "the voice of a stammering child calling unto the Parent."[28] The God that African Christians know and love is a God who vastly exceeds anything any human being could ever fully comprehend or understand and who loves all of creation equally.

Summary

Christianity has been present on the African continent since the earliest years of the movement, but the modern history of African Christianity began about five hundred years ago when the Portuguese introduced the message of Jesus to the sub-Saharan region. Since then, the continent's engagement with the gospel has been filtered through a complex history of interaction with European (and North American) Christianity that was linked with slavery and colonization. Various independent churches have been established, and Africans assumed leadership of most churches in the decades following World War II. The Christian population has expanded enormously in the last fifty years, and by 2030 more Christians will live in Africa than anywhere else in the world.

African Christians speak with their own distinctive voice. At the core of that message is the notion of *ubuntu*, meaning that every human life has value and that all of humanity is interconnected. Christians everywhere refer to the body of Christ and assume that all Christians are connected through the Spirit. African Christians are now reminding Christians all around the world about the importance of these connections, not only within the church but also within human society as a whole.

28. John S. Mbiti, *Concepts of God in Africa* (London: SPCK, 1970), xiv–xv.

4

Latin America

T HE YEAR 2013 MARKED A TURNING POINT in the history of Christianity: the selection of the first non-European pope in more than twelve hundred years and the very first pope from the Americas. On March 13 of that year, Jorge Mario Bergoglio, archbishop of Buenos Aires, became Pope Francis, the 266th pope of the Roman Catholic Church. His elevation symbolizes the globalization of Christianity and marks the coming of age of Latin American Christianity. Fifty years ago, having a pope from Latin America would have been unthinkable. Today it seems, if anything, overdue.

Latin America, as defined in this chapter, includes Mexico, Central America, and the Caribbean in addition to the geographically defined continent of South America. The nations in this part of the world share many historic connections and religious similarities, and one of the key connections is that almost all of these countries have Catholic-majority populations. It is hard to overstate Catholicism's importance in the region. Latin America is home to 40 percent of the world's Catholics, and the Latin American Catholic Church has become a source of renewal and vitality within Catholicism worldwide. One respected scholar has gone so far as to credit Latin America with saving the soul of the Catholic Church worldwide.[1]

1. Edward L. Cleary, *How Latin America Saved the Soul of the Catholic Church* (Mahwah, NJ: Paulist Press, 2010).

73

Christianity in Latin America is not limited to Catholicism, however. Almost 100 million Latin American *evangélico* Christians (Protestant and Pentecostal believers) now live side by side with their Catholic neighbors, and these *evangélico* Christians are reshuffling religious dynamics in the region. *Evangélico* churches can be found almost everywhere, and *evangélico* preachers can be seen on television and heard on radio all across the continent. During the last half century, this new *evangélico* visibility has introduced an element of choice into Latin America that was missing before. Chosen faith tends to be more vibrant than inherited faith, and competition between Catholics and *evangélicos* has been a boon for Christianity in Latin America in general. A quarter of the world's Christians now live here and, with almost 90 percent of the local population identifying as Christian, it is numerically the most intensely Christian of the five major continents.

The History of Latin American Christianity

The history of Christianity in Latin America begins with violence and ends with an emphasis on liberation and justice for all. The pathway from violence to liberation has been convoluted. Despite the many similarities that connect the nations of Latin America, the region also contains a good deal of diversity. Brazil and Ecuador and Panama and Mexico are very different places. The following historical narrative tries to take that diversity into account, but the common and shared story of Christianity is the focus. It begins with an examination of the European conquest of the region and the years of colonial rule. The era of independence and its aftermath (the 1820s to 1900) is then explained, followed by sections on the twentieth century (up to the 1970s) and recent developments.

The Colonial Era (Late 1400s to 1820s)

The gospel was introduced to Latin America through "a violent evangelism" as European military personnel conquered and subjugated the New World to bring it under Christian political rule.[2] The monarchs of Spain and Portugal viewed their action in the region as a religious crusade, and the endeavor had papal approval. In 1455, Pope Nicholas V issued a document called *Romanus pontifex* that gave Catholic rulers permission to seize the lands of "pagans" and to enslave local inhabitants as long as the ultimate goal was

---

2. Luis N. Rivera, *A Violent Evangelism: The Political and Religious Conquest of the Americas* (Louisville: Westminster John Knox, 1992).

conversion. In this violent style of evangelism, savagery and sacred theology went hand in hand. Using rhetoric that most Christians today find disturbing, the sixteenth-century Spanish theologian Juan Ginés de Sepúlveda explained that "terror" could sometimes be a very useful tool in spreading "the light of truth and scatter[ing] the darkness of error."[3] His contemporary, the Spanish historian Gonzalo Fernández de Oviedo y Valdés, suggested rhetorically, "Who can doubt that gunpowder shot off against the heathen is incense for the Lord?"[4]

Church and state were very closely connected in colonial Latin America. A special agreement known as *patronato real* gave the Spanish and Portuguese monarchs almost complete control over the Catholic Church in their newly conquered lands. Political authorities, not the pope, oversaw missionary activity, established dioceses, appointed bishops, and regulated all other matters of church life. Doctrine remained under the purview of the pope, but little else. The Latin American *patronato* system represented an almost total reversal of what many medieval popes had fought for centuries to achieve: independence of the Church from political control. But Rome had no way of imposing its will on a land that was thousands of miles across the ocean, so the *patronato* system became the law of the land, and church and state essentially merged. Colonial Latin America was divided into two Spanish viceroyalties (further subdivided into a variety of *audiencias*) and one Portuguese royal colony called Brazil (see fig. 4.1). The conquest of the Americas was a well-organized and coordinated venture, designed simultaneously to Christianize the region and to enrich the Spanish and Portuguese crowns.

One of the first concerns of the European conquerors was labor, and putting the native people to work for the conquistadores seemed like the simplest solution. The cruelty of this indigenous slave system quickly became known internationally when the outspoken Dominican preacher Bartolomé de Las Casas published his *Short Account of the Destruction of the Indians* in Spain in 1552. The indigenous slave system was abolished that same year.[5] The decision to stop enslaving the native population was partly the result of the Church coming to acknowledge that Latin America's native people were indeed fully human and required respect as children of God. But it was also the result of a precipitous decline in the indigenous population due to overwork and to the introduction of new diseases into the region from Europe. Population loss was

---

3. Quoted in ibid., 220.

4. Quoted in Hans-Jürgen Prien, *Christianity in Latin America*, trans. Stephen Buckwalter (Boston: Brill, 2013), 71.

5. Bartolomé de Las Casas, *A Short Account of the Destruction of the Indians*, trans. Nigel Griffin (New York: Penguin, 1992).

Figure 4.1
Map of Colonial Latin America, c. 1600
(showing Portuguese territory and Spanish
viceroyalties and *audiencias*)

most severe in the Caribbean and along the coast where colonization was the most intense. Mortality rates were lower in mountainous areas where the terrain made colonization more challenging and less profitable. Because of this, significant populations of indigenous people remain today in the Andes (Bolivia, Ecuador, and Peru) and in the highlands of southern Mexico and Guatemala.

The end of indigenous slavery led Spanish and Portuguese settlers to look elsewhere for labor, and their attention turned to Africa. As a result, a massive African slave industry sprang into existence, transporting more than ten million African slaves to Latin America between the years of 1650 and 1860 (see fig. 4.2). Most African slaves ended up in either the Caribbean or Brazil, but some were put to work in Mexico, Central America, and Spanish South America. Racial mixing among Africans, the indigenous population, and Europeans (and later Asians as well) became a distinctive characteristic of the region.

Partly because colonial Latin American society was so racially mixed, racial differences came to play a significant role in both church and society.

Figure 4.2
Latin American Slave Trade, 1650–1860*

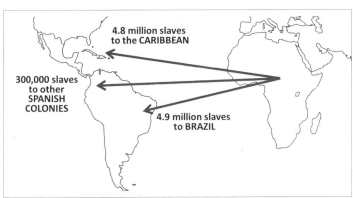

* Estimates of the number of slaves who were transported to the Americas vary considerably. These figures come from the Trans-Atlantic Slave Trade Database, www.slavevoyages.org /tast/index.faces. The numbers in this figure do not include the roughly two million Africans who died during the passage across the Atlantic.

Attention to racial difference was another concern brought to the region by settlers from the Iberian Peninsula (i.e., Spain and Portugal). Iberian attitudes toward race had been formed during the long years of Reconquista (900 to 1492), a time when Christian soldiers slowly took back control of the Iberian Peninsula from Muslims who had conquered the territory in the early 700s. The Muslims who ruled Iberia during the medieval period were known as Moors, and they were mostly darker-skinned people of North African descent. To white Spanish and Portuguese Christians, dark skin became synonymous with heathenism. This was so much the case that even when Muslims (or Jews) converted to Christianity, white Iberian Christians continued to view them as social and spiritual inferiors who were prone to heresy. It is thus not surprising that non-white converts were the main targets of the infamous Spanish Inquisition. For Iberian Christians, *limpieza de sangre* ("purity of blood" meaning, in this case, purity of white European blood) came to be seen as a marker of Christian orthodoxy.

Spanish and Portuguese settlers brought this racist perspective to Latin America, where it mutated into a new, complex hierarchy of race and religion. White Europeans born in Spain or Portugal, called *peninsulares* because they came from the Iberian Peninsula, were at the top of the social pyramid. *Peninsulares* considered themselves to be morally, intellectually, and religiously superior to all others. *Creoles*, people of pure European ancestry who were born in the new world, were a step lower on the social ladder. Located on the next steps down the social order were *mestizos* (people of mixed European and Indian blood), followed by indigenous Latin Americans and mulattos (people of mixed European and African blood), and finally by African slaves (see fig. 4.3).

Figure 4.3
Racial and Religious Social Hierarchy of Colonial Latin America

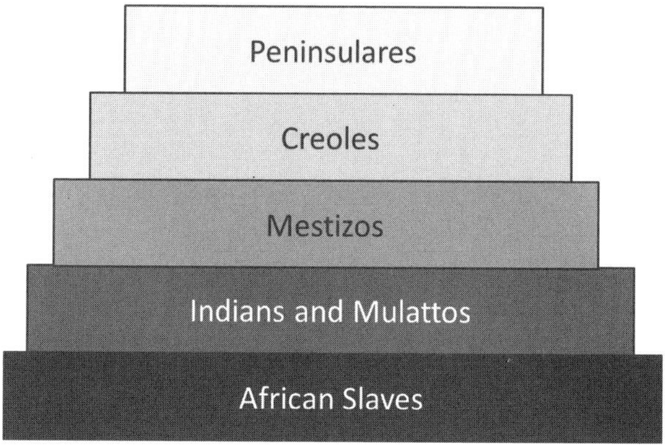

Peninsulares

Creoles

Mestizos

Indians and Mulattos

African Slaves

Christianity as it was experienced by *peninsulares* and *creoles* was very different from Christianity as it was experienced by the other population groups. For *peninsulares* and *creoles*, Latin American Christianity was a more intense version of the type of Catholicism practiced in Europe by their contemporaries. Catholic values defined their lives, the Church calendar determined the rhythm of the year, and there were no pesky Protestants to disturb the peace. Many bishops, priests, and members of the religious orders provided exemplary service to the communities they served. For example, the Jesuit priest Peter Claver (1581–1654) worked in Cartagena for forty years, catechizing and baptizing as many as three hundred thousand slaves, while also attending to the spiritual needs of both the indigenous people and European settlers. But many other *peninsulares* and *creoles*, including members of the priesthood and religious orders, were more interested in their own comfort and power than in serving others. In sum, Iberian immigrant Catholicism in Latin America was the same mixed bag of holiness, avarice, sacrifice, and wealth that could be found in Europe.

The Catholic experience of the non-white, non–Spanish-speaking population was very different. Church leaders typically viewed indigenous people, mulattos, and African slaves as less than fully human, treating them like perpetual children incapable of deep thought or spiritual insight. Members of these lower social classes were often segregated from the European immigrant population, both in church life and in society. Indigenous people were banned from entering some cities. During Mass, members of lower-status groups stood in the wings, back, or courtyard of the church building, while Europeans sat in the sanctuary. In the early days, *mestizos and* mulattos along with Africans and members of the indigenous population were prohibited from joining religious orders. Later they were assigned to special missions or monasteries designated specifically for people of their color and social status. Throughout the colonial period, mulattos and Africans were banned from the priesthood. The ordination of indigenous people and *mestizos* was allowed but was infrequent.

Members of the lower social classes usually received very little in the way of spiritual or theological instruction, but when Christianity was explained to them it was often through comparison or connection with local pre-Christian religious beliefs and practices. This approach was encouraged by Rome because it eased the path toward conversion. In 1558, for example, Pope Paul IV suggested "that the days which the Indians in their rites devote to the sun and to their (other) idols [should] be ascribed to those on which the church celebrates its festivities, in honor of Christ, the true sun, and of his holiest Mother, and of the other saints."[6] Often, sites of local religious rituals were selected as locations for new church buildings in order to maintain a geographic sense of continuity in the religious history of the region. Indigenous people and African slaves added their own fusions to this mix, combining non-Christian religious practices and beliefs with bits and pieces of Christianity to create new ideas and rituals that helped them cope with the disorienting experience of conquest, colonization, and slavery.

Over time, this hybridization of official Catholic theology with the preexisting ideas and practices of local religions and African spirituality became a permanent part of *"popular"* Catholicism, meaning Christianity as created by "the people." Popular Catholicism has flourished in Latin America ever since, especially in *confradias*, local organizations of laypeople devoted to a particular cause or saint. For many Latin American Christians, these local organizations, which are almost always led by the laypeople rather than by the clergy, define the center of their Christian faith, and participating in the rituals of the *confradias* often feels more religiously meaningful than taking part in the formal rituals and sacraments of the Church.

Forms of popular Catholicism in Latin America today vary widely, as do evaluations of the movement. Some varieties of popular Catholicism are clearly syncretistic in the negative sense of that term, inappropriately mixing

6. Quoted in Prien, *Christianity in Latin America*, 87.

Christianity with non-Christian beliefs and practices. Even sympathetic observers such as Samuel Ruiz García, bishop of Chiapas in southern Mexico from 1960 to 1999, recognize that popular Catholicism can sometimes be a "sandwich religion" composed of a "pagan filling" with only a thin veneer of Christianity on the outside.[7] But others have interpreted the rise of popular Catholicism in Latin America as authentic, appropriate, and even spiritually necessary as part of the process of both blending and resisting the cultures thrown together by the colonial enterprise.[8] Evangelical theologians such as Samuel Escobar of Peru similarly acknowledge that "the gospel dignifies every culture as a valid and acceptable vehicle for God's revelation."[9] During the colonial era, differences between European-style Catholicism and popular Catholicism were often stark, but over the centuries the official and the popular versions of Catholicism have significantly intertwined.

Independence (1820s to 1900)

In the early nineteenth century, independence movements were initiated across much of Latin America. The rhetoric of political independence in Latin America was just as idealistic as the rhetoric that characterized the North American Revolution of 1776, but the realities of revolution in Latin America were more modest. The revolution that created the United States was energized by a belief that a new order of human freedom and equality was dawning in human history, while the revolutions in Latin America were much more concerned about simply ending European control over the region. Spain and Portugal had colonized Latin America partly for religious reasons, but also for the purpose of enriching themselves. By 1800, many Latin American leaders thought the second goal had become all-consuming and that Europe was intent on draining the region dry. Simón Bolívar, one of the most outspoken of the revolutionaries, observed that European exploitation of the region had given rise to "hatred . . . in us [that] is greater than the ocean between us."[10]

When Napoleon invaded the Iberian Peninsula in 1807 and toppled the monarchies of Portugal and Spain, the time seemed ripe for independence,

7. Quoted in Todd Hartch, *The Rebirth of Latin American Christianity* (New York: Oxford University Press, 2014), 177.

8. See Alex García-Rivera, *St. Martin de Porres: The "Little Stories" and the Semiotics of Culture* (Maryknoll, NY: Orbis, 1995).

9. Samuel Escobar, "The Global Scenario at the Turn of the Century," in *Global Missiology for the 21st Century: The Iguassu Dialogue*, ed. William Taylor (Grand Rapids: Baker Academic, 2000), 26.

10. Simón Bolívar, *Letter from Jamaica*, September 6, 1815, http://history202.wikispaces .com/file/view/Jamaica+Letter.pdf.

and Latin America revolted. Paraguay claimed its freedom from Spain in 1811, followed by Argentina in 1816, Chile in 1818, Colombia in 1819, Mexico and Peru in 1821, the United Provinces of Central America in 1823, and Bolivia in 1825. Brazil became independent of Portugal in 1822. By 1825, the map of the region had been entirely redrawn (see fig. 4.4).

Figure 4.4
**Political Map of Latin America
after Independence, c. 1825**

In Latin America, most of the new revolutionary leaders were quite content with existing social structures. They sought independence from Europe not for the purpose of promoting greater equality in Latin America but so they, instead of the kings and queens of Europe, could be in charge of society. Most revolutionary leaders also wanted to maintain the religious status quo, adapting the old *patronato* system to fit the new multinational structure of the region. The Catholic Church, however, was unwilling even to talk to the revolutionary leaders. This reaction was largely shaped by the Church's experience during the French Revolution (1789–1799), which had eventually become thoroughly anti-Catholic. Viewed through that lens, the Church considered political revolution to be a sinful act of rebellion against God. As early as 1816, Pope Pius VII was telling the Catholic rulers of Portugal and Spain that it was their Christian duty "to uproot and completely destroy the baleful tares

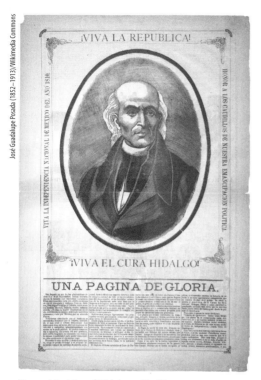

José Guadalupe Posada (1852–1913)/Wikimedia Commons

Figure 4.5. Miguel Hidalgo y Costilla

of riots and insurrections" that were beginning to appear in Latin America.[11]

While the Church hierarchy was decidedly anti-revolutionary, this was not necessarily true of the Catholic Church as a whole. Most Latin American bishops agreed with the pope and fully supported his efforts to squash the revolutions and maintain colonial rule, but the political attitudes of priests and the religious were much more diverse. Some Catholic leaders actively supported the revolutions. Perhaps the most famous was Father Miguel Hidalgo y Costilla, a parish priest from southern Mexico. In September 1810, Hidalgo gathered an army of farmers and marched into battle against the colonial government. He was captured and executed, but today he is honored as the "father of Mexico" (see fig. 4.5).

Conflicting Catholic attitudes toward independence—with the bishops opposing it and Hidalgo and other priests fighting for it—were a precursor of strained church-state relations that soon emerged throughout the region. At first the Church ignored the new nations of Latin America, hoping the independence movement would fail. Many bishops fled the region, and the pope initially refused to appoint any replacements. But this meant the Church was leaderless, and soon it was floundering. Catholic laypeople were living and dying with no access to the sacraments. These pastoral needs had to be addressed, and within a decade or so the Catholic Church was forced to come to terms with the new governments. In 1835, Pope Gregory XVI laid aside the anti-revolutionary policies of his predecessors and opened a dialogue with the political leaders of the region. Gregory hoped to restore some sense of religious orderliness to the continent, and he also wanted to regain some degree

11. Pope Pius VII, *Etsi longissimo terrarium* (1816).

of papal authority over the churches. In exchange for acknowledging papal authority, the pope offered to the new rulers of independent Latin America religious legitimacy and a promise to encourage Catholic laypeople to obey the authorities God had placed over them.

None of Latin America's new political leaders rushed forward to embrace the pope's offer, but eventually some responded positively. In 1852, Guatemala became the first Latin American nation to conclude a *concordat* (a formal agreement) with the pope about the status and rights of the Church within its borders. Ecuador, Honduras, Nicaragua, and Venezuela followed suit in the early 1860s and Colombia in 1887. Some of the largest and most influential Latin American nations remained aloof, however, including Argentina, Brazil, Chile, and Mexico. Church-state relations in these nonconcordat states varied considerably. Argentina granted religious freedom to all its citizens, but it also unilaterally declared Catholicism to be the official religion of the state. In Mexico, church-state relations were always tense, and twice erupted into widespread violence: first in the mid-nineteenth-century War of Reform and then again in the early twentieth-century Cristero Rebellion. In both instances, the results were devastating for the Church. When the Cristero Rebellion began in 1926, there were roughly 4,500 priests in Mexico; when it ended in the mid-1930s, fewer than 400 priests remained to serve the nearly 15 million members of the Catholic Church.

Church-state relations in nineteenth-century Latin America tended to fluctuate wildly based on which party and which specific politicians were in office. Favor was shown to the Church when conservatives were in office, and restrictions were placed on the Church when liberals were in charge. Social issues became flashpoints for conflict. Conservative governments usually let the Church control public education; liberal governments favored secular education, sometimes even preferentially recruiting Protestant teachers in the hope that they would be more secular and scientifically minded than Catholics. Conservatives wanted the Church to oversee marriage; liberals wanted civil authorities to regulate marriage and family matters. Conservative governments typically provided public funds to support the Church; liberal governments usually reduced or cut off such funding, and sometimes they imposed new taxes on Church properties or seized Church lands to enlarge their own budgets.

Caught in these seemingly endless fluctuations between pro-Catholic and anti-Catholic policies, the nineteenth-century Latin American Catholic Church developed a largely defensive posture intended to protect the power and independence of the institutional Church against any and all intrusions by the state. The Church focused on its own institutional needs, and laypeople were encouraged to "pay, pray, and obey."[12] As the century drew to a close, however, attitudes began to change. Pope Leo XIII's encyclical *Rerum novarum* (1891) was an important catalyst for moving the Catholic Church toward a more constructive engagement with society. The pope called on Catholic laypeople and Church leaders alike to become actively involved in public life and to address the many social needs being generated by modern industrialization and urbanization.

Early Twentieth Century

For Latin American Catholics, the twentieth century began in 1899 when Pope Leo XIII convened the first Latin American Plenary Council of bishops. The official goal of the gathering was to reflect on the Latin American implications of *Rerum novarum's* new vision of social Catholicism but, in retrospect, the real significance of the council was that it gathered the bishops of Latin America together for the first time. Until then, bishops had paid attention only to their own dioceses and nations. A new sense of corporate identity was born at the council when the bishops discovered how much they had in common. Latin American bishops have continued to meet under the aegis of the Latin American Conference of Bishops (*Consejo Episcopal Latinoamericano*, which is more typically referred to as CELAM). Today, there is a stronger sense of regional Catholic identity in Latin America than anywhere else in the world.

Already primed by *Rerum novarum* to think proactively about the relationship of faith and society, the Latin American Catholic Church was pushed further by an encyclical issued by Pope Pius XI in 1931. *Quadragesimo anno* encouraged Catholic laypeople to join with priests and bishops and with "all men of good will" to help in the "reconstruction and promotion of a better social order."[13] In response, a new movement called Catholic Action was created. Lay (nonordained) Catholic professionals such as doctors, lawyers, teachers, and government officials were urged to infuse their work with Catholic values and to nudge public ideals and practices in a Catholic direction. Three words summarize the philosophy behind Catholic Action: "see, judge, act." To *see* means viewing the problems of the world realistically, to *judge* means assessing those problems in the light of Catholic social teaching, and to *act* means proactively addressing the world's problems in ways that align with Catholic faith and values.

Eventually, this new perspective on the public responsibilities of bishops and laypeople had a major impact on Latin American Catholicism, but change did not come easily. At the grassroots level, Catholics were often averse to social

12. Hartch, *Rebirth of Latin American Christianity*, 129.
13. Pope Pius XI, *Quadragesimo anno*, 95–96.

involvement. This was especially true for members of the *confradias*, who were much more interested in their own private gatherings than they were in influencing public life. The same could be said about many other Catholic men and women who went to Mass and then simply went home with no interest in changing the world. A 1953 study sponsored by Catholic Action found that most Latin American Catholics were only minimally interested in the Church's social agenda. Blame for this disengagement was attributed in large part to the region's perennial shortage of priests. There were, and still are, fewer priests per parishioner in Latin America than anywhere else in the world.[14]

Latin American Catholics were ultimately forced into social activism, not by the Church, but by the military dictatorships that arose in the region during the three decades following World War II. During the Cold War era, nations across the globe were pressured to align with one of only two political alternatives: communism or democratic capitalism. When Fidel Castro's Communist Party took control of Cuba in 1959, after six years of guerrilla warfare against the pro-US but dictatorial government of Fulgencio Batista, Latin American politicians, business leaders, and military commanders were shocked into action. Anti-communist military dictatorships sprang up all over Latin America, claiming that this style of governance was necessary to prevent the spread of communism (see fig. 4.8). Anyone who raised a voice of protest against these regimes was labeled a communist or a communist sympathizer. Many of these protesters were arrested and killed, and others simply "disappeared." In Argentina, more than ten thousand citizens vanished. In the tiny nation of El Salvador, with a total population of only three million people, thirty thousand citizens were seized and never seen again.

At first, the Catholic Church was uncertain about how to respond. The Church had a long history of teaching obedience to the government and support for law and order. Some Church leaders championed the new military dictatorships and their fight against godless communism, but other priests and bishops, as well as many Catholic laypeople, were troubled by the violence and by the economic inequities that existed throughout the region. Catholic women were especially vocal. In country after country, "mothers of the disappeared" began to object, gathering in front of churches to inquire about their missing sons and daughters and to hold prayer vigils for their safe return. Eventually the Church had to respond.

The issue came to a head at the 1968 CELAM meeting held in Medellín, Colombia. The official reason for this meeting was to discuss how the declarations of the Second Vatican Council (the general council of the worldwide Catholic

14. Hartch, *Rebirth of Latin American Christianity*, 13.

Figure 4.6
Locations of Military Dictatorships in Latin America, 1960–1990

Argentina
Bolivia
Brazil
Chile
Ecuador
El Salvador
Guatemala
Haiti
Honduras
Nicaragua
Panama
Paraguay
Uruguay

Church that took place in the years 1962–1965, referred to as Vatican II) applied to Latin America. The declarations of Vatican II stressed giving special attention to the needs of the poor. Reflecting on the Council's message in light of social, economic, and political realities in Latin America, the bishops concluded that Catholic social ethics should be guided by a "preferential option for the poor." After the Medellín meeting, many Catholic bishops, priests, and devout laypeople began to speak and act more assertively, denouncing the abuses of military governments and calling for democratic reforms. The result was a long list of new martyrs. Catholic social activists were killed by their own governments (or by government-associated death squads) because they expressed concern for the poor. Archbishop Óscar Romero of El Salvador was the most prominent of these martyrs, gunned down in 1980 while saying morning Mass at the Church of the Divine Providence in the capital city of San Salvador.

Liberation theology emerged during this tumultuous time, a new approach to theology that combined social analysis (often from a Marxist perspective) and social action with traditional Catholic teaching. As a movement, liberation theology was held together by the conviction that Christian theological reflection and social action needed to be combined in self-conscious service to the poor. This new relationship between theory and action was called *praxis*. Older Catholic ways of thinking had defined theology as simply explaining doctrine and had viewed moral action as simply putting Catholic rules into practice. Liberation theology combined doctrine and activism in a new way, enlarging the work of Catholic Action and seeking to involve everyone, not just professionals, in the work of transforming society. Most notably, liberation theologians encouraged the poor to speak and advocate for themselves.

In the 1970s, the liberation theology movement inspired the creation of tens of thousands of "base communities," small gatherings of Catholic men and women who met regularly to discuss how the message of the Bible applied to their own experience. Base communities were also settings where people could strategize about how to change the social structures of their own neighborhoods so life would be better for everyone, especially for the poor. Liberation theologians had different opinions about appropriate ways to promote social change. Based on "just war" theory, some concluded that injustice in Latin America was so pervasive and so deeply imbedded in the social fabric of the region that armed rebellion was a reasonable response. However, the overwhelming majority of liberation theologians advocated nonviolent means of social change.

The intensity of the liberationist movement peaked around 1980 and then subsided as democracy was slowly restored throughout the region and as violations of basic human rights declined. Liberation theology and the liberationist cause also lost support because popes John Paul II and Benedict XVI were unsympathetic. In one famous exchange, caught on film on the runway at the Managua airport, Pope John Paul II publicly chided the Nicaraguan Jesuit priest and liberation theologian Ernesto Cardenal for being too involved in politics. Several liberation theologians have been investigated by the Vatican, and some have been officially silenced. Care for the poor remains an important moral concern for Latin American Catholics, but poverty now competes for attention with other matters such as abortion and indigenous rights.

Recent Decades

Up until the mid-twentieth century, Protestants (or *evangélicos*, as they are typically called in Latin America) were so peripheral to Latin American life that they hardly mattered. A few Protestants had moved into the region during the colonial era, but no permanent Protestant communities were ever established. After independence, Protestant numbers slowly increased, but most Protestants were members of ethnic churches (such as German Lutherans, Russian Mennonites, or Italian Waldensians) who moved to the continent hoping to be left alone. They were not missionary minded, and they lived within their own religious and cultural enclaves separate from the rest of society.[15] In 1900, after four hundred years of Christianity in the Americas, Protestants represented only a tiny fraction of the population.

Despite a remarkable worldwide increase in the number of Protestant missionaries during the first half of the twentieth century, very few were sent to Latin America. North American and European Protestants were ambivalent about the continent because, while it was not Protestant, it also was not non-Christian. In the end, most Protestants decided missionary needs were greater in Africa and Asia, where most people had never heard the gospel, so that is where they directed their time, money, and missionary personnel. The one exception to this rule was the Andean nations, especially Ecuador, where there were significant numbers of indigenous people. These groups had never been effectively evangelized by the Catholic Church, so Protestants felt called to become involved in these communities. But the number of Protestants remained small, and in 1950, Protestants still accounted for only about 2 percent of the Latin American population.

But then things began to change. By 1970, 4 percent of the Latin American population was *evangélico*, and by 2000, this number had jumped to around 9 percent. Today, close to 15 percent of the continent's population can be considered *evangélico*, and in places such as Brazil and Nicaragua the percentages are much higher. *Evangélico* growth was so rapid in Guatemala during the 1990s that one scholar projected that, should the growth rate continue, an impossible 126.8 percent of the Guatemalan population would be *evangélico* by the year 2010![16] Almost all of this *evangélico* growth in Latin America has been generated by Pentecostals rather than by traditional Protestants. Pentecostalism had been present in Latin America since the beginning of the twentieth century. The Chilean Methodist Pentecostal Church, founded in 1910, is one of the oldest Pentecostal denominations in the world. But Pentecostal growth remained slow until the 1960s. In 1970, only about 25 percent of Latin American *evangélicos* were Pentecostal, while about 75 percent were traditional Protestants. Today the numbers are reversed. At least 80 percent of *evangélicos* in Latin America are now Pentecostal and only 20 percent or less remain traditionally Protestant.

Given the overwhelmingly Catholic character of Latin America, the rising number of *evangélico* Christians has often been linked with a parallel decline

15. See Justo L. González and Ondina E. González, *Christianity in Latin America: A History* (New York: Cambridge University Press, 2008), chap. 7.

16. David Stoll, *Is Latin America Turning Protestant?* (Berkeley: University of California Press, 1990), 337.

in the Catholic population of the region. In 1970, Catholics still accounted for close to 90 percent of the continent's population; today they represent less than 80 percent. This is not a huge decline, but it caused great concern within the Catholic Church when the trend first became evident in the 1990s. For many Catholic leaders, the reason for this decline was clear: *Evangélico* Christians were "stealing" Catholic sheep. Some prominent Catholic leaders, including the pope, described the situation as an "invasion of the sects" and denounced Pentecostal pastors, in particular, as "ravenous wolves" who were trying to gobble up unsuspecting Catholic laypeople. Catholic bishops warned the Catholic faithful not to be deceived. In some places such as Mexico, devout Catholics nailed signs to their doors that read: "This home is Catholic. We do not accept Protestant propaganda."

While conversion to *evangélico* Christianity clearly did play some role in drooping Catholic numbers, many Catholic leaders now recognize that other factors were also at work, with the region's persistent shortage of priests being at the top of the list. In North America and Europe, the ratio of priests to parishioners is roughly one to 1,500. In Asia, it is one to 2,500. But in Latin America there is only one priest for every 6,500 Catholic believers. What makes these numbers even more problematic is that many of the Catholic priests serving in Latin America are not themselves Latin Americans. A majority of the priests in Bolivia, Chile, Guatemala, Honduras, Mexico, Paraguay, Peru, and Venezuela were born outside of Latin America.[17] This means that the average Latin American Catholic encounters a priest only rarely, and when he or she does see a priest there is only a fifty-fifty chance that he will be a fellow Latin American. While the size of the Catholic Church has decreased slightly as a percentage of the overall Latin American population, the flipside of recent developments is that lay activism and church attendance has increased. As some nominal Catholics drop out of church life or convert to *evangélico* Christianity, those who remain are becoming more devout. The dynamics behind this change are explained in the following section.

Contemporary Latin American Christianity

Latin America is the most urbanized region of the world, and urbanization is expected to increase even more during the next two decades. In 1950, 40

17. R. Andrew Chestnut, "Spirited Competition: Pentecostal Success in Latin America's New Religious Marketplace," in *Spirit and Power: The Growth and Global Impact of Pentecostalism*, ed. Donald E. Miller, Kimon H. Sargeant, and Richard Flory (New York: Oxford University Press, 2013), 76–77.

percent of Latin Americans lived in cities. Today 80 percent of the population is urban.[18] Urbanization has upset the older, agrarian social structure of the region. It has also undermined traditional Catholic ways of faith that were based on stable local communities where children were born, baptized, raised, and confirmed in the same place and where they later worked, married, raised their own children, and died. This is not how life works in the megalopolises of contemporary Latin America, and increasingly this is not how life works in rural Latin America either. The region's new social dynamics have opened space for Pentecostalism to grow and flourish and have forced Catholics to confront the need for choice in matters of faith. These two developments (the rise of Pentecostalism and religious choice) have, in turn, spurred a revival of sorts within the Catholic Church itself—something that no one had predicted.

Pentecostalism

Pentecostalism in contemporary Latin America is a predominantly urban faith that has grown up in the cracks of the broken social order that defines life in the *barrios* (in Spanish) and *favelas* (in Portuguese) of the region. The Catholic presence in these low-income neighborhoods is often minimal. The big Catholic churches are located in richer districts, and the workloads of most priests are already so full that they have no extra time for visiting downtrodden areas. Many of the people living in these poorer parts of Latin America's urban centers have moved there relatively recently, having left the countryside in search of employment in the city. Many of these rural-to-urban migrants end up unemployed or underemployed, lonely because of being separated from their extended families, and in search of support and community. These women and men often find a lifeline in a Pentecostal church.

Most Latin American Pentecostal Christians attribute the movement's growth to the Holy Spirit. They were attracted to Pentecostalism because they felt the presence of God in the lives of other Pentecostal Christians, and they wanted that experience for themselves. This interpretation of Pentecostal growth seems almost self-evidently true given that Pentecostalism itself focuses so strongly on experience. But the growth of Pentecostalism also has sociological dimensions. Perhaps most notably, the movement's unique mix of heated piety and down-to-earth pragmatism resonates with the roiling dynamics of urban poverty. The route to becoming Pentecostal typically begins informally through conversation with a friend, neighbor, or acquaintance who attends

---

18. *World Urbanization Prospects: The 2003 Revision* (New York: United Nations, 2004), 30.

a Pentecostal church or through the conversion of a spouse or other relative. Pentecostalism is not preached by outsiders who visit poor communities but is instead spread by local residents who are living out their faith in their home communities and who invite their neighbors to join them. Pentecostalism is growing among Latin America's impoverished urban masses because it is not just a church *for* the poor but also a church *of* the poor.

Pentecostal churches are also succeeding because they are entertaining. Life in the slums of Latin America's cities can be monotonous and boring; Pentecostal services are lively and fun. People sing, dance, put their hands in the air, praise God, and rejoice together. Pentecostal churches have the additional advantage of being socially comfortable. There are no requirements to wear formal clothes to services at most Pentecostal churches. So the relative socioeconomic status of attendees is not on display. No one is made to feel inferior on the basis of their attire. Pentecostal churches also pray for the sick and suffering, offering the hope of divine healing to people who may not be able to afford any other kind of health care.

Most of the recent growth of Pentecostalism in Latin American has come in the form of neocharismatic churches, which range in size from denominations with only a few hundred members to the massive *Igreja Universal do Reino de Deus* (the Universal Church of the Kingdom of God) with more than five million members. Almost all these churches champion prosperity, promising that God will reward spiritual faithfulness with material gain. Many Pentecostal Christians do indeed climb out of abject poverty, but the explanation is practical as well as spiritual. Pentecostal churches are places where individuals discover skills and talents they never knew they possessed. Members are expected to be active, and these churches operate as meritocracies. If someone can do a task well, then he or she is given responsibility, and no pedigree or educational degree is required. For many people, the result is a nearly miraculous surge of self-confidence.

Pentecostalism's emphasis on disciplined living—being sexually faithful to one's spouse; avoiding alcohol, drugs, and crime; dressing modestly; getting places on time—is another factor in moving out of poverty. These personality traits are highly attractive to employers and provide new converts with the abilities they need to be hired and to keep their jobs. Most Pentecostals do not become as wealthy as their churches suggest they might, but simply making ends meet can be a powerful confirmation of faith. The all-encompassing character of most Pentecostal churches has also made them one of the only viable pathways out of gang membership. Gangs are a major problem in many Latin American cities, and normally the only way to leave a gang is in a coffin. But those who depart because of Pentecostal conversion often survive because the change of lifestyle is so complete that it warrants respect.[19] The holistic nature of Pentecostal church life can, however, eventually become too much for some converts. The main reason people leave the movement is that Pentecostalism simply demands too much time and commitment.

A New Religious Economy of Choice

As the Pentecostal movement has grown in Latin America, Pentecostalism has become much more adept at marketing its message. Radio stations, television networks, newspapers, and other publications proclaim the Pentecostal message loudly every day. From the beginning of the movement, Pentecostals have told their fellow Latin Americans that they need to make a decision for Christ. While this is a familiar concept to Christians from North America, it was—and to some degree still is—a radical suggestion in Latin America. Traditionally, Catholic faith was something one was born into, and that faith was tied to a specific geographic location. In the past, people went to the one and only church that existed in their local parish, and choice was not part of the equation. That is no longer the case. In country after country, Latin Americans are discovering that choice has become an unavoidable dimension of faith. This is partly the result of Pentecostal growth, but it is also part of modernization and globalization. Options are available. Even when a person wants to remain traditionally Catholic, this is now perceived as something that must be chosen.

Brazil is at the forefront of these developments. The fifth-largest country in the world, more Christians live in Brazil than in any other nation in the world with the sole exception of the United States. Home to many European émigrés, it also has the largest African-descended population of any Latin American country. The Brazilian Constitution of 1891 separated church and state, and the nation has been officially secular ever since. Lack of an official state religion did not, however, result in full religious freedom. Catholicism continued to play a huge role in Brazilian life and politics. *Evangélicos* faced discrimination, and Afro-Brazilian religions such as Condomblé and Umbanda were banned. In 1988, Brazil adopted a new constitution that mandated genuine religious freedom for everyone. Catholicism remains the largest religion in the country, but it has no special standing. Religious life in contemporary Brazil is now defined by a four-way competition among Catholics, Pentecostals, practitioners of the newly legal Afro-Brazilian religions, and secularism. At present, Brazil is about 65 percent Catholic, 20 percent *evangélico*, 10 percent

---

19. See Robert Brenneman, *Homies and Hermanos: God and Gangs in Central America* (New York: Oxford University Press, 2012).

religiously unaffiliated, and 5 percent other religions, but this last number clearly under-reports the influence of Condomblé and Umbanda. These two Afro-Brazilian traditions do not have members in the traditional sense of the term, but instead serve clients, who come to their centers only when they need spiritual help or guidance.

The level of religious choice found in Brazil is not yet the norm everywhere across Latin America. Instead, there is a checkerboard pattern. Some nations, such as Chile and Guatemala, are almost as religiously diverse as Brazil. In other nations, such as Ecuador, Mexico, and Peru, Catholicism is so central to the culture that the notion of religious choice hardly enters anyone's thinking. Even so, in Mexico, for example, *evangélicos* now number more than ten million and make up about 8 percent of the total population. The long-term trend seems obvious: Latin America is becoming a region of religious choice. The transition is taking place quickly in some countries and more slowly in others, but it is underway everywhere. Catholicism can no longer assume it has a religious monopoly over the region, and other faiths are flexing their muscles.

The changing situation in Latin America became a matter of concern for the Vatican beginning in the late 1980s. Older ways of becoming and remaining Catholic were breaking down, and new self-chosen ways of being Catholic needed to be developed. Pope John Paul II described this fresh perspective as "the new evangelization." The new evangelization focuses on conversion, with the term *conversion* retaining its traditional Catholic meaning of a lifelong journey toward God. What is new in the "new evangelization" is the overt emphasis on the need for personal choice. As described by the pope in the *Redemptoris missio* (1990), "conversion means accepting, *by a personal decision*, the saving sovereignty of Christ, and becoming his disciple." The target population for the new evangelization is Catholics who have "lost a living sense of the faith, or even no longer consider themselves members of the Church," but who still possess some vestigial sense of being Catholic.[20]

The new evangelization is not composed of a specific package of predefined programs or activities. It is instead characterized by a change of attitude toward those who have drifted away from the Church. Rather than scolding delinquent members, it seeks winsomely to woo them back home to the Church. In essence, the new evangelization represents the dawning awareness that cultural Catholicism—becoming Catholic simply by being raised within a culture that is imbued with Catholic values and rhythms of life—is

20. Pope John Paul II, *Redemptoris missio*, 33, 46, emphasis added.

no longer an adequate strategy for helping Catholics to remain Catholic. To grow spiritually, to progress in the ongoing experience of conversion, is a matter of choice, and Catholics are slowly beginning to believe that, rather than being an impediment to faith, choice can strengthen faith. For this to happen, however, a new Catholic infrastructure of religious organizations had to be built. That has now happened, and the Catholic Church is reaping the benefits. Millions of formerly nominal Catholics have become re-involved in the life of the Church.

Catholic Revival

The Catholic Church's contemporary revival has taken many different forms, but two developments have been especially significant. One is the Catholic Charismatic Renewal, a movement that did not even exist in the year 1960 but that now involves roughly one quarter of all Catholics in the region. The second is the appearance of a plethora of new Catholic "ecclesial movements" and organizations. These lay-led, theme-focused Catholic religious associations have given Latin American Catholics a host of new ways to express their faith.

The Catholic Charismatic Renewal (CCR) began as part of the broad and wide-ranging charismatic movement that swept across the world in the 1960s and 1970s. The Catholic Church's initial reaction to the CCR, especially in Latin America, was negative. Bishops feared that the movement's ecumenical tendencies would undermine Catholic identity and make *evangélico* Pentecostalism seem less strange and more attractive to Catholics. Some bishops also worried that non-ordained charismatic leaders would challenge the spiritual authority of the clergy. In Brazil, bishops fretted that the movement would undermine the Church's commitments to social justice.

None of these worries proved to be warranted. If anything the opposite was true. The initial ecumenical impulses of the broader charismatic movement soon lessened, and by the late 1970s and early 1980s, many Catholic charismatics were re-gathering into their own decidedly Catholic charismatic communities. Church leaders simultaneously discovered that the lay leaders of the movement were not radicals intending to challenge the authority of bishops, and fears that the CCR would undermine social action were simply wrong. As a result, more and more Latin American bishops threw their support behind the CCR. Members of the CCR were typically the most spiritually energized people in their dioceses, and often they were the most resolutely committed to the Church and fervently devoted to the Virgin Mary. With the approval of Church leaders, the CCR's growth has been stunning. The

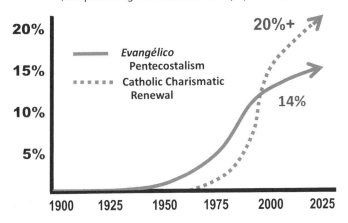

Figure 4.7
**Comparative Growth of *Evangélico* Pentecostalism
and the Catholic Charismatic Renewal**
(as a percentage of Latin American population)

movement is strongest in Brazil, but the CCR has impacted every country in the region.[21] At present, Catholic charismatics in Latin America outnumber *evangélico* Pentecostals four to three (see fig. 4.7).

Additional evidence related to the revival of Catholicism in Latin America is provided by the host of new ecclesial movements (NEMs) that are now flourishing in the region. NEMs are Catholic versions of what Protestants would call Christian voluntary associations or parachurch ministries. They typically focus on one particular concern or "charism" (a specific spiritual gift or a particular calling such as teaching or social justice), and they are generally lay led. The base communities associated with liberation theology were one type of NEM, and local charismatic prayer groups are another. However, the matrix of NEMs in contemporary Latin America spans a huge spectrum of concerns, commitments, and associated spiritualities, ranging from the relatively conservative Opus Dei, which focuses on personal holiness, to the relatively progressive Sant'Egidio Community, which focuses on ecumenical and interreligious dialogue. In between are countless other groups, including the Cursillo movement (sponsoring weekend retreats for personal spiritual renewal), Focolare (dedicated to fostering the unity of all people), the L'Arche Community (providing aid to persons who are intellectually challenged), the Legion of Mary (focusing on works of mercy), Marriage Encounter (seeking

21. Edward L. Cleary, *The Rise of Charismatic Catholicism in Latin America* (Gainesville: University Press of Florida, 2011), 268.

to deepen marriage commitments and marital joy), the Neocatechumenal Way (fostering the spiritual development of adult Catholics), and Regnum Christi (encouraging greater devotion to the Church worldwide).

The current Catholic revival has produced a new marketplace of religious choice within Catholicism itself. Rather than offering only one or two different Catholic options, the Church now provides Latin American laypeople with opportunities to choose from a multitude of different movements, organizations, and styles of worship, each of them embodying different theological emphases and spiritual values. There is plenty of variety inside the Church, and the temptation to convert to *evangélico* Pentecostalism has declined accordingly. This has not eliminated all the challenges facing the Catholic Church in Latin America. The chronic shortage of priests continues, and until that problem is solved there will be plenty of space for *evangélico* churches to attract dissatisfied and disgruntled Catholics. Still, the Christian diversity that has emerged over the past twenty or thirty years is helping both the *evangélico* churches and the Catholic Church to flourish.

Latin American Theology and Liberation

If one word captures the core message of the gospel in Latin America today it is *liberation*. The idea of liberation goes beyond the notion of forgiveness, a frequent emphasis in Christian theology, and points toward a much fuller understanding of the kind of salvation God intends for humankind. Salvation is not about simply being reconciled with God, it is an experience that transforms human beings into something more than they currently are. The Latin American Protestant theologian Elsa Tamez says liberation gives people the power to live with dignity "in communion and solidarity with God and with one another."[22]

In Latin America, the term *liberation* is often linked with liberation theology, a movement (as described above) that was especially prominent in the 1970s and 1980s, when military dictatorships dominated the region. But liberation is a concept with relevance that extends far beyond liberation theology alone. It also refers to liberation from racial prejudice and liberation from the powers of darkness. The idea of liberation is naturally connected to Latin America's long history of socioeconomic injustice, but the full scope of liberation includes cultural and spiritual elements as well. In Latin American theology, all of these dimensions of liberation are viewed as interconnected.

22. Elsa Tamez, *The Amnesty of Grace* (Nashville: Abingdon, 1993), 163.

Socioeconomic Liberation

Latin America's long and continuing history of economic inequality has made issues of poverty and wealth unavoidable. Economic tensions were especially evident during the second half of the twentieth century when military governments terrorized the region, but concerns about socioeconomic injustice track all the way to the earliest days of colonization. In the sixteenth century, Bartolomé de Las Casas was already lamenting the continent's economic inequalities, criticizing wealthy colonial rulers and *encomenderos* (large land owners) for forcing the indigenous people to work their lands for the sole purpose of increasing the owners' already enormous personal wealth. Five hundred years later, Latin American Catholic social activists are still castigating government officials and business titans for oppressing the poor in order to protect the wealth and comfort of the very rich.

Although the influence of liberation theology as a formal movement has waned in recent decades, many of the underlying socioeconomic realities that gave rise to liberation theology remain in place. Latin America continues to be the continent with the greatest disparity between the rich and the poor. Many leaders of all churches are troubled by this enduring inequality, including Pope Francis, the former archbishop of Buenos Aires, Argentina. He made this concern a main theme in his first papal proclamation *Evangelii gaudium* ("The Joy of the Gospel"). Francis argues that "each individual Christian and every community is called to be an instrument of God for the liberation and promotion of the poor."[23] Pope Francis and other contemporary Latin American Christians no longer expect a total restructuring of social life like that espoused by liberation theology, but they do hope those living in poverty will experience at least a "touch of salvation" in the present, and those who are wealthy will become more personally concerned with society as a whole and with the needs of the poor.[24]

While Pope Francis shares many of the sentiments expressed by liberation theologians, he believes that the movement's heavy reliance on religious, social, and political theory can sometimes undermine compassionate action as much as encourage it. Ideas, he says, can easily get disconnected from social realities, and when they do they "give rise to ineffectual forms of idealism and nominalism, capable at most of classifying and defining, but certainly not calling to action."[25] Instead of focusing constantly on justice, Francis emphasizes face-

23. Pope Francis, *Evangelii gaudium*, 187.
24. Ivone Gebara, *Out of the Depths: Women's Experience of Evil and Salvation* (Minneapolis: Fortress, 2002), 114.
25. Pope Francis, *Evangelii gaudium*, 232.

to-face interactions with those in need and small acts of solidarity with the poor who cross our paths every day. The pope says compassion is necessarily "fleshy."[26] It requires physical contact with people, experiencing their voices, their looks, their smells, their joys, and their sorrows firsthand. Francis is attuned to social structures and to the long history of mistreatment of the poor in Latin America, but he insists that concern for the poor must result in personal relationships with the poor and not rely only on structural change. The point is to help both the rich and the poor rediscover their shared humanity. His goal is to help not only the poor but also "those who are in thrall to an individualistic, indifferent and self-centered mentality to be freed from those unworthy chains and to attain a way of living and thinking that is more humane, noble and fruitful, and which will bring dignity to their presence on this earth."[27]

One Latin American church leader who is almost universally recognized as a saint is Óscar Romero, the assassinated archbishop of El Salvador. His eloquence on the topic of poverty and social violence was impressive partly because it was so thoroughly unexpected. When Romero was appointed as archbishop in 1977, he was a bookish padre with little stomach for political confrontation, and everyone assumed he would remain steadfastly neutral with regard to public conflicts. But once appointed archbishop, Romero began to speak out. When his calls for justice went unheeded, he publicly denounced the violence of the state and the greed of the wealthy. Finally he begged, and then he ordered, Catholic soldiers not to kill their fellow citizens. The result was his own assassination, but his words live on, calling Christians in Latin America and everywhere else to remember the poor and to remember that salvation has material implications for the present as well as spiritual ramifications for the future (see textbox, Latin American Theology: Óscar Romero).

Liberation and Race

From the earliest days of European colonization, Latin American society was shaped by racist attitudes imported to the New World from the Iberian Peninsula (as described earlier in this chapter). Racism became part of Latin American culture, and race continues to shape social and interpersonal relations today. It is not uncommon to hear Latin American society described as a "pigmentocracy."[28] This enduring racial prejudice became newly obvious

---

26. Ibid., 90.
27. Ibid., 208.
28. See Edward Telles and Liza Steele, "Pigmentocracy in the Americas: How Is Educational Attainment Related to Skin Color?," *AmericasBarometer Insights* 73 (2012).

Latin American Theology: Óscar Romero

Hope in History: Liberation for Both the Poor and the Wealthy

Óscar Arnulfo Romero y Galdámez was the Catholic archbishop of San Salvador (in El Salvador) from 1977 to 1980. He was assassinated on March 24, 1980, while saying Mass at a small chapel on the grounds of a local Catholic hospital. No one was ever charged with his murder, but it is widely believed that the killer was part of a paramilitary death squad who opposed Romero's religious and political views. This excerpt comes from one of his last sermons.

> The church has to proclaim good news to the poor. Those who, in this-worldly terms, have heard bad news, and who have lived out even worse realities, are now listening through the church to the word of Jesus: "The kingdom of God is at hand; blessed are you who are poor, for the kingdom of God is yours." And hence they also have good news to proclaim to the rich: that they, too, become poor in order to share the benefits of the kingdom with the poor. Anyone who knows Latin America will be quite clear that there is no ingenuousness in these words. . . . What is found in these words is a coming together of the aspirations on our continent for liberation, and God's offer of love to the poor. This is the hope that the church offers, and it coincides with the hope, at times dormant and at other times frustrated or manipulated, of the poor of Latin America. . . .
>
> The real world of the poor also teaches us about Christian hope. The church preaches a new heaven and a new earth. It knows, moreover, that no socio-political system can be exchanged for the final fullness that is given by God. But it has also learned that transcendent hope must be preserved by signs of hope in history, no matter how simple they may apparently be.*

*Óscar Romero, *Voice of the Voiceless: Four Pastoral Statements and Other Statements* (Maryknoll, NY: Orbis, 1995), 180, 184.

in 1992, when the five hundredth anniversary of Columbus's "discovery" of the Americas sparked protests by indigenous peoples across the region. A new resurgence and recovery of indigenous identities has been underway ever since.[29] This movement aims to reduce prejudice and to reassert the goodness and value of indigenous perspectives and ways of life.

When Latin American Catholics think about racial liberation, most turn instinctively to the Virgin Mary for inspiration, and especially to the Virgin of Guadalupe, an apparition of Mary that took place in December 1531, just eleven years after the conquest. The person to whom Mary appeared was Cuauhtlatoatzin (more widely known by his baptismal name of Juan Diego),

29. See Edward L. Cleary and Timothy J. Steigenga, eds., *Resurgent Voices in Latin America: Indigenous People, Political Mobilization, and Religious Change* (New Brunswick, NJ: Rutgers University Press, 2004).

a poor indigenous worker who lived near Mexico City. Cuauhtlatoatzin's experience is chronicled in a document called the *Nican Mopohua*. Cuauhtlatoatzin was passing by a hill called Tepeyac (a former Aztec holy site) when he heard someone call out to him. When he ascended the hill in response to this call, he was surprised to see someone who looked like a dark-skinned indigenous woman. She told him, "I am the Ever-Virgin Holy Mary, Mother of the God of Great Truth. . . . I am your merciful mother and the merciful mother of all the nations that live on this earth. . . . I will hear their laments and remedy and cure all their miseries, misfortunes, and sorrows."[30] The message to Cuauhtlatoatzin was confirmed when the image

Figure 4.8. Virgin of Guadalupe as imprinted on Cuauhtlatoatzin's *Tilma*

was miraculously transferred to his *tilma*, an all-purpose cloth used by the local population as both a cloak for warmth and a tarp for hauling goods and produce to market. That *tilma* now hangs in the massive Basilica of Our Lady of Guadalupe in Mexico City, where it is visited by millions of pilgrims every year (see fig. 4.8).

The Virgin's message was powerful. It was a proclamation of divine care and compassion for everyone, a bold declaration that all the people of the world are equal in God's sight. During the years of conquest and European occupation that followed, perceptions of the Christian God had been thoroughly distorted by violence. The Christian God seemed more like a warrior deity demanding submission to Europe than like the loving creator of all humankind. This was a misunderstanding of the gospel, but it made sense in the context of conquest and also in light of local religious customs that

30. Virgilio Elizondo, *Guadalupe: Mother of the New Creation* (Maryknoll, NY: Orbis, 1997), 8.

sometimes required human sacrifice to a violent God as part of efforts to maintain the existence of the world.

Taking the form of a woman with brown skin and wearing local dress, the Virgin of Guadalupe gave Cuauhtlatoatzin a message of hope and love for all the peoples of the world. In an act that translated her egalitarian proclamation of God's love into observable action, Mary ordered Cuauhtlatoatzin to convey her message to the bishop—reversing the social order—so that a lowly indigenous farmer became God's messenger to a white *peninsulare* bishop. This was unheard of, and it took another miracle—flowers blooming out of season—to get the bishop finally to agree to a meeting.

In the story of Guadalupe, the harsh and violent image of God that had been imported to Latin America from Spain was tempered and corrected by Mary's care and compassion, and the racism of Spanish Christianity was demolished by Mary's own complexion. She did not appear as Mary in the abstract or as Mary the European maiden; she was the Virgin of Guadalupe who communicated God's love and compassion to all of Latin America's native people. Many other appearances of the Virgin in colonial Latin America confirmed Guadalupe's message, with Mary being honored by the name of La Negrita in Costa Rica, Our Lady of Aparecida in Brazil, Our Lady of Caridad del Cobre in Cuba, and by many other names in other countries.

The Catholic priest and theologian Virgilio Elizondo says that the appearance of the Virgin to Cuauhtlatoatzin is perhaps "the most prodigious event since the coming of our Lord and Savior, Jesus Christ." He explains, "At that unique moment in the history of our planet, God intervened to open up the possibilities for the eventual unity of all peoples. Human beings wanted to conquer, divide, and dominate—spiritually and/or physically—but God wanted to convert, unite, liberate, and create a common home for everyone."[31] God, speaking through the Virgin of Guadalupe, de-racialized Christianity and placed all the people of Latin America (and by extension all the people of the world) on equal ground alongside one another (see textbox, Latin American Theology: Virgilio Elizondo).

The gracious and liberating story of the Virgin of Guadalupe, with her message of God's equal love for all people of the world, has important theological implications. It is a story about how Mary intervened in human history, and it raises questions about the role of Mary in the history of salvation. Most Catholic and Orthodox Christians believe Mary is an active spokesperson

31. Ibid., 134. Elizondo's views echo to some degree the philosophy of José Vasconcelos Calderón, who suggested early in the twentieth century that a new "cosmic race" was being created in the *mestizaje* of Latin America. Vasconcelos did not, however, tie this idea to the Virgin of Guadalupe.

Latin American Theology: Virgilio Elizondo

Guadalupe: Rehumanizing the Dehumanized

Virgilio Elizondo serves as parochial vicar of St. Rose of Lima parish in the Catholic archdiocese of San Antonio, Texas, and also as professor of pastoral and Hispanic theology and fellow of the Institute for Latino Studies at the University of Notre Dame in South Bend, Indiana. Elizondo is one of the world's most outspoken *Guadalopanos* (promoters of the message of the Virgin of Guadalupe), which is evident in this excerpt explaining the significance of her appearance at Tepeyac, near Mexico City.

> The conversion process associated with the "spiritual conquest" demanded that the Indians give up their existence without ever being fully recognized as equal to the European Christians. Converted Indians would become cultural mestizos and would thus join the ranks of the mestizo homeless of the Americas. . . .
>
> At Tepeyac no one is to be rejected. Tepeyac becomes the most sacred space of the Americas precisely because of the unlimited diversity of peoples who experience a common home there. Precisely because everyone is welcomed there and experiences a sense of belonging, is listened to with compassion and senses the energy of true universal fellowship, the face of God is clearly seen while the heart of God is experienced intimately and tenderly. This is what makes Tepeyac so sacred—it is not a sacredness that scares, separates, and divides but the sacredness of the holiness of God that allures, brings together, and unites.
>
> In the events of Tepeyac, the process of unjust dehumanizing segregation by sex, race, class, and ethnicity is totally reversed not by providing a finished humanity but by initiating a new process by which a truly new humanity recognizing the legitimacy, beauty, and dignity of each and every human group might gradually develop and come to be. Within the new process, mestizaje will be transformed from a source of shame and dislocation to a source of belonging and pride in each of the ancestral lines.*

* Virgilio Elizondo, *Guadalupe: Mother of the New Creation* (Maryknoll, NY: Orbis, 1997), 109, 112–13.

for God in this world and that she is also a powerful purveyor of God's grace to those in need. She is the Mother of the Church, and she plays an essential role in God's plan of salvation. By contrast, many Protestant and Pentecostal Christians worry that assigning any significant role to Mary related to salvation or divine revelation runs the risk of minimizing the work of Jesus. Because of these theological differences, Mary has often been left out of global ecumenical conversations about Christian unity and cooperation. But in Latin America, Mary cannot be ignored. This means that any fruitful global conversation about following Jesus faithfully in the world today must include the Mother of Jesus (or the Mother of God as most Catholic and Orthodox Christians would say). Mary can no longer be conveniently ignored.

Spiritual Liberation

Demons and demon possession rarely appear as topics in books of systematic theology, but belief in demons and in their ability to control individuals is widespread. This is true even in the United States, where a 2012 survey found that 63 percent of eighteen- to twenty-nine-year-olds believe that "invisible, non-corporeal entities called 'demons' can take partial or total control of human beings."[32] These beliefs are even more widespread in Latin America, and churches in Latin America are accordingly reclaiming a third vision of liberation: liberation from the powers of evil. The need to confront demonic powers has prompted the Catholic Church to begin offering annual courses for priests on "Exorcism and Prayers of Liberation." Official Catholic teaching is that demon possession is a very rare occurrence. The Church says that most people who think they are demon possessed are mentally ill and in need of psychiatric or psychological assistance. Exorcism has traditionally been seen as a last resort, to be used only after all other avenues of treatment have been exhausted. But opinions are changing in the Latin American Catholic Church, and they are changing partly because of the new prominence of Pentecostalism.

Many Pentecostals see exorcism not as a last resort but as a powerful weapon to be used whenever it is needed in the battle against Satan and the forces of evil. In some Pentecostal circles, ministries of exorcism and spiritual deliverance are part of normal church life and are routinely offered as sources of liberation for all who are spiritually oppressed. The Universal Church of the Kingdom of God actually calls its rituals of exorcism "*cultos de libertação*," services of liberation. The Pentecostal perspective on demon possession is much closer to opinions on the ground in Latin America than the Catholic stance, and it has been a factor in Pentecostalism's rapid growth.

Fighting demons is not the ultimate goal of spiritual liberation, however, even for Pentecostals. The broader goal of spiritual liberation is to free individuals from everything and anything that prevents them from being the people God wants them to be. Liberation in this sense of the term is not so much liberation *from* oppression as much as it is liberation *for* spiritual growth and vitality. Maritza León, a Pentecostal pastor in the Christ is Coming Church, calls this broader and more positive understanding of spiritual liberation "integral liberation," a focus on God's love and acceptance and on the experience of being transformed by the Holy Spirit. Spiritually liberated individuals "feel recognized by God and everyone else. No longer

32. "Halloween Poll Results," Public Policy Polling, October 30, 2012, www.publicpolicy polling.com/main/2012/10/halloween-poll-results.html.

Latin American Theology: Maritza León

The Divine Design and the Work of the Holy Spirit

Maritza León is an ordained minister in the Christ Is Coming Church (Iglesia Cristo Viene), a Pentecostal denomination in Venezuela. She was one of roughly fifty participants in the first consultation between Latin American Pentecostals and the World Council of Churches in Lima, Peru, in November 1994. This excerpt from her presentation at that meeting emphasizes the breadth of the Holy Spirit's liberating work in individual lives and society.

> Pentecost came 50 days after the Passover and was a celebration of dedication to the God of Liberation. . . . It is there that the Holy Spirit began its action among faith communities, from where he goes out to sow and reap living offerings to God, of whom we are ambassadors in this mission. . . .
>
> When believers feel they are subjects participating actively in the extension of the Kingdom of Heaven they adopt the attitude of praise in the complex reality in which they live, because this is part of the mission. And they begin to understand that it is not the organized church which fills temples through the appeal of its programs but the Holy Spirit making living temples of those who were human wrecks of sin, pain, misery and oppression; penetrating all layers of life and making us accept that the key point is to take the Divine Design with human support, and not the human plan which seeks divine sustenance.
>
> The Divine Design goes on amidst opposition: Jesus himself was sent out in the midst of total opposition, in the family, in the society (he was called a son of adultery), in the political realm (he represented another kingdom with another system, whereas Herod was the link with the system of the world which Christ came to break down). In the religious sphere (because he came to abolish the ceremonial law of the Old Testament with his new covenant, established through his sacrifice once and for all) and above all this he brought integral liberation with the sword of the Spirit, the Word of God, which instead of killing brings life.*

* Maritza León, "A Pentecostal Perspective on Evangelism," accessed January 16, 2015, www.pctii .org/wcc/leon94.html.

rejected, they feel accepted. They get their personal dignity back."[33] This kind of liberation is important to Pentecostals and also to Catholics. Almost all the churches in the region agree that spiritual liberation is as important as liberation from economic oppression and racial prejudice, and most see the three as intimately intertwined (see textbox, Latin American Theology: Maritza León).

33. Samuel Olson, quoted in "Roundtable on the Future of Pentecostalism," in *Religion in Latin America: A Documentary History*, ed. Lee M. Penyak and Walter J. Petry (Maryknoll, NY: Orbis, 2006), 377.

Summary

Christianity in Latin America began violently, with the conquest of the region followed by the forced Christianization of its people. But while religion played a major role in the rhetoric of colonization, the primary purpose of colonization was wealth accumulation—wealth for Spain and Portugal and wealth for the white colonial rulers and landowners. From the beginning, Latin America was a land where a few were rich and many were desperately poor. The revolutions of the early nineteenth century that severed Latin America's ties with Europe did little to moderate the social structure of the region, but they did dramatically complicate church-state relations. Catholicism remained the faith of the overwhelming majority of the region's population, but politically the nations of Latin America often swung back and forth between pro- and anti-Church groups. In this volatile context, a main concern of the Church was defending its own rights. Beginning in the early twentieth century, the Latin American Catholic Church developed a more positive self-identity and a more socially proactive stance, and in the 1960s and 1970s the Church began to confront the social inequalities of the region and to speak out on behalf of the poor. By that time, however, many Latin Americans were looking elsewhere for spiritual guidance and help. The *evangélico* Pentecostal movement exploded in the 1980s and 1990s, and there were predictions that the whole continent might become post-Catholic. In recent years, the Catholic Charismatic Renewal and a variety of other new ecclesiastical movements have drawn many people back to the Catholic Church.

One of the great gifts that Latin American Christianity brings to the global Christian community is the ability to speak honestly about its own past and its continuing failures, including matters of social and economic oppression and liberation. Latin Americans know that Christianity was imposed on the continent violently and that the Church has been complicit in the structures of inequality that dominate the region. Latin American Christians also recognize that liberation involves both socioeconomic and spiritual dimensions of life. Liberation frees people from everything that holds them back from being the people God wants them to be, and liberation in this sense applies to both the rich and the poor.

5

Europe

In October 2004, twenty-five European countries debated (and ultimately rejected) a new constitution for the European Union (EU). The draft constitution's preamble stated that "pluralism, non-discrimination, tolerance, justice, solidarity, and equality between women and men" were the core values of Europe derived from the unique "cultural, religious, and humanist inheritance" of the continent.[1] The little phrase "cultural, religious, and humanist inheritance" ignited a furor. Some people were appalled that God and Christianity were not mentioned by name. Some questioned how Europe could be understood without acknowledging its Christian past. Others were troubled by religion appearing in the document at all because they consider Europe's contemporary values to be the fruit of a successful secular transformation. Did these modern European values signify a new and robust flowering of Christian moral teachings, or were they markers of secularism's victory over Christianity?

There is no arguing that Christianity's influence in Europe has declined dramatically, and it is fair to describe contemporary Europeans as the least religiously active Christians anywhere in the world. Less than 10 percent attend worship services weekly, and levels of belief in God are low. But a quarter of the world's Christians still live in Europe, and some expressions of Christianity in Europe are flourishing. Every year, millions of pilgrims flock to places such

1. "Treaty Establishing a Constitution for Europe," October 29, 2004, http://www.cvce .eu/en/collections/unit-content/-/unit/d5906df5-4f83-4603-85f7-0cabc24b9fe1/0a763119-b665 -4710-9a3d-2a931285fd0c/Resources#6ea22f22-4455-431f-a30d-c1e719c6aa43_en&overlay.

as Lourdes (France), Fatima (Portugal), the shrine of Padre Pio (Italy), and Santiago de Compostela (Spain); millions more participate in Catholic ecclesiastical movements such as Focolare, Opus Dei, and Sant'Egidio. Protestantism continues to be upheld in the formal state churches of Denmark, England, Finland, Iceland, and Norway. And Orthodox Christianity is experiencing a revival in both Russia and elsewhere in Central and Eastern Europe, after decades of persecution under communist regimes.

Two hundred years ago, Europe ruled the world and governed the global Christian movement. Now it is merely one center of Christianity alongside many others, and European Christianity is clearly diminished. Despite this change of status, Europe continues to play an important role within Christianity worldwide. European theologians and biblical scholars are globally influential, and Rome remains the spiritual axis of the Catholic Church. Europe is the home of the World Council of Churches, and it is the heartland of Eastern Orthodoxy. European Christianity has been provincialized—it no longer dominates the world Christian movement—but the distinctive values and viewpoints of European Christianity continue to resonate in the global conversation about what it means to be a follower of Jesus today.

The History of European Christianity

The history of Christianity in Europe has been studied more deeply and intently than any other region of the world, so it is impossible for any overview of the region to capture all the many important stories that could be told. This section explores the role of Christianity in the creation of European culture (beginnings to 1450); presents the new Christian map of Europe created during the Protestant Reformation (1450–1650); examines the two and one-half centuries (1650–1900) when three religiously defined regions of Europe (Orthodox, Catholic, and Protestant) followed very different historical trajectories; and describes the key events of the twentieth century, when the three European traditions reengaged one another in the midst of two world wars, the Holocaust, the rise and fall of communism, and secularization.

Christianity and the Creation of Europe (Beginnings to 1450)

Christianity was introduced to Europe in the first century, when the apostle Paul received a call from God to move beyond the Roman province of Asia Minor (Turkey) across the Aegean Sea and preach the gospel in Macedonia. Both Paul and the apostle Peter later traveled to Rome, and the combined efforts of these two hugely influential early Christian leaders gave Rome a preeminence within the worldwide Christian movement, which it has maintained ever since. During the fourth and fifth centuries, both the city of Rome and the empire that was named after it became officially Christian. This process began with the conversion of the emperor Constantine in the early 300s, was dramatically advanced under the rule of Theodosius I (379–395), and was completed and codified in law by Theodosius II (402–450). Christianity, which had begun as a small network of believers with no political influence, became the governing philosophy of the world's most powerful empire. Power was wedded to piety, and that marriage of church and state shaped all of Europe's subsequent Christian history.

At the time when the Roman Empire first became Christian, the idea did not exist of a place called "Europe." The Roman empire was a water-based domain circling the Mediterranean Sea, and the area of land now known as Europe was simply the northern hinterland. It had no name. The event that set the stage for Europe to emerge as a separate and distinct region of the world was the barbarian invasion of the western half of the Roman Empire during the 400s.[2] Migrating Germanic tribes defeated the Roman army and then flooded into the region. The result was a much-reduced Roman Empire. Only the eastern half remained, and it was soon renamed the Byzantine Empire (see fig. 5.1). The western half of the old Roman Empire became the blank canvas upon which a new European regional identity would eventually be drawn.

Many of the so-called "barbarians" (a Roman term of derision for people unable to properly pronounce Latin) who lived in the nameless region that would later become Europe were Christians of a sort, but they held some beliefs that most Roman Christians considered heretical. In particular, Arianism, the idea that Jesus was not fully divine but was instead a semi-divine intermediary between God and humankind, had been introduced to these Germanic tribes in the mid-300s by the Arian missionary Ulfilas. This theological perspective was condemned at the Council of Nicaea in 325, and during the 400s and 500s, these formerly Arian tribes slowly gave up their Arianism and adopted Catholic Christianity instead. During the following five centuries, the rest of the region's non-Christian people adopted Catholic Christianity too, and Catholicism (which was already taking on a slightly different understanding of Christianity than Eastern Orthodoxy) became part of the territory's emerging identity.

Another crucial step in the development of Europe as a distinct geographical region of the world was the rise of Islam. The Prophet Muhammad died in

---

2. On this period as a whole, see Peter Brown, *The Rise of Western Christendom: Triumph and Diversity, A.D. 200–1000* (Oxford: Wiley-Blackwell, 2013).

Figure 5.1
The Roman Empire in 400 and 500

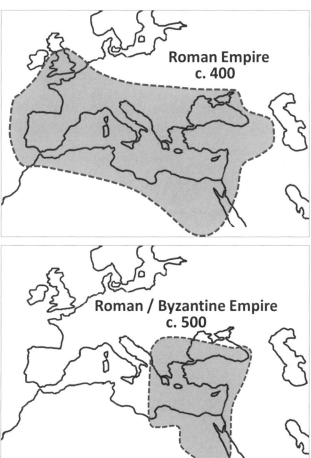

the year 632, and within a hundred years his followers had conquered almost all of the Middle East and North Africa, shattering the sea-based geographic network that had defined the old Roman Empire. With Muslims ruling the southern and eastern regions of the Mediterranean, the Byzantine Empire was reduced in size to little more than modern-day Turkey and Greece; what is now Western Europe became a third distinct region seeking an identity. During the late eighth and early ninth centuries, this western territory would become largely united in the form of Charlemagne's "Holy Roman Empire," which included most of what is now France, Italy, Switzerland, Germany, Austria, Belgium, and the Netherlands (see fig. 5.2).

Figure 5.2
European-Mediterranean Regional Map, c. 800

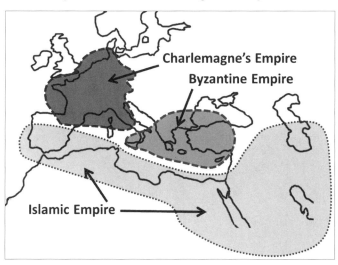

Charlemagne's domain became the nub of what would later expand into Western Europe as we know it today. What originally set this region apart was its Catholic identity, which was defined over against both the Islamic territories of North Africa and the Middle East and the Orthodox Byzantine Empire. Charlemagne tried to negotiate a treaty with the Byzantine Empire that would have united all the Christian lands in the north in opposition to Islam, but his proposal was rejected; and that rejection solidified the reality of Europe as a bifurcated region with a Catholic zone in the West and an Orthodox zone in the East.[3]

During Charlemagne's time, Scandinavia was still pagan, and so was most of Eastern Europe. Northern Europe was not fully Christianized until around the year 1000, which is also the time when Christianity was introduced to southern Russia (now Ukraine). Muscovite (northern) Russia and the Baltic states of Lithuania, Latvia, and Estonia were not converted to Christianity until the 1200s. The missionary efforts that spread Christianity into these new areas combined persuasion, political negotiation, and force or the threat of force. Once any particular region became officially Christian, the followers of pagan religions usually lost their rights, as did any Christians holding divergent or heretical (i.e., non-mainstream) views. A small number of Jews

3. See Andrew Louth, *Greek East and Latin West: The Church A.D. 681–1071* (Crestwood, NY: St. Vladimir's Seminary Press, 2007).

also lived precariously in Europe, subject to frequent persecution and inter-mittent expulsions from the lands where they lived. As Europe coalesced, it was religion and not physical geography that determined its boundaries: Europe was Catholic Christendom, the land where Catholic Christians were in charge.[4]

The culture of high medieval Europe (the period after 1000) was thor-oughly Christianized. Christianity dictated the annual calendar, Christian ceremonies marked the major transitions of life (birth, adulthood, marriage, coronations of rulers, and death), Christian art and architecture dominated the visual world, Christian moral teachings were encoded in the law, and Christian ideas formed the grid through which scholars viewed the world. Absolutely convinced of the rightness of its own values, Catholic Europe also became religiously aggressive, actively exporting its faith and way of life through military interventions in Muslim Spain, the Middle East, and the Baltic. Levels of personal religiosity are harder to assess, but the avail-able evidence points to a mix of compassion and cruelty, and of faith and magic that would trouble many contemporary Christians. While Europe was solidly Christian territory during these years, the era's Christian practices were not always exemplary.

A New Map of Christian Europe (1450–1650)

The dissolution of the Byzantine Empire after the fall of Constantinople in 1453 and the explosive rise of Protestantism redrew the religious map of Europe in the two centuries between 1450 and 1650.

The Great Schism of 1054 is typically cited as the time when Catholicism and Orthodoxy broke apart, but Catholic-Orthodox relations continued to be relatively cordial for at least another century. The real break between these two traditions came in 1204, when Catholic Crusaders attacked the Orthodox city of Constantinople, plundered the city's churches, and settled down to rule the region for the next seventy years. Many Orthodox Christians were compelled to become Catholic. Greek rule was restored to Constantinople in 1261, and Orthodoxy slowly recovered, but the struggling Byzantine Empire remained under threat from the ever-expanding Islamic Ottoman Empire. So, despite animosities between Catholic and Orthodox Christians, the Byzantines turned to the West once again in the early 1400s looking for help. The cost of that hoped-for assistance was becoming Catholic, and at the Council of Florence-Ferrara (1439), the Byzantine emperor John VIII Palaiologos agreed

4. See Richard Fletcher, *The Barbarian Conversion: From Paganism to Christianity* (Berkeley: University of California Press, 1997).

to acknowledge the primacy of the pope in exchange for Western military assistance. The promised military aid never arrived, however, and Constantinople fell to the Ottomans fourteen years later. Russian Orthodox Christians interpreted the Byzantine Empire's collapse as divine punishment for having consorted with Catholic heretics. Catholic and Orthodox Christians (especially Russians) no longer thought of each other as different followers of the same faith but as implacable religious antagonists.

The rise of Protestantism produced even greater animosity within Europe's Christian community. Protestantism emerged in the early sixteenth century following a series of earlier attempts at reform.[5] Protestantism offered a comprehensive theological critique of Catholicism, and it garnered enough support from local political rulers to be protected until the movement became too big to crush. "The Reformation," as it later came to be called, was triggered by Martin Luther, an ordained German monk who had existential, pastoral, and philosophical concerns about Catholic Christianity. He wanted to feel forgiven for his sins, but nothing in the Catholic tradition gave him the confidence to believe God had genuinely forgiven him. He thought the selling of indulgences (guarantees of reduced punishment in purgatory) was spiritually harmful to local parishioners. And he questioned how a religious tradition could correct its errors when its only source of authority was the tradition itself. Luther found the solution for all of these problems in the same place: the Bible. Luther said the Bible was the Christian's sole source of religious authority, and its message was one of unmerited (and unpurchasable) grace accessed through faith alone. Luther's new insights were summarized in three short phrases: *sola gratia*, *sola fide*, *sola scriptura* (salvation by grace alone through faith alone based on the authority of the Bible alone).

Originally, Luther did not intend to be a revolutionary. He wanted to reform the Catholic Church, not undermine it. But his new theology removed the need for any priestly mediation between God and humankind, undermining the authority of the Church, and the egalitarianism of his views caused some to question the authority of political rulers as well. Not surprisingly, both church and state reacted negatively. The pope excommunicated Luther in 1521, and later that year Emperor Charles V summoned Luther to appear at the Diet (the imperial court) in Worms, Germany. If Luther had been born fifty or a hundred years earlier, or if he had been living in Italy or Spain, he would probably have been declared a heretic and summarily executed. But

---

5. On the Reformation era as a whole, see Diarmaid MacCulloch, *The Reformation* (New York: Penguin, 2005).

Luther was from Saxony, and the local Saxon ruler, Frederick the Wise (who had almost been elected emperor himself), decided that neither the emperor nor the pope was going to eliminate a Saxon scholar who was as interesting and well known as Luther. Frederick was a Catholic and remained a Catholic all his life, but he was also Luther's protector. Several other European rulers joined Frederick in defense of the Protestant cause, and many of these monarchs became Protestants themselves. Soon England and Scandinavia were under Protestant governance, and so were various subregions of what is now Germany and Switzerland.

From its earliest days, the Protestant movement was internally diverse. Luther had opened a door, and a host of other Protestant reformers were soon rushing through it, championing their own differing visions of what Protestantism ideally should be. Anabaptists in Switzerland and the Netherlands read the Bible more literally than Luther did and began advocating for pacifism and adult baptism. Faustus Socinus started preaching a Unitarian Protestant version of the gospel in Poland. Huldrych Zwingli championed a decidedly humanistic form of Protestantism in Zurich before he was killed in battle in 1531. The Reformer with the greatest international influence was John Calvin, the first person to write a comprehensive, systematic theology for the Protestant movement. Calvinism (or Reformed theology) was soon being preached everywhere in Europe. (Calvin's message even won over Cyril Lucaris, an early seventeenth-century Orthodox patriarch of Constantinople, who sent several young Orthodox theologians to Switzerland and the Netherlands to study with Reformed professors.)

As the Protestant movement expanded, tensions with Catholics increased. Violence ensued, and for a hundred years, from roughly 1550 to 1650, Western Europe was embroiled in a continent-wide religious civil war. The fighting was not continuous, and allies sometimes changed sides, but the results were disastrous. The bloodiest fighting took place during the Thirty Years War (1618–1648), and the carnage was so great that the belligerents were finally forced to the bargaining table. The Peace of Westphalia that ended the war settled on a simple solution: each local ruler would determine which form of Christianity would be allowed in his or her domain. The ultimate result of this governing principle was that Europe was divided into three religiously homogenous regions (Orthodox, Catholic, and Protestant) with only a little territory left over where these traditions mixed (see fig. 5.3). Counting heads in 1650, about half of Europe's population would have been Catholic, one-third Orthodox, and one-sixth Protestant. Those percentages, and the religious map of Europe, have remained basically the same ever since.

Figure 5.3
Religious Map of Europe in 1650 (and Today)

Separate Histories (1650 to 1900)

From 1650 to 1900, the three religious regions of Europe—Orthodox Eastern Europe, Catholic Western Europe, and Protestant Northern Europe—existed side by side with little interaction among them. There were only a few limited regions in Europe where different kinds of Christians mixed. Germany was one of them. German-speaking Europe consisted of a variety of different principalities, duchies, kingdoms, and other territories. Some of them were predominantly Catholic, while others were Protestant. As the process of German unification moved forward in the 1800s, Catholics and Protestants had to learn how to interact and even cooperate with each other. Protestants, Catholics, and Orthodox Christians also rubbed shoulders in the Baltic region. In general, however, the histories of Orthodox, Catholic, and Protestant Europe unfolded separately.

Eastern Orthodoxy

The fall of Constantinople in 1453 changed the political geography of Eastern Orthodoxy. The Balkans and remnants of the Byzantine Empire were subsumed into the Islamic Ottoman Empire, and Russia became the only Orthodox territory still under Christian rule. Orthodox Christians in Russia soon developed a theory on the progression of history. The first Rome (Rome in Italy) fell because of pagan worship, and the second Rome (Constantinople) fell because of its heretical alliance with Catholicism. Moscow, by God's decree, was the third and final "Rome"—the center of true Christianity on earth—and it was from Moscow that the millennium (God's rule over the world) would slowly expand until it covered the globe. This messianic sense of Russia's role in Christian history continues to inform Russian Orthodoxy and the Russian nation today.

The actual history of Russian Orthodoxy between the years 1650 and 1900 was much less glorious than this messianic theology would suggest. In the mid-1600s, Russia developed plans to invade the Ottoman Empire and to liberate the Orthodox Christians living there from Muslim rule. Ecclesiastically, the hope was to reunite the Russian and Greek Orthodox churches, even though the Russian and Greek liturgical traditions had slowly diverged. Anticipating this event, the Russian Orthodox patriarch Nikon (1652–1658) suggested that some Russian liturgical practices might be modified to make them more compatible with Greek customs. That suggestion met with strong opposition, and when the contemplated invasion of the Ottoman Empire did not occur, it produced a massive schism within the Russian Orthodox Church. Nikon's anti-Greek opponents left the church. Later called "Old Believers," they continued to fight each other over the minutiae of Orthodox liturgy for decades, eventually splitting into two large groups and numerous smaller ones. Many of these divisions still exist within Russian Orthodoxy today.

Partly because of these divisions within the Orthodox Church, the Russian tsars of the eighteenth century—especially Peter the Great (1682–1725) and Catherine the Great (1762–1796)—decided to exercise greater control over the nation's religious life. Peter and Catherine were enamored with Western Europe, and they wanted to remodel the Russian state and its church to be more like the West. Peter was attracted to Lutheranism, so much so that in 1712 he appointed a Lutheran minister as the Orthodox bishop of his new capital of St. Petersburg. In 1721, Peter took a step further, abolishing the ecclesiastical office of the patriarch (the spiritual head of the Russian Orthodox Church). and placing the Church under the control of a layperson, a royal appointee called the *Oberprocurator*. Catherine tightened state control over the Church even more. A friend of the French Enlightenment thinker Voltaire, Catherine was suspicious of Church power. She seized much of the land still owned by the Orthodox Church, forcing the clergy to become more dependent on government support. Yet Catherine was also a cheerleader for Orthodoxy in opposition to Catholicism. When Russia joined with Prussia and Austria in 1772 to defeat and partition Poland, Catherine supported the forced conversions of Catholics to Orthodoxy, a policy that heightened already existing Catholic-Orthodox animosities.

The history of Orthodox Christianity outside of Russia is very different. Rather than following a trajectory of ever-expanding state control over the church, the Orthodox churches of non-Russian Eastern Europe experienced increasing freedom from external control. For most of the sixteenth, seventeenth, and eighteenth centuries, Eastern Europe was part of the Islamic Ottoman Empire. During these years, significant limitations were put on all the churches in the empire, including the fact that all the different Orthodox churches in the region were required to place themselves under the control and direction of the Patriarchate of Constantinople. The patriarch was not particularly respectful of Orthodox cultural differences, and many non-Greek-speaking Orthodox Christians came to resent the patriarch's interference in their ecclesiastical affairs. When the Ottoman Empire began to fall apart, these different Orthodox communities seized this opportunity to re-establish both their political independence and their ecclesiastical autonomy. The two were often intertwined, with political independence sometimes preceding and sometimes following ecclesiastical independence. In Greece, political independence came in 1832 and ecclesiastical freedom in 1833. Romania, by contrast, announced its churchly independence in 1865 and regained its political independence in 1877. Eventually, all of the different nations of Eastern Europe and all of their respective churches followed the same path, giving rise to the various independent, autocephalous ("self-headed") Orthodox churches that exist in the region today.

CATHOLICISM

By 1650, Catholic Europe had come to accept the permanence of Protestantism. Some territory had been lost in the north, but Catholicism continued to control at least two-thirds of Western Europe from Spain in the west to Poland in the east and from Ireland in the north to Italy in the south. The bonds between church and state remained strong in these predominantly Catholic nations, even though some of these countries had negotiated concessions from the pope that gave them considerable control over the Catholic Church within their domains. The pope himself was a political ruler—monarch of the Papal States, a sizeable territory in central Italy owned by the Church since the sixth century (see fig. 5.4)—so the art of political compromise came naturally.

On a more spiritual level, the Catholic Church was feeling increasingly secure in its competition with Protestantism. Rather than debating theological ideas, which many Protestants would have relished, the Catholic Church juxtaposed its own aesthetic sense of holiness to the austerity of standard Protestant worship. This was the age of baroque, with gilded churches, stained glass windows, and burning incense signaling the sacredness of Catholic space

Figure 5.4
Papal States, c. 1700

and where the Eucharist itself became a kind of holy pageant highlighting Christ's presence in the bread and wine. Catholic worship was meant to convey a sense of being transported to heaven. It was far different from the stark and imageless, sermon-centered worship of Protestantism. In comparison to Catholicism, Protestantism could seem dull to the point of being hardly religious at all. And that was precisely the point; Catholic aesthetic splendor trumped Protestant doctrinal diatribe.

Catholicism's post-Reformation stance is sometimes referred to as "throne and altar" because it mixed political loyalty to the monarch with spiritual devotion to the sacraments. The approach was successful for many years, but in the late 1700s Catholicism came under attack in a new way. The Age of Reason (the Enlightenment) was dawning, and across Europe people turned their attention away from faith—especially mystical and authoritarian faith—and looked toward science and rationality for guidance about how to live their lives and structure society. In 1789, these new tendencies, taken to the extreme, erupted with deadly violence in the French Revolution. King Louis XVI was executed in 1793. Revolutionaries also seized Church lands, called for the de-Christianization of the nation, and tried to create a new religion of Reason that would replace Catholicism as the public faith of the nation. Monasteries were closed, and thousands of priests fled the country. An entire generation of

French children was raised with little or no Christian instruction. Even more alarming, the new Republic of France seemed intent on exporting its gospel of secular liberty into the rest of Catholic Europe. Napoleon took control of France in 1799 and made himself emperor in 1804. His consolidation of power undermined revolutionary ideals in France, but he continued to export those ideals outside France because they served his political purposes. In all the regions he conquered (see fig. 5.5), connections between throne and altar were severed.

Napoleon was defeated at the Battle of Waterloo in June 1815, and the Congress of Vienna tried to restore European politics and national boundaries to something like their pre-Napoleonic existence. The Catholic Church also tried to recover its old power and prestige within European society. Neither attempt was particularly successful because too much had changed. The Catholic Church accordingly settled into a stance of long-term opposition to anything that it deemed to be modern. Pope Pius IX (in office from 1846 to 1878), who was also known as *Pio Nono* in Italian, was caricatured in the English press as "Pope No-No" because he so consistently denounced all things new. In the *Syllabus of Errors*, issued in 1864, he famously rejected the preposterous idea that "the Roman Pontiff can, and ought to, reconcile himself, and come to terms with progress, liberalism, and modern civilization." Trying to hold onto the Papal States further complicated matters and kept the papacy on

Figure 5.5
**Napoleon's Conquered Territories
and Allies, c. 1810**

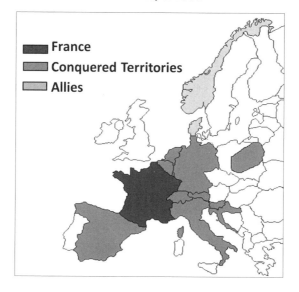

the defensive. Invaded and dismantled several times between 1799 and the mid-1800s, the Papal States were permanently incorporated into the newly unified nation of Italy in 1870, though the Catholic Church did not give up its claim to the territory until 1929.

Some Catholic scholars and theologians tried to carve out a middle ground between the radicalism of the revolution and Pio Nono's ultraconservatism, and it was this middle path that the Church eventually followed. The modern world was not going away, and the Catholic Church slowly began to direct its attention toward the plight of the poor in a rapidly industrializing Europe. New Catholic political parties arose to support the rights of workers against abusive business owners, and religious orders and other Catholic associations and organizations were created to serve the needs of workers. Pope Leo XIII's encyclical *Rerum novarum* (1891) said it was the responsibility of Catholics everywhere "by every means in their power [to] strive to secure the good of the people."[6] This statement marks a remarkable transformation in the papacy itself. In the early years of the nineteenth century, popes were still trying to hold on to political power and their cozy relationship with royalty; by the end of the century they had relinquished that desire and had become spiritual spokespersons for the masses. The forces of modernity bemoaned by Pio Nono had effectively become a blessing in disguise. As the popes lost political power, the spiritual nature of the office was reaffirmed. A similar turn toward the spiritual is evident in the proliferation of new Catholic religious orders, especially women's religious orders, that were created in Europe during the nineteenth century. As the political world became more complicated and secular, European Catholics funneled their religious energies into spiritual devotion and service to others.

PROTESTANTISM

The experience of European Protestants between 1650 and 1900 was less tension-ridden than either Orthodoxy or Catholicism, but it was also more internally pluralistic. European Protestantism was housed in government-sanctioned state churches in England (Anglicanism), in Scandinavia (Lutheranism), and in smaller states and provinces across the region that now comprises Germany, Switzerland, Belgium, and the Netherlands (mostly Reformed churches, but some Lutheran). By 1650, all of these churches had begun articulating their slightly different theologies with great precision and detail. This was the age of Protestant *Confessionalism*, when each of the various Protestant subtraditions composed written confessions of faith defining the

---

6. Pope Leo XIII, *Rerum novarum*, 63.

beliefs and doctrines that members of those churches were supposed to affirm. Protestantism had burst onto the scene in the early 1500s with an explosion of new insights and emphases, and there was no doubt that many of these assertions needed to be tamed, evaluated, reconfigured, and systematized. But by the mid-1600s, many European Protestants felt as if the vitality of the movement was being drowned in a sea of words.

Pietism was one reaction to the perceived ossification of the movement. Rather than emphasizing doctrine and belief, pietism put the accent on inner experience. The goal was conversion of the heart, not the head. "True Christianity," as Pietists sometimes called their stance, focused on loving God, resisting sin, and serving others with gladness and joy. Pietists thought that arguing about doctrinal differences, as so many Confessionalists were prone to do, was detrimental to faithful Christian living.

Pietists were not religious revolutionaries. They had no desire to dismantle any of the Protestant state churches; instead, they wanted to breathe new life into them. Most Pietists accordingly remained members of their various state churches, but they created small cell groups within those churches where "true" believers could gather for prayer, Bible study, and mutual encouragement. Even in England, where Pietism in the form of Methodism eventually split off from the Anglican state church, separation was not the original goal. John Wesley, the founder of the Methodist movement, was an ordained Anglican priest who intended for his network of spiritually energized Anglican Christians to remain within the Church of England. But after Wesley's death, tensions between the Anglican leadership and Wesley's followers led to the formation of a new Methodist Church, which later divided into a variety of different Methodist denominations.

Pietists never attained a majority in any of the historic Protestant churches, but they influenced all of European Protestantism nonetheless, and nowhere more spectacularly than in the Protestant missionary movement. The different Protestant churches of Europe had initially shown no interest in foreign missionary work. The focus instead was on establishing Protestantism at home in Europe. Pietism challenged this attitude, and by the late 1700s pietistically oriented Protestants from a wide variety of European Protestant traditions (Anglican, Baptist, Lutheran, Methodist, Moravian, and Reformed) were engaging in missionary activity around the world. Pietism's emphasis on "saving the lost" would eventually leaven all of European Protestantism.

Another broad movement that developed within European Protestantism in reaction to Confessionalism was Christian *rationalism*. Rather than stressing the existential dimensions of Christianity as Pietists had, rationalists focused their attention on morality and the reasonableness of faith. Like Pietists, most

Protestant rationalists maintained membership in their various state churches, but they ignored whatever they deemed too petty or divisive or outdated. They viewed Christianity as the natural faith of all humankind, a perspective that any reasonable person would see as true. Protestant rationalism was mostly a movement of the educated elite, but university-educated ministers often transmitted at least some of their views to parishioners through their sermons. Taken to an extreme, Protestant rationalism could border on being post-Christian, more oriented toward science and common sense than anything specifically Christian. But most rationally oriented Protestants did not go that far. What set them apart as Christians was their reasonable approach to Christianity in contrast to being either unwarrantably dogmatic (Confessionalism) or unduly subjective (Pietism). John Locke's *The Reasonableness of Christianity* (1695) exemplifies this stance. All three varieties of Protestantism—Confessionalism, Pietism, and rationalism—can be found in contemporary European Protestantism, but rationalism is probably the most influential.

Protestantism remains more focused on ideas and beliefs than either Catholicism or Orthodoxy, so it is unsurprising that the rise of modern philosophy and science has had a deep impact on the movement. In fact, European Protestantism helped drive these developments. For example, Immanuel Kant, who is frequently credited with launching the modern philosophical movement, was a Lutheran. Similarly, it was Charles Darwin, a ministerial student in the Church of England, who developed the theory of evolution, with his new views of biology being grounded on a Christian sense of respect for all creatures, whether living or extinct.

Rather than fighting against new intellectual insights and theories, European Protestants generally embraced them and adjusted their religious beliefs to bring them into alignment with the best of modern thought. It was not uncommon, for example, to hear European Protestant preachers say that evolution was God's way of doing things. Some Protestant theologians voiced resistance to modern ideas, but there was nothing in European Protestantism that came close to Catholicism's nineteenth-century rejection of modern learning. Protestantism had a similarly easy time adapting to modern democracy. Rather than either resisting democracy or linking democracy with the abolition of monarchy, most of Protestant Europe slowly embraced democracy without feeling any need to end their monarchies.

The Twentieth Century

The nineteenth century ended on a positive note for all three Christian traditions. Protestants had moved smoothly into modernity, Catholics had stopped fighting modernity and were seeking to be agents of care and compassion in newly industrialized Europe, and Orthodox Christians were regaining control over their nations and churches in Eastern Europe. Hope was in the air, and most Christians in Europe assumed the future would be significantly better than the past. The twentieth century dashed those hopes. Rather than bringing peace and progress, it was an era of warfare, violence, persecution, and genocide. And it was a century of decline for Christianity in Europe.

The First World War (1914–1918) never should have been fought. The immediate trigger was the assassination of Archduke Franz Ferdinand of Austria, which set off a cascade of escalating military responses. The deeper roots of the war lay in the military ideal itself (the manly glories of battle) and in inflated national and ethnic pride that pushed Europeans toward confrontation at the slightest hint of disrespect. Once the war began, the churches quickly got into the business of hyping it. German Protestant theologians portrayed the war as a holy crusade for Christ and the German nation. Russian Orthodox leaders argued that the war was necessary to defeat the Western European antichrist and to defend Mother Russia. French Catholics sewed images of the Sacred Heart of Jesus to their national flag, indicating that faith and the nation were one. Anglican bishops told British soldiers to kill Germans whether they were good or bad or young or old in order to save the world from Teutonic dictatorship.[7] Almost all the war rhetoric, on all sides, mixed God, glory, and gutsiness into a hot soup of righteous fervor. For ordinary foot soldiers, none of it made much sense. Harry Patch, the oldest survivor of the war who died in 2009 at the age of 111, said bluntly, "What the hell we fought for, I now don't know."[8]

The barbarity of the war was shocking. More than ten million soldiers died along with five million civilians, and many millions more were maimed and wounded. Pope Benedict XV, one of the few religious leaders to speak against the war, called it "the suicide of civilized Europe." Who, he asked, could imagine that the belligerents, so full of hatred for one another, were "all of one common stock, all of the same nature, all members of the same human society?"[9] Who could imagine they were all followers of the same Lord Jesus Christ? How could followers of Christ hate one another so much?

After the war, these questions prompted a radical reconsideration of theology all across Europe. For German-speaking Protestants, the writings

7. Philip Jenkins, *The Great and Holy War: How World War I Became a Religious Crusade* (San Francisco: HarperOne, 2014).

8. Nigel Blundell, "Last Survivor Re-lives the Horrors of Passchendaele," *The Daily Mail*, July 28, 2007.

9. Jenkins, *Great and Holy War*, 65.

of the Swiss pastor Karl Barth became especially important. His reformulation of Protestant theology stressed the sinfulness of humankind and the "otherness" of God, a God who could never be corralled into the confines of any nationalistic, war-mongering ideology. In Catholic Europe, a group of French theologians (including Jacques Maritain, Yves Congar, Pierre Teilhard de Chardin, and Henri-Marie de Lubac) developed a new theological approach (*nouvelle théologie*) that reaffirmed the radicalness of the gospel, suggested firm limits on the power of the state, and championed the dignity of all persons regardless of national or ethnic identity. These were important responses, and they helped the churches of Europe dissociate themselves from the mindless nationalism that had shaped their behavior during the war. But for many ordinary believers, people who did not read academic texts about Christian theology, the more common response was disillusionment with the churches and with religion in general. To some degree, modern European secularism was birthed by the First World War.

Christians in Eastern Europe did not have as much time as those in the West to reflect on the meaning of World War I. Especially in Russia, the much more immediate concern was communism. The First World War destabilized the government of Russia, and Tsar Nicholas II was forced to abdicate in March 1917. A power vacuum resulted, and the Communist Party seized the moment, taking control of the government in October 1917. The communist vision of society was vastly different from that of tsarist Russia, and, once in power, Russia's communists orchestrated a major restructuring of political and economic life. They were atheists who believed religion caused many of the world's ills, and they launched a massive attack on the Orthodox Church. Over the next three decades, most of the nation's churches were closed, hundreds of monasteries were destroyed, thousands of priests were arrested or killed, and Russian Orthodoxy itself was driven to the brink of extinction. The only small ray of hope during these years was the reestablishment of the patriarchate, the ecclesiastical office that had been abolished by Peter the Great in 1721. Patriarch Tikhon was elected just before the Communist Party took control, and he was deposed from the office in 1923 by Premier Joseph Stalin. The office itself remained intact, however, and was later filled by Ivan Stragorodsky, who was installed as Patriarch Sergius in 1943.

The punitive terms of the peace treaty that ended World War I made World War II almost inevitable. The second World War began in September 1939, when Germany invaded Poland, and soon all of Europe was involved in another bloody conflagration. It looked like World War I all over again, but one thing was different: religion played a much smaller role. World War II was not a crusade. Many Christians considered it a "just war" that had to be fought, but the spiritual swagger of the first war was absent.

The most important religious concern associated with World War II was not passion for the war but lack of passion in protecting Jews and other vulnerable people (including Gypsies, the disabled, gay men, and prisoners of war) from mass execution by the Nazis. Between 1939 and 1945, six million Jews were killed along with three or four million non-Jews. The Holocaust, the systematic effort to exterminate the Jewish race, is a terrible chapter in human history and, more specifically, in Christian history. Some scholars say the Nazi movement was a direct outgrowth of Christian anti-Semitism, while others argue that the roots of Nazism were more pagan than Christian; but it is undeniable that many European Christians supported the Holocaust, and many others passively acquiesced. Only a handful of Christians hid Jews, helped them escape, or actively resisted the Nazi death machine. Even Dietrich Bonhoeffer, who is well known for participating in an attempted assassination of Hitler, was not primarily focused on protecting Jews but on thwarting Hitler's attempts to control the church.

It is not just the failure of Christians to intervene that haunts the European Christian psyche but also the failure of God to stop the event. Many questioned how an omnipotent God could have allowed the Holocaust to happen. One of the most common theological responses was to argue that God does not control history, even though God encourages and promotes certain developments within history. The Holocaust, therefore, was an expression of sin and human choice, and not God's will. Many European Protestant theologians also suggested that God was not indifferent to what had happened. God feels the pain of the world, and God somehow suffered along with the victims of the Holocaust. Wrestling with the Holocaust has been a special focus of German theology, and Jürgen Moltmann's *The Crucified God*, first published in 1973, declares that theology can never be the same after Auschwitz.

Catholic theology since World War II has been less explicitly tied to the war, but no less radical in its revisioning of the gospel. The declarations of the Second Vatican Council, which met four times between October 1962 and December 1965 (see fig. 5.6), is a case in point. Vatican II was not convened for the purpose of coming to grips with the war, but the council reflected a significant shift in how Catholics define themselves and their faith. In contrast to older attitudes that drew clear lines of difference between Catholics and everyone else, Vatican II said, "The joys and the hopes, the griefs and the anxieties of the men of this age, especially those who are poor or in any way afflicted, these are the joys and hopes, the griefs and anxieties of the followers of Christ. Indeed, nothing genuinely human fails to raise an echo in their

Figure 5.6. Bishops entering St. Peter's Basilica for opening of Vatican II

hearts."[10] Prior to Vatican II, most Catholics believed that God felt the pain of Catholics, but the council said that God felt the pain of the whole world. As a result, Catholics were encouraged to reach out to everyone who was suffering, regardless of race, ethnicity, nationality, or religion. The council even argued that non-Catholics deserve respect both as human beings *and as people of faith*, declaring that "the Catholic Church rejects nothing that is true and holy in [other] religions. She regards with sincere reverence those ways of conduct and of life, those precepts and teachings which, though differing in many aspects from the ones she holds and sets forth, nonetheless often reflect a ray of that Truth which enlightens all men."[11] Before Vatican II, Catholics (and most other Christians as well) had viewed Jews as enemies of Christ or even as Christ killers, an attitude that helped make the Holocaust possible. After World War II, those views were mostly jettisoned.

For all their efforts to update Christianity after World War II and to make it more positive in orientation and more attuned to modern life, the churches of Western Europe have not been successful in holding on to their members. Instead, the general trend in Western Europe has been one of serious decline in terms of both Christian practices (such as going to church) and Christian

10. Pope Paul VI, *Gaudium et spes* (1965), 1.
11. Pope Paul VI, *Nostra aetate* (1965), 2.

beliefs (such as belief in God). To some degree this decline can be attributed to disillusionment with religion in general after two world wars, and to some degree it may be a function of the sheer busyness of modern life when too many other matters call for attention. But these factors do not completely explain the decline, because Western Europeans began turning away from Christianity even before World War I. The Law of Separation enacted in France in 1905 imposed a policy of *laïcité* (governmentally enforced secularization) on public life, and church attendance records from Great Britain show that weekly attendance at Sunday services was already below 20 percent in 1900. Christianity in Western Europe has been declining ever since.

Christianity in Eastern Europe faced a very different challenge after World War II. The armistice that ended the war gave Russia a free hand in Eastern Europe, which translated into communist domination for everyone behind the "iron curtain" that divided Europe in half (see fig. 5.7). Nations to the west of the line were politically democratic, nations to the east were communist, and there was little interaction between the two. Christians in the communist-dominated East were subjected to the same kind of persecution that Christians in Russia had endured since 1917, but religious conditions varied from nation to nation. Albania declared itself an officially atheistic state in 1976 and religion was banned entirely, while Poland was so devoutly Catholic that churches had to be tolerated to some degree. In all the countries where communists were in charge, churches were closed, pastors and priests

Figure 5.7
**The "Iron Curtain" That Divided Europe
from 1946 to 1990**

were harassed, arrested, and sometimes killed, and Christianity itself was marginalized as much as possible.

Communism collapsed in Eastern Europe in 1990 under the weight of its own moral and political deficiencies, and many of the churches in the region helped with its demise. Since then, there has been a revival of religious faith in the region, and especially of Orthodoxy. New churches are being built, monasteries are being reestablished, and people are flocking to worship. However, Christianity in Eastern Europe can still be nationalistic and confrontational. The Balkan Wars of the 1990s pitted Orthodox Christians, Catholics, and Muslims against one another. This war had many contributory causes, but the religio-ethnic "cleansing" that was at its core reveals how much faith can still be allied with hatred and violence. A similar but less violent religious confrontation is currently taking place in Russia, where the Orthodox Church has pressured the postcommunist government to impose significant restrictions on non-Orthodox Christians such as Baptists and Pentecostals. The Russian Church and the Russian government are now closely aligned, and Russian Orthodoxy's historic perception of itself as the Third Rome, the champion and protector of true Christian faith, is back on full display.

Contemporary European Christianity

It is often said that Christianity is dying in contemporary Europe. That is an overstatement, but the sentiment is understandable given the dynamics of religious life in Europe today. There are some signs of spiritual vitality in the region, but the overall pattern is one of deep and pervasive decline. Because this is the case, secularization is the first topic discussed below. A second topic addressed in this section is immigration, a new development that is rapidly changing the religious composition of the region. The final topic concerns sex and procreation and its impact on both church and society.

Secularization

In its simplest definition, *secularization* means that religion is less visible, less pervasive, and less influential than it was in the past. This trend is blatantly visible in Europe, where massive medieval cathedrals stand empty all week and only a handful of parishioners appear for Sunday worship, with the faithful few clustering in the front of the sanctuary or in a small side chapel. The word *God* appears less often in public documents, prayers are invoked less frequently at public events, and churches make the news only if violence or scandal is involved. But it is not just behavior that has changed; beliefs have changed too. Today, only about half of Europeans say they believe in God (see fig. 5.8). Precise percentages depend on how the question is framed. In France, for example, when people are asked if they believe in God defined simply as a force governing the universe, about 65 percent say yes, but only 35 percent believe in God when God is defined as a "person."[12]

Figure 5.8
Percentage of the Population Believing in a Personal God*

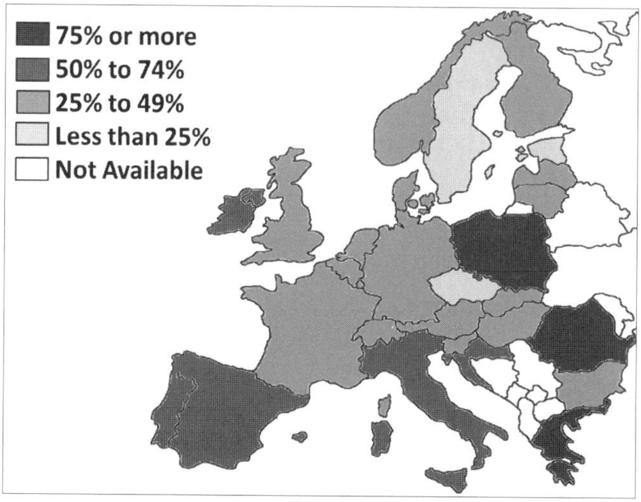

* Based on data from Eurobarometer, Public Opinion Analysis, European Commission (website), http://ed.europa.eu/public_opinion/index_en.htm

Some European nations are very secular, others are decidedly not, and most of Europe falls somewhere in between. In more secular countries such as France and Sweden, inviting a person to attend church on Sunday is a social faux pas. In contrast, nearly half of Poles attend Mass every week, and though that proportion is 15–20 percent less than it was twenty years ago, Poles are still among the most religiously active Christians on earth. Two generalizations can be made about overall patterns. First, secularization is deeper and more evenly dispersed across Protestant Europe than in either Catholic or Orthodox Europe. Second, Eastern Europe is generally less secular than Western Europe, even though Eastern Europe experienced decades of forced secularism under

12. Eurobarometer, Public Opinion Analysis, European Commission (website), http://ed.europa.eu/public_opinion/index_en.htm, accessed August 29, 2014.

Figure 5.9
East and West Historical Trends 1900 to Present*

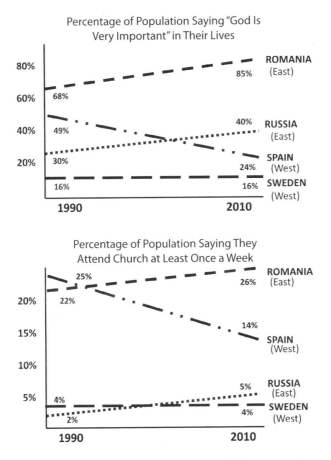

Percentage of Population Saying "God Is
Very Important" in Their Lives

80%   ROMANIA
                                                    85%   (East)

60%   68%

40%   40%   RUSSIA
      49%   (East)

20%   30%   SPAIN
                                                    24%   (West)
      16%   16%   SWEDEN
                                                          (West)
      1990   2010

Percentage of Population Saying They
Attend Church at Least Once a Week

         25%   ROMANIA
                                                    26%   (East)
20%   22%

15%   14%
                                                          SPAIN
                                                          (West)
10%

                                                    5%   RUSSIA
5%   4%   (East)
                                                          SWEDEN
                                                    4%   (West)
      2%
      1990   2010

* Statistics from the World Values Survey, www.worldvaluessurvey.org/wvs
.jsp, accessed 25 July 2014.

communist rule, while Western Europe became secular with no coercion at
all. The difference between East and West is evident in the number of people
saying God is very important in their lives and in church attendance figures.
In Western Europe, the numbers are holding steady or decreasing. In Eastern
Europe, they are slowly rising (see fig. 5.9). Eastern Europe's recovery from its
forced secularization under communism has surprised scholars. In the 1960s
and 1970s, most sociologists and historians assumed that secularization was
a one-way path that could never be reversed, but Eastern Europe shows that
assumption is wrong.

Secularization is not just about observable changes in behaviors and expressed beliefs; it is also a state of mind. Secularization encourages a practical, this-worldly, nonmysterious, moral approach to life, and European Christianity generally fits this bill. Decades ago, the German theologian Dietrich Bonhoeffer wrote a series of letters from prison in which he mused that Europe might be entering a religionless age. Rather than being disturbed, Bonhoeffer thought this might be a reason for Christians to rejoice. Overconfident religiosity, he said, can easily become dangerous, and religious people sometimes assume that God is theirs to manipulate. Bonhoeffer hoped that secularization would free Christianity from its penchant to see the world through us-versus-them lenses and would enable Christians to more easily discover Christ in all of life. Bonhoeffer was not alone in viewing secularization as a potentially positive development. This same attitude is evident, for example, in the support European Christians gave to the Universal Declaration of Human Rights passed by the United Nations in 1948. The document is directed toward "all members of the human family." God is not mentioned at all, but this very secular declaration has perhaps advanced Jesus's command to "do unto others as you would have them do unto you" more successfully than any statement issued by any church. If such an outcome is the result of secularization, then many European Christians would welcome a more secular world.

Immigration and Faith

Europe is currently undergoing significant demographic changes as a result of immigration. More than 2.5 million immigrants now arrive in Europe every year, coming mostly from Africa and Asia. The most visible immigrants, and for Europeans the most problematic, are Muslims. Muslims have been present in Eastern Europe for centuries, ever since the Islamic Ottoman Empire conquered most of southeast Europe in the 1400s. The situation has not always been amicable, as evidenced by the Balkan Wars in the 1990s, but it is familiar. The presence of Muslims in Western Europe is, by contrast, a recent phenomenon. In 1950, only a handful of Muslims were living in Western Europe; today there are about 20 million, many of them lower-wage workers. Germany, France, and the United Kingdom each have Muslim populations in excess of three million. Paralleling where these countries established colonies around the world, most of Germany's Muslims come from Turkey, most of France's from North Africa, and most of the United Kingdom's from India and Pakistan. In Western Europe as a whole, Muslims now account for about

5 percent of the total population, a number expected to rise to more than 7 percent by 2030.[13]

As is typical of immigrants worldwide, most new arrivals seek housing near family members and friends. This clustering has resulted in the growth of sizeable Muslim neighborhoods in some European cities. Muslims now represent 20 percent or more of the population in Amsterdam, Marseille, Rotterdam, and Stockholm, and they account for 10–20 percent of the population in Antwerp, Birmingham, Brussels, Frankfurt, London, Paris, Utrecht, and Vienna. In France, the number of religiously practicing Muslims is now roughly equal to the number of Catholics attending Mass every week. In Paris, so many Muslims gather for Friday prayers that the city's mosques can no longer accommodate them. Prayer mats are spread out on the streets around the mosques, with the devout blocking traffic for the duration of their prayers.

In Western Europe as a whole, the social (and sometimes legal) rule is that individuals can practice whatever faith they choose in private, but the public sphere is supposed to be religiously "naked," devoid of all obvious religious symbols. France, in particular, is a place where religion has been considered a thoroughly private affair for most of the twentieth century, so the visibility of Islam there is disturbing to many. Muslims, and especially Muslim women who cover their faces with veils when in public, flout the written and unwritten rules about public secularism. Some of the most intense recent debates about religion have centered on whether Muslims girls should be allowed to wear headscarves in public schools. So far, the answer in most of Western Europe has been no; but Europe's Muslim communities are unhappy with that response, and the issue is far from settled. Even more troubling to many French citizens is the way that some radical Muslim extremists seem to repudiate core Western European values. This was evident in the 2015 attack on the headquarters of the *Charlie Hebdo* magazine during which a number of satirical cartoonists were killed, ostensibly for drawing derogatory pictures of the Prophet Muhammad. This attack fueled the view held by some European Christians that Islam and modern Western culture are simply incompatible. That is not necessarily true, but the perception is very real.

Europe's contemporary encounter with Islam is forcing Western Europeans to think about religion and secularism in new ways. For the most part, secularization in Western Europe has advanced almost unconsciously, as individuals have drifted away from church often without thinking. Because this has taken place so unreflectively, many Christian attitudes and habits of life

13. *The Future of the Global Muslim Population* (Washington, DC: Pew Forum, 2011), 122, 124.

Figure 5.10. Africa-based World Flaming Gospel Church International (Uppsala, Sweden)

have remained subliminally part of European culture even as the region as a whole has become progressively secular. The visible presence of Muslims in Europe is now reminding many Europeans of how culturally Christian they still are, at least in contrast to Islam. For many secular Europeans, this is an awkward exercise in dawning self-awareness. Whether it will result in a self-conscious return to faith or a more explicit rejection of religion is another unsettled religious question.

Fewer than half of Europe's new immigrants are Muslim, however. Christian immigrants from Africa and Asia now exceed the number of Muslims entering the region. Currently, 39 percent of new European immigrants are Muslim, and 42 percent are Christian.[14] Christian immigration has not been the topic of much debate in Europe, but it is reshaping religious life in Europe at least as much as Muslim immigration is challenging it. African or Asian congregations can now be found in all the major cities in Western and Eastern Europe. Some of these churches are small storefront operations with only a handful of worshipers attending (see fig. 5.10), but others draw huge crowds for Sunday worship. The Kingsway International Christian Centre in the United Kingdom was founded in 1992 by a Nigerian pastor named Matthew Ashimolowo, and it currently attracts more than 12,000 worshipers weekly to its Prayer City site in Chatham. Many of the church's members are people from Africa or the African diaspora, but the number of white Britons attending is increasing as well.

A similar phenomenon can be observed in Eastern Europe, where, for example, the largest church in Ukraine is the Embassy of the Blessed Kingdom of God for All Nations, pastored by the Reverend Sunday Adelaja. In the late 1980s, Adelaja moved from Nigeria to Kiev to study engineering on a

14. *Faith on the Move: The Religious Affiliation of International Migrants* (Washington, DC: Pew Research Center, 2012), 54.

scholarship from what was still a communist government. Instead, he started a church, reaching out especially to drug addicts and the city's homeless. Adelaja's career has had its ups and downs, including accusations of financial fraud, but none of these accusations have ever been proved in court. Today, the church claims one hundred thousand members; some are African immigrants, but many are ethnic Ukrainians. Ashimolowo and Adelaja's churches are both Pentecostal, as are many of the other immigrant churches now found in Europe.

Immigrants continue to arrive in Europe in large numbers, so it is likely that Europe will become more religiously and culturally diverse in the years ahead and that Pentecostalism, which has traditionally been only slightly represented in the region, will grow in size and visibility. These two trends may have the effect of making Europeans more religiously self-aware and perhaps even more self-consciously Christian. Already, about 10 percent of the Catholic parishes in France use the Alpha Course, a charismatically oriented introduction to Christianity developed by Holy Trinity Anglican Church in London, to teach their members about their faith and how to share it with others.[15] Europe is clearly a secular place at present, but immigration is opening space for new religious conversations and visibility.

Marriage, Children, Families, and Sex

Families and faith have been inseparable from the beginning of Europe's Christianization, and they are still linked today. More than 90 percent of the Christians in Europe belong to churches that practice infant baptism. This includes the Catholic Church; all the Orthodox churches; all the Scandinavian Lutheran churches; the Reformed churches in Germany, the Netherlands, Scotland, and Switzerland; the Church of England; and even the Methodists. Europeans are defined by their faith traditions long before they have any individual choice in the matter. Baptism is both one's record of birth and one's membership card in the church. Or at least that is the way things worked in the past. Today, only 30 percent of children in France and 50 percent in Sweden are baptized, and baptism numbers are declining across the continent.[16]

Weddings are changing too. Weddings with a priest and church bells used to be ubiquitous, but now they are not. In Sweden, for example, only 40 percent

15. Personal conversation with Dominique Marie Jean Rey, bishop of Fréjus-Toulon, France, January 28, 2014.

16. "Swedes Depart Church in Droves," *The Local: Sweden's News in English*, May 27, 2010, www.thelocal.se/20100527/26878; and "France before the Drop in Vocations and Baptisms," *Revelation Secular*, June 7, 2014, http://apocalisselaica.net/en/varie/cristianesimo-catto licesimo-e-altre-religioni/la-francia-davanti-al-calo-delle-vocazioni-e-dei-battesimi-nuovi-modi -di-essere-chiesa.

of weddings are now performed in churches. Perhaps more important, many Europeans are not getting married at all, not even when children are on the way. The number of children born out of wedlock has skyrocketed. In England in 1980, about 10 percent of births were to single mothers; today the number is 50 percent. In Italy, the proportion of children born to single mothers jumped from 4 percent in 1980 to more than 20 percent today. In Ireland, the percentage rose from 5 percent to more than 30 percent. In Norway, rates shot up from 15 percent to 60 percent. And, married or not, European women are having fewer babies than in the past. For any given population group to maintain its numbers, each woman must give birth on average to at least two children. European-born Europeans, in contrast to recently arrived immigrants, are currently averaging only about 1.5 children per woman. This means that the number of white Europeans is declining and, if birth rates remain this low, the rate of decrease will accelerate significantly in the future. Some commentators have suggested that Europeans seem intent on committing "demographic suicide."[17]

Pope John Paul II had both a diagnosis and a cure for Europe's fertility problem. He said that falling birthrates in Europe signaled a "troubled relationship with [the] future" and identified the underlying problem as a "dimming of hope" brought about by Europe's loss of "Christian memory and heritage." John Paul blamed Europe's "culture of death," including legalized abortion, embryonic research, and euthanasia, for the decline in childbearing, and he said the cure necessarily involved a rediscovery and recovery of Europe's "true identity," meaning its Christian heritage. Only a new culture of life and solidarity could restore hope and the "proper ordering of society." The pope stated his case plaintively, "Europe, as you stand at the beginning of the third millennium, '*Open the doors to Christ! Be Yourself. Rediscover your origins. Relive your roots.*'"[18] For Pope John Paul II, the institution of marriage is the single most important human symbol for understanding the mystery of salvation, and sexual intercourse (or what he called the "language of the body") is the "great analogy" of God's love for humankind—a love that, like God's, must always be open to the creation of new life. For him, the dissolution of marriage and declining birthrates in Europe are not just social or moral problems, they are theological problems as well.

Both John Paul II and his successor Benedict XVI spoke out insistently against anything they thought undermined the traditional family, including birth control, abortion, gay rights, the full equality of men and women, and the general laxness

17. George Weigel, *The Cube and the Cathedral: Europe, America, and Politics without God* (New York: Basic Books, 2005), 21.

18. Pope John Paul II, *Ecclesia in Europa* (June 28, 2003), 7, 95, 111, 114, 120. Emphasis in original.

of European sexual mores.[19] They were expressing what they thought was best for the Catholic Church, for Europe, and for Christianity in general. But their blunt declarations—that Europe can be saved only by a massive return to Christianity and by stricter laws against things such as abortion and gay rights—have not had the desired effect. Rather than nudging Europe closer to Christianity and closer to traditional marriage and family practices, the heavy-handed politicking of the Catholic Church has pushed many Europeans farther away.

Public confidence in the Church has plummeted in recent years, especially in Spain and Poland, two traditionally Catholic nations, largely because of the Church's sexual politics, including the Church's poor handling of the priestly sex-abuse crisis. As recently as 1995, half the population of Spain said they had confidence in the Catholic Church, but today it is only a quarter. In the 1990s, according to the World Values Survey, almost every Pole would have trusted the Catholic Church, and 80 percent continued to say that in 2005; but only 58 percent indicate that they trust the Catholic Church today. There is a growing perception that the Catholic Church is more concerned with its own rules and social power than it is with truth, fairness, and social equality. Pope Francis is trying to reverse this trend. When asked about homosexuality, for example, he famously replied, "Who am I to judge?" Emphasizing the more compassionate and understanding side of the Catholic Church may improve its reputation in the years ahead, but given the depth of feelings on this issue, it will likely take more than words to significantly moderate anti-Catholic sentiment.

European Theology and Truth

Compared to Christians elsewhere, Christians in Europe have always placed great emphasis on "truth," on the correspondence between Christian claims and reality itself. European Christians have wanted not merely to have faith in the Bible and Christian tradition but also to demonstrate that Christianity is *true*. The twentieth-century French philosopher and Christian convert Simone Weil asserted that a Christian who was forced to choose between Christ and truth should always opt for truth: "Christ likes us to prefer truth to him because, before being Christ, he is truth. If one turns aside from him to go toward the truth, one will not go far before falling into his arms."[20] Weil's expression of confidence in truth versus Christ would be almost unthinkable for Christians in many other parts of the world, but in Europe it is commonplace.

---

19. See John Paul II, *Man and Woman He Created Them: A Theology of the Body*, trans. Michael Waldstein (Boston: Pauline Books, 2006).

20. Simone Weil, *Waiting for God* (New York: Harper and Row, 1973), 69.

Europe's commitment to seeking truth has been enormously important in the development of Christian theology. This section examines three of Europe's truth-related contributions to global Christianity: respect for reason, with rationality defined largely in terms of classical Greek philosophy; an appreciation for scientific methodology and for relating Christian faith to empirical evidence as revealed by modern science; and awareness of how limited and partial humanity's grasp of truth will always be, a perspective articulated both by ancient Orthodox writers and by contemporary postmodernists.

Respect for Reason

Christianity did not begin as a philosophical movement or as a vision of life based on reason. The New Testament expresses more than a little doubt about the helpfulness of reason and argument. The apostle Paul, in particular, warned his followers not to be deceived by "fine-sounding arguments" or by "hollow and deceptive philosophy, which depends on human tradition . . . rather than on Christ" (Col. 2:4, 8). However, Paul himself was a superb debater who had mastered the argumentative skills of Jewish biblical interpretation and who was not averse to using Greek philosophical ideas and concepts when they helped him explain the significance of Christ to others. His rhetorical skill is evident in the sermon he preached in Athens on Mars Hill (Acts 17:22–31). While Paul did not want converts to be led astray by *cleverly deceptive* arguments or by *hollow* philosophy, he clearly considered *good* arguments and *sound* philosophy to be compatible with Christian faith.

What Paul's life and writings only imply, Augustine of Hippo (354–430) stated boldly. Faith and reason cohere. Trust in God and clear thinking go hand in hand. For Augustine, like Paul, faith came first and reason came second, but the first required the second. The shorthand phrase to describe this relationship, which was first coined by Augustine and resuscitated by Anselm 650 years later, was "faith seeks understanding." Augustine's vision of faith and reason was based largely on the thinking of the Greek philosopher Plato. Like Plato, Augustine saw reason as working mostly from the top down. Gaining an understanding of the most important big facts about the world provides a vantage point for making logical sense of all the smaller, particular things and events in the world. For Augustine (and for Plato), knowledge of the big facts about the world was gained through some form of revelation (or faith), and the job of the philosopher or theologian was then to explain all the smaller truths about the world in light of that larger revelation (faith seeking understanding).

Thomas Aquinas (1225–1274), who lived eight hundred years after Augustine, added a second dimension to European Christian thinking about truth by utilizing the ideas of a different Greek philosopher, Aristotle. Aristotle essentially turned Plato's philosophy upside down. Instead of seeing the search for truth as a top-down process, Aristotle argued that truth was uncovered from the ground up. For Aristotle, knowing truth begins with understanding fundamental facts about the world and how it functions—things that can be known through the five senses. Larger or more encompassing truths about the world are generated by reflecting on the connections that exist among all those smaller facts or fragments of truth. Aristotle rejected revelation; what mattered for him was argument and proof.

As a Christian, Aquinas disagreed with Aristotle's rejection of revelation, but he embraced Aristotle's notion that a person could reason from smaller truths to larger truth. Aquinas believed knowledge of God came to most human beings through revelation, but he thought the existence of God could be proven on the basis of evidence-based, logical thinking. By joining reason with revelation, mere belief could be turned into solid, demonstrable knowledge. This became the new goal of theology in Western Europe, not only to explain but simultaneously to prove the truthfulness of Christianity. This vision of theology stimulated the development of Christian doctrine and also gave rise to the European university system. Speaking at a German university in 2006, Pope Benedict XVI confirmed this connection, arguing that Greek-style reasoning is intertwined with the core message of the gospel and, conversely, that the Christian gospel is integral to the reason-based, truth-seeking context of the modern university (see textbox, European Theology: Pope Benedict XVI).

Ever since the time of Aquinas, proof and reason have played major roles in European theology. This inclusion of reason has not been without its critics. Questions about it were raised within a few decades after Aquinas's death by a theologian named Duns Scotus (1265–1308), who believed knowledge of God was above and beyond human reason and that the only way to know anything about God was through God's own self-revelation in Jesus and the Bible. The Protestant Reformer Martin Luther, who was influenced by Duns Scotus, is also sometimes cited as a critic of reason. Luther often employed coarse language to make his points, and he once crudely exclaimed that reason was a whore, capable of proving any assertion whether it was genuinely true or not. However, when Luther was hauled before the governing council of the Holy Roman Empire and told to officially withdraw his Protestant views, he famously replied, "Unless I am convinced by Scripture *and plain reason* . . . I cannot and I will not recant anything for to go against conscience is neither right nor safe."[21] Clearly, reason was an important element in Luther's faith.

---

21. "Luther at the Imperial Diet of Worms (1521)," accessed January 16, 2015, www.luther.de/en/worms.html, emphasis added.

European Theology: Pope Benedict XVI

Faith and Reason: An Indissoluble Bond

Pope Benedict XVI, formerly Cardinal Joseph Ratzinger, a German theologian, headed the Vatican office charged with maintaining doctrinal purity for twenty-four years (1981–2005) under the pontificate of John Paul II, and he then became pope in 2005. In 2013, he resigned from office, the first pope to do so since the fifteenth century. This excerpt is from a talk he delivered at the University of Regensburg shortly after becoming pope. In it, he strongly affirms European Christianity's partnership with Western (Greek) philosophy, so much so that he says the two have become permanently wedded.

> Is the conviction that acting unreasonably contradicts God's nature merely a Greek idea, or is it always and intrinsically true? I believe that here we can see the profound harmony between what is Greek in the best sense of the word and the biblical understanding of faith in God. . . .
>
> This inner rapprochement between biblical faith and Greek philosophical inquiry was an event of decisive importance not only from the standpoint of the history of religions, but also from that of world history—it is an event which concerns us even today. Given this convergence, it is not surprising that Christianity, despite its origins and some significant developments in the East, finally took on its historically decisive character in Europe. . . .
>
> In the light of our experience with cultural pluralism, it is often said nowadays that the synthesis with Hellenism [Greek philosophy and reason] achieved in the early Church was an initial enculturation which ought not to be binding on other cultures. The latter are said to have the right to return to the simple message of the New Testament prior to that enculturation, in order to enculturate it anew in their own particular milieu. This thesis is not simply false, but it is coarse and lacking in precision. The New Testament was written in Greek and bears the imprint of the Greek spirit, which had already come to maturity as the Old Testament developed. True, there are elements in the evolution of the early Church which do not have to be integrated into all cultures. Nonetheless, the fundamental decisions made about the relationship between faith and the use of human reason are part of the faith itself; they are developments consonant with the nature of faith itself.*

> * Pope Benedict XVI, "Faith, Reason and the University: Memories and Reflections," University of Regensburg, September 12, 2006, www.vatican.va/holy_father/benedict_xvi/speeches/2006/september /documents/hf_ben-xvi_spe_20060912_university-regensburg_en.html.

Europeans have had a penchant for seeing *systematic* theology as the best way of doing theology. Systematic theology is the rational examination of Christian belief, seeking to explain how every Christian tenet is related logically and necessarily to every other Christian belief. The goal of systematic theology is not just to explain individual doctrines, but to develop an entire system of thought or worldview. Because reason and logic are so central to this endeavor, training in philosophy is usually a prerequisite for becoming a theologian in Europe.

Not all European Christians have adopted this systematic, philosophical point of view. Some European Christians have opted for a more existential, nonrational (though not necessarily irrational) understanding of faith. Many of these Christians, like Christians in other parts of the world, fear that too much emphasis on reason can dilute faith to the point of being nothing more than what society deems acceptable. The Swiss Protestant theologian Karl Barth (1886–1968) was especially adamant on this point, describing God as thoroughly untamable and more than willing to transgress what European society took to be reasonable. But reason has a way of insistently reasserting itself, especially in a place as highly educated as Europe. As the rest of global Christianity becomes similarly invested in university education and intellectual inquiry—a trend that is already well underway—issues of truth and reason will likely become more prominent, not less, in the Christian movement worldwide.

Faith and Science

If rationality focuses on *how* people think, science focuses on *what* they think, on what they consider to be empirically true and provable. Scientists seek carefully and systematically to document their findings and to publish them so that their accuracy and reliability can be examined and tested by others. Science is not a matter of merely believing this or that about the world; science makes empirical claims about the world, and every such claim is open to public criticism and experimental falsification. Science at its best is not about *defending* beliefs or opinions at all. Instead, it is about *discovering* how the world really works, regardless of whether those discoveries confirm or contradict any previously held beliefs or opinions.

Modern science, with its evidence-based methodologies, was born in Europe, and the history of science and its relationship to Christianity has occasionally been tense. In some sense, Christianity's belief in the orderly nature of the universe is the foundation of modern science, and to this day science can largely be characterized as the search to discover the inner orderliness of the universe. So science and Christianity share some common attitudes, but conflict can occur when new findings from science contradict, or seem to contradict, what the Bible says or what the churches have traditionally taught. The condemnation of Galileo Galilei in 1633 is the most well-known example of this kind of conflict. Galileo was declared a heretic because he promoted the discovery that the Earth revolves around the sun. Speaking with confidence that quickly proved unwarranted, the Catholic Church declared that Galileo's "proposition that the Earth is not the center of the world and immovable" was absurd and theologically erroneous.[22] Within a few decades, the Church was forced to admit its mistake. Ever since, science has generally been out in front and theology has followed behind. Science decides what is considered to be true about the world, and theologians and church leaders then modify their views to keep them in line with advances in science.

This process of theological adaptation has not always worked smoothly. One particular topic that has generated a great deal of friction is the theory of evolution. Up until the nineteenth century, virtually all European Christians would have taken the Genesis account of creation as a straightforward statement of fact: God spoke, the world came into being, and all of it happened in the space of six, twenty-four-hour days. Then, in the nineteenth century, European scientists began to develop a different explanation for how the world took shape. First in geology and then in biology, scientists articulated a longer, slower, and much less God-dependent explanation for how the Earth was formed and how life came into existence. Life was not created in a flash, but instead evolved over millions of years from simple-celled organisms to more complex forms of life, driven by a process of random mutations and environmental adaptation. This theory of evolution, which most scientists now consider to be factual beyond any reasonable doubt, has troubled some Christians because it raises so many questions about how to understand God, human life, and God's involvement in the world.

Some Christians have thoroughly condemned the idea of evolution, while others have embraced the new, scientific vision of the history of life on Earth. In the United States, many Christians reject the ideas of evolution altogether, saying evolution is simply wrong, the Bible is right, and that settles it. Only about 40 percent of Americans today agree with the statement that "human beings, as we know them, developed from earlier species of animals." Opinions in Europe are starkly different. Roughly 60 percent of Eastern Europeans and 80 percent of Western Europeans believe that humankind evolved from earlier species of life.[23] In 1996, Pope John Paul II acknowledged that evolution is much more than a mere hypothesis and can now be assumed to be an empirical fact. Most European Protestants, including the famous Anglican writer

22. Quoted in Giorgio de Santillana, *The Crime of Galileo* (Chicago: University of Chicago Press, 1955), 307.

23. See Jeff Hecht, "Why Doesn't America Believe in Evolution?," *New Scientist*, August 20, 2006, www.newscientist.com/article/dn9786-why-doesnt-america-believe-in-evolution.html.

European Theology: Evelyn Underhill

Seeing the World as God Created It: The Sanctity of Science

Evelyn Underhill was a layperson in the Church of England, a prolific writer who wrote thirty-nine books and hundreds of articles about Christian faith and spirituality. She died on June 15, 1941, a date now commemorated each year in the Anglican Church calendar. This excerpt from her commentary on the Nicene Creed focuses on the importance of science in developing a proper Christian understanding of creation, including both the natural world and ourselves.

The universe in its wholeness, and with all its disconcerting contrasts—the world of beauty, the world of science, the world of love, and those mysterious deeps of being of which the spirit can sometimes in prayer discern the fringe—these, visible and invisible, the very heavenly and the very earthly, are the creations of the Divine Charity; the living, acting, overflowing generosity of God. . . .

It is easy to be both sentimental and theological over the more charming and agreeable aspects of Nature. It is very difficult to see its essential holiness beneath disconcerting and hostile appearances with an equable and purified sight; with something of the large, disinterested Charity of God.

To stand alongside the generous Creative Love, maker of all things visible and invisible (including those we do not like) and see [the world] with the eyes of the Artist-Lover is the secret of sanctity. St. Francis did this with a singular perfection. . . . So too that rapt and patient lover of all life, Charles Darwin, with his great, self-forgetful interest in the humblest and tiniest forms of life—not because they were useful to him, but for their own sakes—fulfilled one part of our Christian duty far better than many Christians do. . . .

This loving reverence for life is not to stop short even at the microbe and the worm. It must be extended to ourselves, and the qualities, tendencies and power which God has implanted or brought forth in us. We have to discriminate between our natural passions, which are a true part of His creative material, and the way we handle them, which is left to us. It is no proof of spirituality to discredit the fiery energies which He has implanted in the natural order, and in [us].*

* Evelyn Underhill, *The School of Charity* (Harrisburg, PA: Morehouse, 1991), 13–15.

Evelyn Underhill, have reached the same conclusion (see textbox, European Theology: Evelyn Underhill).

Why do Christians in Europe think so differently about evolution than Christians in North America and most of the rest of the world? Some argue that this is because of the way Europe has distanced itself from religion in general. Europe is more secular than any other place on earth, and Europe's embrace of science may be one of the driving forces behind its secularity. But most Europeans, including most Christians, think that reimagining

Christianity in light of modern science is simply how theology ought to work.

The Limits of Reason

The emergence of postmodernism in the last three or four decades has forced a thorough rethinking of what *truth* means. European scholars, including Jacques Derrida and Michel Foucault, have questioned whether anything can really be known with certainty, suggesting instead that much of human knowledge is rooted in habit, opinion, interpretation, and power (including the power of some people or societies to impose their views on others). Less cynically, postmodernists recognize that there is slippage in all the ways people talk about the world. Words and concepts can never capture all of reality. In the 1930s, long before postmodernism existed, the British poet and Christian apologist T. S. Eliot wrote his poem "Burnt Norton" about the way words strain and sometimes break under the pressure put on them. Words slip and slide and refuse to stay in place; they decay into imprecision. Reality in all its fullness ever eludes us, Eliot mused, and all our attempts to nail down truth are inevitably only partially successful. This does not mean that reason and science no longer matter, but that truth is always contestable.

Humanity's inability to grasp truth has long been a conversation thread among European intellectuals, but Christians in Western Europe were prone to brush this problem aside. Western European Christians tended to trust their words and their perceptions of reality and believed, along with Aquinas, that many of the central truths of Christian faith, although revealed by God, could also be proved through science and logic. Such an assumption was never made by Christians in Eastern Europe, where Orthodoxy has been and still remains the dominant Christian tradition. Most Orthodox Christians think the truth problems of the West began with Augustine and only got worse with Aquinas and Luther. Rather than acknowledging that all creatures are incapable of understanding the Creator, Western European Christians arrogantly assumed they could explain God and God's world in categories of their own devising. For Eastern Orthodox Christians, this is tantamount to idolatry, worshiping humanity's own ideas about the world rather than worshiping the Creator of the world with appropriate humility. Pavel Florensky, one of the most articulate Orthodox theologians of the twentieth century, asks bluntly how the fullness of God and God's relationship to the world could possibly "be packed into a narrow coffin of logical definition?" Rather than seeking cognitively to understand God and God's mystical presence in the world, it is far better to explore the truth of the human condition existentially through worship and meditation.

Florensky says immediate experience is the only way to know the deep truth of what it means to be human, to be created in the image of God, and to live in a world created by God.[24] Many other Orthodox theologians have echoed this point, including Kallistos Ware, who was a professor at Oxford University for more than three decades (see textbox, European Theology: Kallistos Ware).

Something very similar to this postmodern and Orthodox understanding of the elusiveness of truth is starting to be embraced by some Christians in Western Europe. For example, Lesslie Newbigin, a Reformed theologian, missionary, and ecumenical activist, has recently argued that all of the West's supposedly timeless, universal, rational, and scientific truths "are only meta-narratives that falsely claim to explain the human story as a whole." These so-called "truths" are simply the intellectual products of one particular human culture. He says the certainty promised by Western reason and science is a myth, nothing more than a story that overly confident Western Europeans tell themselves about who they are and what they know. For Newbigin, a proper understanding of truth begins elsewhere, not with science or reason but by accepting the truthfulness of the gospel story and the light it sheds on the human condition. He says that "even in the darkest hours . . . the story that the church tells continues to exercise its power both to correct and reform and to convince and convert the world."[25]

For both postmodern Christians and Orthodox Christians, "true truth" (if such a phrase makes sense) is the truth of our own fallibility and of humanity's need for divine aid. This newer postmodern and simultaneously older Orthodox European Christian vision of truth is grounded in commitment and participation and not in abstract knowledge or rationality. For Christians in the West, this perspective offers a modified self-understanding that might make it easier for them to enter into dialogue with Christians from other regions of the world. At the same time, it poses the risk of sliding into a relativism that rejects the importance of science and rationality and declares that anyone can believe whatever he or she wants to believe regardless of evidence and reason. This live-and-let-live intellectual stance may lessen social tensions, but it also means that testimony—telling one's own story without making any claims about what may or may not be true for others—becomes the only appropriate form of religious speech. Social tranquility is an important concern, but ultimately, truth is public. Truth cannot be reduced to personal opinion or personal commitment alone. Proof, argument, evidence, and logic still matter.

24. Pavel Florensky, *The Pillar and Ground of Truth: An Essay in Orthodox Theodicy in Twelve Letters*, trans. Boris Jakim (Princeton: Princeton University Press, 2004), 7.

25. Lesslie Newbigin, *Proper Confidence: Faith, Doubt and Certainty in Christian Discipleship* (Grand Rapids: Eerdmans, 1995), 74, 78.

European Theology: Kallistos Ware

Knowing God beyond Words and Concepts

Kallistos Ware, formerly known as Timothy Ware, is an English bishop in the Eastern Orthodox Church under the Patriarchate of Constantinople. Author of numerous books on Orthodox faith and practice, he served as the Spalding Lecturer of Eastern Orthodox Studies at the University of Oxford from 1966 to 2001. This excerpt describes the Orthodox Christian emphasis on apophatic theology, a way of knowing that stresses the limitations of the human mind.

The Greek Fathers [early Christian theologians] liken man's encounter with God to the experience of someone . . . standing at night in a darkened room: he opens the shutter over a window, and as he looks out there is a sudden flash of lightning, causing him to stagger backwards, momentarily blinded. Such is the effect of coming face to face with the living mystery of God. . . . [T]here seems nothing for us to grasp; our inward eyes are blinded, our normal assumptions shattered.

Recognizing that God is incomparably greater than anything we can say or think about him . . . we need to use negative as well as affirmative statements saying what God is not rather than what he is. Without this use of the way of negation, of what is termed the apophatic approach, our talk about God becomes gravely misleading. All we affirm concerning God, however correct, falls far short of the living truth. If we say that he is good or just, we must at once add that his goodness or justice are not to be measured by human standards. If we say he exists, we must qualify this immediately by adding that he is not one existent object among many, that in his case the word "exist" bears a unique significance. . . .

Yet . . . the apophatic way of "unknowing" brings us not to emptiness but to fullness. Our negations are in reality super-affirmations. Destructive in outer form, the apophatic approach is affirmative in its final effects: it helps us to reach out, beyond all statements positive or negative, beyond all language and all thought, towards an immediate experience of the living God. . . . It is to know God not as a theory or an abstract principle, but as a person.*

* Kallistos Ware, *The Orthodox Way* (Crestwood, NY: St. Vladimir's Seminary Press, 1979), 13–15.

This is obviously the case in Europe, but given the ever-advancing global spread of science and technology, it seems likely that truth will become a bigger, not a smaller, concern for Christians around the world in the years and decades ahead.

Summary

There is nothing geographic that requires Europe to be considered a different continent than Asia. The two continents share a single landmass. What originally demarcated Europe as a separate region of the world was its religion, and that religion was Christianity. The process of Christianizing Europe took about seven centuries, from roughly 500 to 1200, and when it was done Europe had become the most Christian place on earth. Europe has never been unified around one version of Christianity. It has always been divided into a Catholic West and an Orthodox East, and since the 1500s it has included a third northern region that is predominantly Protestant. Disagreements over the differing versions of Christianity have sometimes become violent. It is only since the mid-twentieth century, after World War II, that Europe has become a relatively unified and peaceful territory, and this development took place at the same time the continent was becoming more secular. Three-quarters of Europe's population continues to identify itself as Christian today, but Europeans are the least religiously active Christians in the world.

In contrast to other regions of the globe, European Christians have always been concerned about the truthfulness of the gospel. They have wanted to know not merely what the Bible teaches, but also how those teachings relate to reason and empirical evidence. In those instances when the Christian message has been shown to be out of sync with reason and the findings of science, European Christians have been comfortable reinterpreting the Christian message to bring it into alignment with truth as they understand it. This is an important and necessary task, since no one wants to believe things that are obviously not true, but sometimes European definitions of truth have seemed too precise and narrow to accommodate all of reality. In recent decades, many European Christian scholars have reformulated their thinking to allow more room for mystery and multiple ways of knowing. Nonetheless, the role of truth in Christian faith and practice remains a hallmark of European Christianity.

6

Asia

On April 28, 2014, officials in the Chinese city of Wenzhou (in Zhejiang province) gave the final order to demolish the massive Sanjiang (Three Rivers) Church that had recently been built on the outskirts of town at a cost of nearly $5 million. Eight stories tall, the church was positioned prominently—some said too prominently—near a local highway. Plans for the site's future development included a retirement home for the aged, and much of the funding had come from the adult children of church members who were no longer living in China but wanted to provide a place for their elderly parents to live. Various reasons were given for Sanjiang's demolition, ranging from general building-code violations to specific complaints about the ostentatious cross on top of the building. Some say the destruction of the church is part of a larger and increasingly well-organized anti-church movement within China. More likely, this incident was meant to be a shot across the bow of the Wenzhou Christian community as a whole.

Wenzhou is an east coast port city with about two million people, and it is sometimes called the "Jerusalem of China" because so many Christians live there. Some estimates run as high as half the population.[1] Wenzhou is full of churches, so no one thought constructing another one would be an issue. The demolition of the Sanjiang Church was especially unexpected because it was associated with the China Christian Council (CCC), the official state-approved

1. See Nanlai Cao, *Constructing China's Jerusalem: Christians, Power, and Place in Contemporary Wenzhou* (Stanford, CA: Stanford University Press, 2011).

wing of the Protestant movement in China. Many church buildings in China, including some almost as large as the Sanjiang Church, do not belong to the CCC. These non-CCC churches exist in a "gray zone" of government religious policy, neither officially approved nor officially condemned. Their continued existence is largely predicated on the personal support of local state officials.[2] But CCC churches have usually been considered safe from destruction—or at least they were until recently. Hundreds of other churches in Zhejiang province were torn down about the same time, reminding local Christians that religious groups perceived as getting too large, too loud, and too influential can be smacked down by the government whenever it wants.

This story is about China, but it is illustrative of Christianity's status in Asia as a whole. Many Asian Christians live insecurely at the edges of society, where they are pestered by both the state and their neighbors. Sometimes this harassment explodes into overt persecution; often it does not. The reaction of Wenzhou's Christians to rumors that the Sanjiang church was about to be demolished is also representative of Asian Christianity; church members flocked to the site to protect the building. Their protest was ultimately unsuccessful—and most knew that would be the outcome before they arrived—but they went anyway. The same spirit can be observed elsewhere in Asia. Despite the precariousness of their lives, Asian Christians are often quite bold in their expressions of faith. They are not looking for a fight, but they are not cowering either.

It is, of course, hard to generalize about any place as large and diverse as Asia. The dynamics of faith and life in the Middle East are very different from the dynamics of faith and life in India or Indonesia or Kazakhstan or Japan. But the region's assortment of diverse experiences is one reason why studying Asia is so important for understanding Christianity worldwide. Asian Christians know that Christians come in many different sizes and shapes and practice their faith in different ways. Asian Christians also know from their own experiences that being faithful to Christ does not guarantee either success or survival.

The History of Asian Christianity

Christianity began in Asia, and it remained a predominantly Asian religion for many centuries. Jesus was Asian, and so were all his immediate followers. When the movement began to move outward from Jerusalem in the decades after Christ's death and resurrection, the gospel spread eastward into Asia almost as quickly as it spread westward into Europe and Africa. The apostle

2. See Fenggang Yang, *Religion in China: Survival and Renewal under Communist Rule* (New York: Oxford University Press, 2012).

Figure 6.1. Traditional
burial site for St. Thomas
(Mylapore, India)

Thomas may even have carried the message of Jesus as far east as India (see
fig. 6.1). It was in Asia, too, that Christianity first became the official faith of
an entire nation, when, in 301, the Armenian state adopted Christianity as
its official religion. Today Christianity is often described as a foreign religion
in Asia, but that is simply inaccurate. Up until the year 900, more followers
of Jesus lived in Asia than anywhere else. The success of Christianity in Asia
has been uneven, however. Asian Christian history has been characterized
by a series of fluctuations between expansion and contraction, which is very
different from historic growth patterns in Europe, Africa, and the Americas.[3]

Christianity's First Expansion (Beginnings to 500)

Christianity's first flourishing in Asia began with the origins of the movement and continued until about the year 500. Christianity was born in Asian

3. See Samuel Hugh Moffett, *A History of Christianity in Asia* (Maryknoll, NY: Orbis,
2005), 2:634.

Palestine and then moved deeper into Asia into what is now Iran and Iraq. The largest of the ancient Asian churches, the Church of the East (also known as the Nestorian Church), was centered in the Persian Empire. It was not easy to establish Christianity in Persia. The Persian Empire was religiously Zoroastrian, and most Zoroastrians considered Christianity to be a diabolical faith, literally on the side of evil. Persia's Zoroastrians believed that humanity was engaged in a great spiritual battle between the forces of evil and death and the forces of goodness and life. Human actions influenced the trajectory of this cosmic battle, and Zoroastrians interpreted some Christian practices as aiding the forces of evil. Early Christianity's emphasis on celibacy was a problem because Zoroastrians viewed having children (producing life) as an important way to fight evil and death. Zoroastrians were also troubled by the Christian practice of burying their dead. Zoroastrians believed that corpses were impure and that allowing them to touch the ground polluted the earth, so they placed their dead on raised platforms where wild birds came and ate the remains. Zoroastrians tried to crush the Christian movement, and many more Christians were killed in Persia than were ever put to death in the Roman Empire. But killing Christians did not stop the movement, and eventually a modicum of mutual toleration emerged between Christians and Zoroastrians.

Meanwhile, relations between Persian Christians and Christians in the Roman Empire were deteriorating. As the Church in the Christian Roman Empire defined its doctrines with ever more precision, a split with the Christians of Persia became almost inevitable. The central issue in this Great Division between Persian and Roman Christianity focused on how best to define the relationship between the human and the divine in the person of Christ. Roman Christians wanted to connect the two dimensions quite closely, but Persian Christians wanted to maintain a clear distinction between them so Christians could realistically model their lives on the humanity of Jesus. Around 500, the two traditions separated, declaring each other heretical.

A third, separate and distinct Christian tradition was also birthed during this Great Division: Miaphysitism. In contrast to both the Roman Church and the Church of the East, Miaphysite Christianity moved in the direction of fusing the human and the divine natures together in Christ, so much so that it sometimes seemed (at least to outsiders) as if Christ's divinity entirely overwhelmed his humanity. The Miaphysite tradition was (and still is) housed in several different churches, including two located primarily in Asia: the Armenian Apostolic Church and the Syrian Orthodox Church, which is sometimes called the Jacobite Church. (The Coptic and Ethiopian Orthodox churches are also Miaphysite.)

A Second Flourishing (500–1000)

The second age of Christian growth in Asia began after the Great Division that divided the Christian movement in three, and it lasted until about 1000. During this time, Christianity was carried further east, following the Silk Road (a trade route that connected the Mediterranean world with Central Asia and the Far East) all the way to China (see fig. 6.2). In 635, a Church of the East missionary named Alopen arrived in the Tang Dynasty capital of Chang'an (near present-day Xi'an). Alopen was a Christian monk, but he likely went to China as part of a Persian government delegation seeking to increase trade between the two empires. His faith impressed the Chinese emperor, and Alopen was given permission to preach the gospel throughout China. He immediately began the work of translating Christianity into the language and culture of Tang Dynasty China.

To communicate the gospel in this new cultural setting, Alopen decided to follow a path developed by another missionary religion, Buddhism. Buddhism, which originated in northern India, had entered China four centuries earlier, and it was the only non-Chinese religion that had attracted a significant following. Buddhism's success was based on building monasteries and on preaching and publishing poetical sermons called *sutras*. Alopen adopted this strategy, establishing a string of monasteries across China and writing Christian sutras. In keeping with the theology of the Church of the East and in harmony with Chinese culture, these sutras used metaphors of health and healing (rather than of guilt and forgiveness) to explain salvation. One sutra implored God to "shower us with Your Healing Rain . . . give life to what has

Figure 6.2
Alopen's Path to China (c. 650)

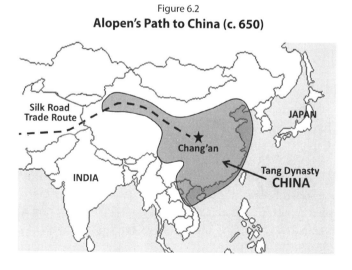

withered, and water the roots of kindness in us."[4] A Chinese *stele*, a stone monument, erected in 781 shows that Alopen's approach was successful. Calling Christianity the "religion of light," the inscription says, "The principles of this religion [are] purely excellent and natural . . . beneficial to all creatures [and] advantageous to humankind."[5] With this reputation, it is not surprising that the Church of the East was able to gain a foothold in other Asian contexts as well, including most of Central Asia, Tibet, and possibly even coastal Southeast Asia, Indonesia, and Japan.

A First Contraction (650–1100)

As Christianity was enjoying its second period of flourishing in East Asia, it simultaneously entered into its first recession in the Middle East. The overall situation was something like paddling a boat that is beginning to leak. The boat of Asian Christianity was still advancing—new cultures were being engaged and new understandings of faith were emerging—but simultaneously holes were appearing in its hull. Christianity in Asia was starting to sink even as it continued to move ahead.

The most significant factor in Christianity's first Asian recession was the rise of Islam. Islam emerged in the early 600s in the Hejaz (the western half of what is now the Saudi Peninsula) under the leadership of the Prophet Muhammad. Like Judaism and Christianity, from which it drew inspiration, Islam was a monotheistic religion that worshiped the one and only God of all creation. But unlike Christianity and Judaism, Islam claimed to be a faith without a history. The Qur'an, the revelation received by the Prophet, was viewed as the infallible word of God, eternally written in heaven (in Arabic) and only later revealed, word by word, to Muhammad. Islam itself was understood to be the original religion of humankind as practiced by Adam and Eve. This pure and ancient faith in God became corrupted over time and had to be periodically rearticulated by prophets such as Moses, Abraham, and Jesus. Muslims believe that the original faith of humankind had been finally restored in fullness by the one Prophet who stood above all other prophets, Muhammad. Compared to Judaism and Christianity, Islam is a simple and straightforward faith. It has no priests, no hierarchy, and no

4. Martin Palmer, *The Jesus Sutras: Rediscovering the Lost Scrolls of Taoist Christianity* (New York: Ballantine, 2001), 204.

5. For a translation of the monument's inscription, see "East Asian History Sourcebook: Ch'ing Tsing: Nestorian Tablet: Eulogizing the Propagation of the Illustrious Religion in China," Fordham University, accessed January 17, 2015, www.fordham.edu/halsall/eastasia/781nestorian .asp.

hard-to-grasp doctrines like the Trinity or the simultaneous humanity and divinity of Christ. The personal requirements are also clear: submit to God, honor the Prophet, pray five times a day, give alms to the poor, fast during the month of Ramadan, and, if possible, visit the city of Mecca at least once during one's lifetime for the annual celebration of the Hajj. For many Middle Easterners, this was an appealing alternative both to the polytheism of traditional Arab society and to the constant theological squabbling that characterized so much of ancient Christianity.

Muhammad made little or no distinction between personal faith and public life. Human existence was a seamless whole that included both, so the border between religion and the state was decidedly porous. Muhammad himself was as much a political and military leader as he was a religious prophet. In 630, just two years before his death, he defeated his last local enemies and united the Arab people into a single *ummah* (community of faith) under his rule. After his death, the Arab nation, now united under Islam, launched a series of military attacks on its imperial neighbors. The Persian Empire quickly collapsed and so did parts of the Byzantine (or Eastern Roman) Empire. Most Byzantine territory in the Middle East was conquered by 637, Egypt (also part of the Roman Empire) fell in 639, and the Persian Empire was decisively defeated in 651. Damascus became the new capital of the rapidly spreading Islamic movement.

In all Arab-conquered lands, Christianity began to decline, slowly at first and then more rapidly. The earliest Muslim rulers were not particularly eager for Christians to convert. They were busy consolidating their hold on newly conquered lands and collecting taxes from non-Muslims. This policy changed under the Abbasids, who took control of the movement in 750, intent on making their empire thoroughly Islamic. Christians and Jews were given some leeway to practice their religions because Muhammad himself had considered them "People of the Book" (something akin to being religious cousins to Muslims), but increasing pressure was placed on them to convert. Many did, for reasons that varied from person to person. Sometimes Christians converted to Islam in order to make their lives easier, sometimes they became Muslims because of intermarriage, and sometimes they simply found Islam to be less internally contentious and more religiously appealing than Christianity. Regardless of motivation, the Christian community in Asia began to shrink, and by 1100 it had been reduced to roughly half its former size.

The rise of Islam was not the only factor in this first recession of Asian Christianity. Resistance to Christianity was also emerging elsewhere, especially in China. In the mid-800s, the Tang Dynasty turned inward, becoming suspicious of everything that was not traditionally Chinese. Buddhism was banned in 843, and Christianity in 845. By the end of the century, there were almost no Christians anywhere in Chinese territory.

A Third Brief Flourishing (1000–1300)

Despite these negative developments, Asian Christianity still managed to experience a modest new flourishing between the years 1000 and 1300. Two factors drove this short-lived advance. The first was lay activism. Local Christian merchants traveling on the Silk Road continued to share their faith with the people they met, and some local tribes converted to Christianity. The second factor was the work of Catholic missionaries, who began to make their way into the region in the thirteenth century. John of Plano Carpini arrived in Central Asia in 1245, and dozens more missionaries followed. Some prominent members of the ruling family of the Mongol Empire converted, and for a time it looked as if the Great Khan himself, the leader of the empire, might become a Christian and declare Christianity the religion of his realm, just as Constantine had done a thousand years earlier in Rome. But instead of becoming a Christian, the Mongol emperor Ghazan, who ruled from 1295 to 1304, converted to Islam. Shortly after, he began a massive persecution of Christians, and this brief third period of flourishing came to an abrupt end.

A Second Catastrophic Recession (1100–1500)

What Ghazan began, others continued, and eventually most of Central Asia and parts of the Middle East became Christian wastelands. The deep history of this development goes back to the Crusades of the 1100s and 1200s. The Crusades were a series of military attacks on the Muslim Middle East by the armies of Catholic Western Europe. Their objective was to reconquer the Holy Land and free it from Muslim domination. The First Crusade, launched in 1095, captured most of what is now Syria, Lebanon, Israel, and Palestine, and these territories came under Christian rule. The Crusaders could be vicious, and when they seized Jerusalem, every Muslim man, woman, and child in the city was slaughtered, along with many Jews and local non-Catholic Christians. According to one report, ten thousand people were massacred in the temple area alone, where the assailants had to slosh through ankle-deep blood to complete their task. The victory was celebrated all throughout Europe in both poetry and art (see fig. 6.3).[6]

6. Fulk of Chartres, *Gesta Francorum Jerusalem expugnantium* ["The Deeds of the Franks Who Attacked Jerusalem"], in *Parallel Source Problems in Medieval History*, ed. Frederick Duncan and August C. Krey (New York: Harper & Brothers, 1912), 113.

Figure 6.3. Medieval European portrayal of siege of Jerusalem (1099)

The First Crusade caught the Muslim Middle East off guard, but that would not happen again. Under the military leadership of Ṣalāḥ ad-Dīn Yūsuf ibn Ayyūb (known as Saladin in the West), the armies of Islam reorganized and recaptured almost all of the Middle East by 1175. New Crusades were organized; as late as the 1400s more were being planned, but none were successful. The Crusades permanently damaged Muslim attitudes toward Christians, leading many Muslims to view Christianity as a ruthless and bloodthirsty faith. Some made a distinction between the "Franks," as they called the Crusaders, and their own home-grown, local, longtime Christian neighbors. But many Muslims did not, and local Christians were frequently seen as potential "terrorists." Official policies regulating Christianity became more restrictive, and violence against Christians became more common. Christian numbers declined throughout the Middle East. Much of the region was politically unstable during these years, which also took a toll on Christians. Empires rose and fell, and political boundaries changed frequently. This kind of political volatility typically makes life harder for everyone, but minority populations usually experience more hardships than others. Christians were clearly in the minority and their suffering was accordingly more intense.

The final purge of Christians came during the reign of Timur Leng (1370–1405). Timur was a ruthless tyrant so cruel than many Muslims refused to acknowledge him as a fellow Muslim. His goal was to conquer all of Central Asia, and 15 to 20 million people were killed in the process of reaching that goal. Timur held special animosity for Christians, however, and targeted them for extinction. By the end of his rule, Asian Christianity had almost been wiped out. Some Christian communities continued to exist in the places that are now Lebanon, Syria, eastern Turkey, northern Iraq, and southern India. But Christianity was completely obliterated in Central Asia all the way from Baghdad to Samarkand (in what is now Uzbekistan).

The Fourth Flourishing (1500–1700)

The fourth flourishing of Christianity in Asia was associated with the entrance of European Christians into the region in the early sixteenth century. This is when Europe first began to flex its global military and economic muscles, and Portugal took the lead. A Portuguese delegation arrived in India in 1498 to scope out the land. Twelve years later they returned, seized the city of Goa on the southwest coast of India, and established a Portuguese colony. The Portuguese went to India partly because of rumors that Christians lived there, and they were looking for allies in the fight against Islam. When the Portuguese arrived, they did indeed find Christians, but they quickly realized that local Indian Christianity differed considerably from European Catholicism. Rather than being embraced as fellow followers of Jesus, the Christians of India were treated as heretics in need of correction. Using the full powers of both the colonial government and the church, the Portuguese did all they could to reeducate these Indian Christians and to force them to accept European Catholic Christianity. At the Synod of Diamper (1599), Indian Christianity was condemned, and all the ancient Indian Christian writings that the Catholic inquisitors could find were collected and burned. Indian Christians who refused to accept Catholic teaching were subject to trial, punishment, and sometimes death.

Spain joined Portugal in the effort to colonize East Asia in the mid-1500s. The Spaniards were more nuanced in their evangelistic approach. The Philippines was the first center of Spanish activity in Asia, and from the beginning, concern for the indigenous population was mixed with the process of conquest. Spanish Catholic missionaries, in particular, often sided with the

Filipino people against the colonial government. These same missionaries embraced the local culture, translating the Catholic catechism into the indigenous languages of the region almost as soon as they arrived. The military conquest of the Spanish Philippines was not without strife, but it was a much more positive encounter than in India. The local population even eventually came to appreciate the Spanish military presence because it helped block the northward advance of Islam from the southern islands of the archipelago.

The greatest contributors to this fourth expansion of Christianity in Asia were the Jesuits, a Catholic religious order (also known as the Society of Jesus) that was founded in 1534. The Jesuits were primarily a teaching order. In the wake of the Protestant Reformation, their goal was to *explain* Christianity, not merely to proclaim and enforce it. The goal was to intellectually inoculate European Catholics against the false doctrines of Protestantism by persuading them of the truth of Catholic faith. The Jesuit commitment to education was not limited to Europe, however, and in non-European settings the Jesuits' educational approach to faith prompted them to take local cultures seriously. Rather than denouncing what they found problematic in the religions and cultures of the places they were sent, Jesuits appropriated local practices and beliefs for the purpose of explaining Christianity to the people they encountered.

The Jesuits went many places, but they were especially active in Asia. The first Jesuit missionary in Asia was Francis Xavier, who arrived in India in 1542. He quickly moved out of Portuguese territory in order to distance himself from the Portuguese and their coercive approach to missions. He later traveled to Indonesia and Japan. A host of Jesuit brothers followed in his wake. Robert de Nobili picked up the work in India, Alexander de Rhodes settled in Vietnam, and Matteo Ricci went to China (see fig. 6.4). Wherever they went, the Jesuit approach was basically the same: they studied the high culture of the society, became credentialed as local scholars, and explained Christianity in the terms of those cultures hoping that local intellectuals would convert. In many cases they did, and those conversions opened the door a little bit wider for other Jesuit missionaries. The Jesuits had little patience for superstition and magic, but they readily accommodated moral customs such as the veneration of the ancestors and easily adopted indigenous terms for God.

This contextualized and culturally sensitive approach to Christian missions was positively welcomed almost everywhere the Jesuits served in Asia, and this same basic practice continues to be the model for successful missions in most of Asia today. The Jesuit approach has been criticized for valorizing high culture over the culture of the masses, and these critics have a point. In India, for example, the Jesuits connected with the Brahmin caste, the highest in the

Figure 6.4. St. Joseph's Catholic Church (Beijing, China) (founded by Jesuits in the 1650s; rebuilt in 1904)

Indian social order, and they often adopted Brahmin-like attitudes toward the rest of society, even condoning separate masses for lower-caste converts so that upper-caste Indian Christians would not be contaminated by coming into contact with members of the lower castes. Despite their tendency to favor the elite, educated members of Asian society, Jesuit missionaries in Asia were overwhelmingly successful at achieving their goals. Many Asians became followers of Jesus in China, India, and Vietnam, and especially in Japan.

A Third Recession (1600–1800)

The third recession of Christianity in Asia began in Japan, precisely where the Jesuits had been most successful, and it began violently. In 1614, the Tokugawa shoguns who ruled Japan banned Catholicism, saying Christians had brought disorder to the region. About one thousand of the perhaps two hundred thousand Catholics in Japan were put to death, some by public crucifixion. No visible Christian movement survived that purge, but underground churches continued to worship Jesus, honor Mary, and carry on the "Kirishi-tan" faith as best they could. Descendants of these Christians, numbering in the tens of thousands, were rediscovered in the Nagasaki region in the mid-1800s.

This third withering of Asian Christianity was accelerated by intra-Christian rivalries among Catholic missionary orders. By the mid-1600s, Dominicans and Franciscans were expressing concern about the Jesuits' willingness to accommodate local cultures. They were especially disturbed that Jesuits al-lowed their converts to participate in rituals honoring the ancestors. These missionary opponents of the Jesuits eventually took their case to the Vatican and convinced the pope to rule against them. In 1715, Pope Clement XI de-clared in the papal bull *Ex illa die* that "whether at home, in the cemetery, or during the time of a funeral, a Chinese Catholic [is] not allowed to perform the ritual of ancestor worship."[7] The Jesuits made the counterargument that veneration of the ancestors was not "worship" at all, but rather a means of showing respect for the dead. But the pope was unconvinced and the papal declaration stood.

This decree damaged Catholic missions across Asia, and in many places Catholic missionaries were banned from preaching and teaching. The Chi-nese emperor Kangxi (1661–1722) expressed his own opinion bluntly, "I have concluded that the Westerners are petty indeed. It is impossible to reason with them because they do not understand larger issues as we understand them in China. . . . To judge from this proclamation, their religion is no different from other small, bigoted sects of Buddhism or Taoism. I have never seen a document which contains so much nonsense. From now on, Westerners should not be allowed to preach in China."[8] Clement's ruling forbidding Catholic participation in Chinese ancestral rites remained in effect until 1939, when Pope Pius XII changed the policy in a statement entitled *Plane compertum est*. The Church now essentially agrees with the Jesuits, and Catholics are allowed to take part in these ceremonies as long as they do not themselves have "the intention of rendering religious worship."[9]

The Fifth Flourishing (1800 to Present)

The fifth and most recent flourishing of Christianity in Asia began around 1800 and is still underway. Catholics have been heavily involved in this new

7. Pope Clement XI, *Ex illa die*, in *China in Transition, 1517–1911*, trans. Dun Jen Li (New York: Van Nostrand Reinhold, 1969), 24.

8. Ibid.

9. "Plane compertum est," in Robert A. Hunt, *The Gospel among the Nations: A Docu-mentary History of Inculturation* (Maryknoll, NY: Orbis, 2014).

resurgence of Asian Christianity, but Protestants and, more recently, Pentecostals have also participated.

Before 1800, only a few intrepid Protestant missionaries had traveled to Asia. Two of the most notable were the German Lutheran pietists, Bartholomaeus Ziegenbalg and Heinrich Plutschau, who arrived in the Danish settlement of Tranquebar in southeastern India in 1706. Their work was noted for its egalitarianism. Contrasting the equality of the gospel with the inequality of the Indian caste system, the Tranquebar Mission required all Christians to worship together regardless of caste. Ziegenbalg was also known for his translation work, which tried to make the Christian message as accessible as possible in the local language (see fig. 6.5).

In the late 1700s, waves of European Protestant missionaries began to arrive in Asia. The trailblazer was William Carey, a Baptist missionary from England. His book *An Enquiry into the Obligation of Christians to Use Means*

Figure 6.5. Page from Ziegenbalg's Tamil translation of the New Testament (1713)

for the Conversion of the Heathens (1792) changed Protestant perceptions of missions forever. Carey moved to Calcutta (now Kolkata), India, in 1793 and was initially refused a residency permit because the British colonial government did not want any religious dissenters (i.e., non-Anglican Christians) such as Carey and his Baptist associates stirring up trouble in the territory. Carey accordingly moved upriver and established his mission in the Danish settlement of Serampore, fifteen miles north of Calcutta.

The Carey mission was driven by four concerns that became the hallmarks of Protestant missions in Asia: evangelism, the translation of the Bible, education, and social justice, focusing especially on the rights of women and children. Carey and his team were not particularly successful in the task of evangelism—only a handful of Indians converted under their ministry—but they succeeded in achieving their other three goals. Under Carey's oversight, portions of the Bible were translated into more than thirty local languages, and by 1820 the mission's primary schools enrolled nearly ten thousand students. Under the leadership of Carey's associate Hannah Marshman, the mission also helped to end the practices of *sati* (the ritual burning of widows) and to reduce the frequency of female infanticide.

Back home in England, Carey became the model of the heroic Protestant missionary who traveled into the most remote parts of the world to preach the gospel. Trying to emulate his model, thousands of other European missionaries were soon circumnavigating the world to bring the gospel to "the lost" wherever they were found. There is a downside to this story, however. Carey's wife, Dorothy, never wanted to go to India, but she followed along anyway. The loneliness she experienced in India combined with the harshness of life (including the death of her five-year-old son from dysentery) eventually broke her. She suffered from severe depression for years before she died in 1807.

Catholic and Protestant missionary efforts in Asia were often hindered by local opposition. Most Asian nations did not want foreign preachers roaming their lands and tried to keep them out, in part because they were desperately trying to resist being colonized by Europe. In the middle of the nineteenth century, Europe dramatically expanded its colonization efforts in the region. Dutch rule over Indonesia was tightened, and so was British control of India and the Middle East. France also tightened its grip on the lands that are now Cambodia, Laos, and Vietnam (see fig. 6.6). Several Asian nations, including China, held Europe at bay, but the "gun-boat diplomacy" of England, France, and the United States—using military force to open ports for trade with the West, including the infamous Opium Wars with China in the 1840s and 1850s—terminated this resistance. China became a quasi colony, and the

Figure 6.6
European Colonies in Asia (late 1800s)

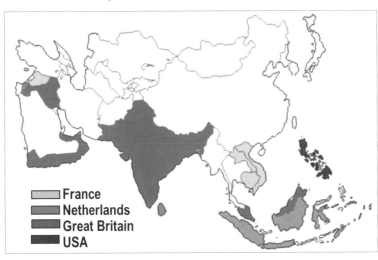

terms of surrender dictated by Western governments gave both Western opium sellers and Christian missionaries the freedom to travel wherever they wanted in the country. Many missionaries did not like being so closely associated with colonial power, and they certainly did not like being linked to the sale of opium, but they seized the opportunity to evangelize China and the rest of Asia nonetheless. For many Asians, Christianity and colonial subjugation seemed like two sides of the same coin, providing some warrant for the notion that Christianity was a foreign religion that had no legitimate place in Asia.

Not all Asians rejected Christianity, however. Some embraced the gospel and became Christian evangelists. The names of most early indigenous Asian evangelists are unknown, but one of the remembered few is a Confucian scholar from Guangzhou named Liang Fa. Liang was considering becoming a Buddhist when he was hired in 1815 to be a printer's assistant for William Milne, one of the first Protestant missionaries in China. After long conversations with Milne, Liang decided to become a Christian instead. Baptized in 1816, he soon began preaching on his own and published a substantial work on Christianity entitled *Good Words to Admonish the Age* in 1832. Liang was profoundly troubled by the British Opium War against China, but he held on to his Christian faith and continued to preach until his death in 1855.

One person who read Liang's *Good Words* shortly after it was published was a man named Hong Xiuquan. A few years later, in 1837, Hong had a dream that he took to be a special revelation from God, and Liang's writings helped him interpret (or, more accurately, to misinterpret) that dream. Hong eventually came to believe that he was the younger brother of Jesus, sent into the world to restore true Christianity and to rule China. On the basis of subsequent dreams and revelations, Hong set about the work of "correcting" the many different errors he believed had crept into the biblical text. He also began promoting his Great Peace (Taiping) movement to cleanse China from all its sins and to overthrow the hated Manchu government. By 1850, Hong had attracted a huge following and formed his own alternative government, including a well-armed military. By the time the Taiping Rebellion was crushed in 1864, 25 million people had died in the fighting.

In retrospect, it is easy to say that the Taiping movement was heretical and utterly misguided, but it was a Jesus-related movement that came very close to taking control of all China. Similar but less successful messianic, Christian-influenced movements have continued to emerge in various parts of Asia. Some groups are still quite active today, including the Unification Church (recently renamed the Family Federation for World Peace and Unification) founded by Sun Myung Moon in South Korea in 1954 and a Chinese group called Eastern Lightning, which teaches that a woman named Yang Xiangbin is Jesus returned to earth today. The Eastern Lightning movement believes strongly in spiritual warfare, and one member was recently arrested for beating a woman to death in a McDonald's restaurant in Beijing because he was convinced the woman was the devil incarnate.

China has always tried to control religion within its borders, and movements like Eastern Lightning and the Taiping movement make the desire to control Christianity understandable. The anti-Christian Boxer Rebellion (1899–1901) even hoped Christianity could be expelled from China for all time. But Christianity has continued to grow in China throughout the twentieth century. This expansion was slowed by the rise of the communist-led People's Republic of China in 1949, and during the time of the Cultural Revolution (1966–1976) it looked as if Christianity might be crushed. The goal of the Cultural Revolution was to eradicate any old ideas and habits that were holding back national development, and religion was at the top of that list. Every religious organization in the country was shut down, and religious practices were forced underground. But instead of destroying Christianity, the Cultural Revolution ironically prompted growth. The need to meet in small, scattered groups produced a huge cohort of new Christian leaders, and when restrictions on religion were lifted in the 1970s these new leaders leaped into action, creating new congregations and house churches all across the country.

In Asia, as in Africa and Latin America, much of the recent growth of Christianity has been Pentecostal in orientation. Today Pentecostal churches predominate in China and in most of East Asia. Pentecostalism has two great advantages in Asia. First, it burst on the scene after the worst excesses of the colonial era were over, so it is not associated with European control to the same degree as the Catholic and Protestant churches. Second, Pentecostalism's experiential focus allows cultural boundaries to be crossed more easily than is the case for churches that insist on strict doctrinal conformity. The result has been nothing less than an explosion of Christianity in the region. There were roughly 20 million Christians in Asia in 1900; today that figure is approaching 400 million. Christianity is expanding at a rate three or four times faster than the growth of the Asian population as a whole. One-third or more of Asia's Christians are now Pentecostal.

A Fourth Regionally Limited Recession (1900 to Present)

Despite the flourishing of Christianity in East Asia during the last century, Christianity has been decimated elsewhere, especially in the Middle East. This decline began in 1915 with the Armenian genocide, a massive and well-organized persecution of Christians in Turkey that resulted in deaths of at least one million people (see fig. 6.7). That genocide reduced the Christian population of the Middle East by almost half, and the number of Christians in the region has taken another nosedive during the last twenty-five years. Two

Figure 6.7. Armenians being rounded up for execution during Armenian genocide (1915–1921)

American-led Gulf Wars, the Arab Spring, and the increasing influence of Islamist radicals in the region (represented by groups such as ISIS, Al-Qaeda, and Hamas) have made the lives of Christians much more precarious. Persecution abounds. Christians accounted for about 15 percent of the population of the Middle East in 1900; today they represent only 3 percent, and the numbers are still declining. The land where Jesus once walked has become a Christian wasteland during the same time that Christianity has been growing by leaps and bounds across the rest of the globe.

Contemporary Asian Christianity

Making sense of Christianity in contemporary Asia is no easy task. Asia is a huge continent where every generalization has countless exceptions. The following discussion of Christianity in contemporary Asia accordingly begins with a description of Asian diversity. It then examines the prevalence of persecution in Asia and explores the impact Asia may have on the world Christian movement as a whole in the years ahead.

Asian Diversity

Asia is a vast region that includes one-third of all the land in the world. It is also home to more different cultures and languages than the rest of the world combined. Asia is called a continent, but it is a very different kind of "continent" than Africa, Latin America, Europe, or North America. Asia is so diverse that it may be helpful to view the region as consisting of four different subcontinents rather than as a single massive supercontinent. This approach also helps explain the experiences of Asian Christians, who face very different situations depending on whether they live in Islamic West Asia, Hindu South Asia, religiously mixed Southeast Asia, or Buddhist/secular East Asia (see fig. 6.8).

Islamic West Asia

Islamic West Asia comprises twenty-five countries, and Muslims are the dominant population in twenty-three of them. (The nations of Georgia and Armenia, located northeast of Turkey between the Black Sea and the Caspian Sea, are the exceptions.) The size of the Christian community in Islamic West Asia is tiny, and it is slowly getting smaller. Christians comprised 5 percent of the population in 1970 and 4 percent today. Lebanon, which had a Christian majority in 1970 (60 percent of the population), is only one-third Christian today.

Figure 6.8
The Four Asias

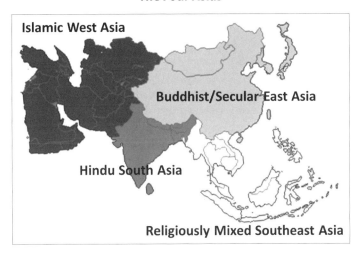

There is, however, one exception to this regional trend. The number of Christians residing in the six oil-producing Gulf nations of Bahrain, Kuwait, Oman, Qatar, Saudi Arabia, and the United Arab Emirates (UAE) is increasing, but this is solely because of the recruitment of "guest workers" for manual labor and domestic service. A significant number of these temporary workers are Christians, many of them from the Philippines, which has an extensive government-sponsored program for placing Filipinos in employment outside the country. In several Gulf nations, Christians now account for almost 10 percent of the population. Since these guest Christians are locked into low-paying jobs roughly equivalent to indentured servitude—passports are typically confiscated, and workers cannot travel without approval of employers—they have had almost no impact on the religious ethos of the region, which remains thoroughly Islamic. Guest workers have, at best, limited opportunities to gather for Christian worship, and they have little or no power to influence society.

HINDU SOUTH ASIA

Christians are no more numerous in Hindu South Asia than they are in Islamic West Asia—about 4 percent of the population in both—but Christians in South Asia live in a very different environment. The great majority of these Christians (95 percent) live in India, where Christians are distributed unevenly across the country. In the south, in Kerala, where Christians constitute one-third of the population, Christians live quite comfortably. Christianity has been present here since the first century, and Kerala's Christians have enjoyed, and continue to enjoy, relatively high social status. Christians in the neighboring state of Tamil Nadu are also sizeable in numbers and doing well. A similar situation exists in the northeast region of the country where Christians, most of them Baptists, represent roughly 90 percent of the population in the states of Nagaland, Mizoram, and Meghalaya (see fig. 6.9).

Figure 6.9
Where Christians Live in India
(Christian percentage of population by state)

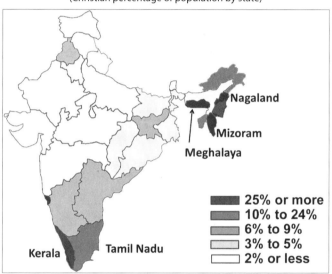

Christians living elsewhere in India are not so fortunate. About 75 percent of all the Christians in the country are Dalits. Dalits, who used to be called "untouchables," continue to exist at the very bottom of the Indian social hierarchy, and they are often treated horribly. Christianity has helped many Dalits gain a new sense of their own worth as persons, but becoming Christian often makes Dalits even more vulnerable to mistreatment by neighbors with higher social standing. Even within India's churches, prejudice against Dalits continues to be a problem.

Religiously Mixed Southeast Asia

Christianity is generally thriving in Southeast Asia. It is especially robust in the Philippines, which is now home to more than 90 million Christians. In terms of the region as a whole, Christians account for 20 percent of the population if the Philippines is included. But even if the Philippines is excluded Christians still make up 10 percent of the total population. Christianity in

Southeast Asia tends to be overrepresented in ethnic minority groups and underrepresented in the majority ethnic groups. In Thailand, for example, only 2 percent of the majority Thai people are Christian (most are Buddhist), but more than 30 percent of the minority Karen people are Christian. In Malaysia, less than 1 percent of the majority Malay people are Christian (almost all Malays are Muslim), while half of the minority Dusan people identify as Christian. The contrast is not as great in Vietnam, where 7 percent of the majority Vietnamese population is Christian, but this is still significantly lower than the 20 percent of the Vietnamese ethnic minority population that is Christian. This same pattern can be found in Indonesia, where Christians make up less than 1 percent of the large Madurese ethnic group and only 10 percent of the equally large Javanese population, but Christians represent more than 40 percent of Indonesia's minority Chinese immigrant community.

In sociological terms, converting to Christianity has become a way to solidify minority-group identity. In Thailand, for example, when members of the minority Karen people convert to Christianity, this reaffirms their Karenness, over against the majority Thai population. Conversion for someone from the majority Thai population involves a very different social dynamic. When a member of the Thai community converts, it often means breaking with one's family and Buddhist culture. Conversion is an act that requires courage and may entail suffering. Whether or not an individual becomes a Christian is never wholly determined by sociological considerations, but these differing social dynamics help explain why Christian growth has been far greater among minority groups.

Buddhist/Secular East Asia

Christianity is growing more quickly in the six nations of East Asia—China, Japan, Mongolia, North and South Korea, and Taiwan—than anywhere else in Asia. In 1970, just slightly more than 1 percent of the population was Christian; today the number is approaching 10 percent. In East Asia, in contrast to Southeast Asia, almost all Christians are members of majority ethnic groups, simply because these nations are so overwhelmingly homogeneous. Minority groups represent only a tiny fraction of the overall population.

The environment for Christianity is quite different in each of these nations. The extremes are represented by North and South Korea. In South Korea, Christians account for about 30 percent of the population, and in general they are highly respected. Six of South Korea's eleven presidents have been Christians. In North Korea, the situation could hardly be worse. North Korea is a communist state committed to state atheism, and Christianity is forbidden along with all other religions. Perhaps as many as two hundred thousand Christians remain in the country, but the actual number is unknown because no one can publicly admit to being a Christian. Many of North Korea's Christians have been imprisoned for their faith.

Japan and China fall somewhere in between these Korean extremes. In Japan, Christianity accounted for perhaps 2 percent of the population in 1900, and roughly 2 percent are still Christian today. Christianity has a generally good reputation—as many as half the weddings in the country use a "Christian" order of service—but very few Japanese feel compelled to actually become Christians themselves. In China, by contrast, Christianity has grown tremendously in the last fifty years, from an estimated one and a half million Christians in 1970 to as many as 100 million today, distributed unevenly across the country (see fig. 6.10). Despite the rising popularity of Christianity in China, or perhaps because of it, Christianity remains suspect in the eyes of many Chinese government officials.

Figure 6.10
Where Christians Live in China
(percentage of local population that is Christian*)

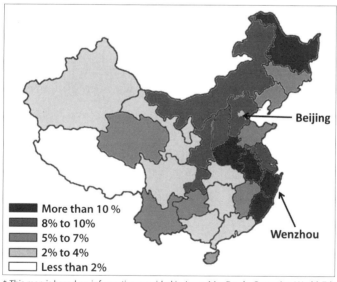

* This map is based on information provided in Jason ManDryck, *Operation World*, 7th ed. (Colorado Springs: Biblica, 2010).

Persecution

One of the few incontrovertible facts of life in Asia is that Christians are more likely to be persecuted or have their religious liberties restricted here than anywhere else in the world. The Christian organization Open Doors publishes a World Watch List each year that identifies places where Christians face persecution; in recent years, Asian nations have almost always topped the list. In 2014, nine of the top ten countries on the list were Asian: North Korea, Syria, Iraq, Afghanistan, Saudi Arabia, Maldives, Pakistan, Iran, and Yemen. The high prevalence of persecution in Asia is corroborated by a recently published Pew Research Center study that looked at government restrictions on religious activity and at nongovernmental social hostility toward religious groups and individuals worldwide. According to the Pew report, Asia is by far the most dangerous place for Christians to live. Twenty-six countries in Asia (two-thirds of all the nations in the region) were deemed to be both politically restrictive of religion and socially hostile to Christians. By comparison, only nine countries in Africa (less than 20 percent of the total) fell into this category, three in Europe, and one in Latin America.[10]

As with everything else in Asia, the persecution of Christians varies by subregion. In Islamic West Asia, it is a crime to leave Islam and convert to Christianity. Conversion is *apostasy*, the willful forsaking of truth for error, and apostasy is a crime punishable by death—though the death penalty is rarely imposed. It is much more common for converts to be harassed and jailed than to be executed. But the threat of death remains, possibly by order of the state or possibly at the hands of one's neighbors. It is not just apostasy that matters, however; any perception, no matter how unfounded, that a Christian has insulted the Prophet or desecrated the Qur'an or demeaned Islam in some other way can trigger persecution. Simply being a Christian is enough to promote hostility, a fact made horribly evident in the behavior of the militants who call themselves the Islamic State (also known as ISIS or ISIL). In Iraq and in several other countries where ISIS has a presence, Christians have been ordered to leave the territory or risk execution—and contrary to the pattern elsewhere in Islamic West Asia, ISIS follows through on its threats. This was sadly illustrated in the recent history of the Iraqi city of Mosul. Christians and Muslims had lived together in Mosul in peace for centuries, but when ISIS invaded, the entire Christian population was either driven away or executed.

In Hindu South Asia, the persecution of Christians has increased in recent decades, due largely to the emergence of a new political philosophy known as Hindutva. Followers of Hindutva have sometimes been described as Hindu fundamentalists. They would like India to be thoroughly and consistently

---

10. *Rising Tide of Restrictions on Religion* (Washington, DC: Pew Forum on Religion and Public Life, 2012).

Hindu, and the presence of Muslims and Christians is seen as problematic. The issue of conversion has been a prominent flashpoint for conflict. Most Hindus consider conversion to be evil because it is a moral and religious duty to live appropriately within the conditions of life into which one is born. Changing faith is construed as an attempt to circumvent the principle of *karma*, the idea that people are reborn into the state of life they deserve based on how they lived their previous lives. Many Indians assume that people change religions only for the sake of personal gain. During the last fifteen years, many Indian states have passed anti-conversion laws that make it a crime to encourage conversion by promising benefits. In some instances, Christian pastors and missionaries have been arrested for promising that Christians will go to heaven when they die. Pentecostal Christians who are convinced God wants to bless everyone with good health and material well-being are frequently at risk, and some Christian evangelists have been attacked by irate mobs. Infamously, an Australian missionary and his two young sons were burned to death as they slept in their car in Manoharpur, in the state of West Bengal, in 1999. In the Indian state of Odisha (formerly Orissa), hundreds of Christians were killed, dozens of churches were burned, and thousands of Christian homes were destroyed by rampaging mobs in 2008.

In Southeast Asia, the persecution of Christians is sometimes as much about politics as it is about faith. In Myanmar, for example, many of the hill tribe people have been seeking independence and resisting the dictates of the central Burmese government for decades, and the government has often responded with force. Many of these minority ethnic communities now have sizeable Christian populations who interpret the government's harassment as a form of anti-Christian persecution. This is not unreasonable, given the anti-Christian attitudes of many Burmese Buddhists. In Indonesia, tensions between Muslims and Christians have been heightened in recent years by the radical Islamic organization Jemaah Islamiah. Over the last two decades, there have been numerous incidents of violence in Indonesia, especially on the islands where the Christian and Muslim populations are roughly equal in size. Religion is a contributing factor in clashes, which are exacerbated by economic competition and long-simmering ethnic rivalries. Restrictions on religious freedom are another form of persecution that Christians experience in Southeast Asia. In 2014, the Malaysian Federal Court ruled that Christians could no longer use the word *Allah* when speaking about God because it might "confuse" Muslims. Though the decree was presented as a way to reduce religious tensions in the country, most Malaysian Christians thought the real goal was to intimidate Christians and undercut their efforts to share the gospel.

In East Asia, the persecution of Christians tends to be more overtly political than it is elsewhere. In North Korea, all aspects of public life are rigidly controlled by the state, and any expression of religious faith that catches the attention of the authorities is severely punished. A similar situation existed in China in the 1960s and 1970s, and China continues to closely monitor religious groups today. But while there are significant restrictions on Christianity in China, one rarely encounters overt persecution of the sort that used to occur. Government officials remain suspicious of any group, religious or not, that garners too much support or becomes too visible. The government's caution is informed by the Taiping Rebellion as well as by other religiously inspired protests by Buddhists and Muslims. While most Chinese Christians would welcome more freedom of religious expression, they also understand that some level of state control may be necessary in a nation of more than one billion people.

Asia and the Future of Christianity

One hundred years ago, almost everyone thought the future of Christianity would continue to be dominated by European Christianity. Christianity was expanding its reach around the world, and most missionaries assumed the Christianity they were planting elsewhere would end up looking a lot like Christianity in Europe or North America, Europe's transatlantic partner in global evangelism. Given the massive transformation of Christianity that has taken place in the last fifty years, no one any longer considers European Christianity to be the biggest player in world Christianity. A sizeable majority of the world's Christians—two-thirds of them—now live in Africa, Latin America, and Asia, and their forms of faith and life sometimes look very different from Christian practices in the global North (Europe and North America). The demographics point to Asian Christianity as a rapidly emerging powerhouse. An enormous number of Christians now live in Asia—almost 400 million in all, which is 100 million more Christians than live in North America. On any given Sunday, there are probably more Christians in church in Asia than there are in all of Europe. Three Asian countries now make the "top-ten" list of the countries with the greatest number of Christians (see fig. 6.11).

These are impressive facts, but even more significant is how much room there is for Christian growth in Asia, much more than anywhere else in the world. Less than 10 percent of the Asian population is currently Christian, compared with 50 percent of Africa, 75 percent of both Europe and North America, and 90 percent of Latin America. Major growth in Christian

Figure 6.11
The Ten Countries with the Greatest Number of Christians
(total number of Christians in each country)

numbers on the other four continents is unlikely, but even a little uptick in the Asian Christian population could radically change global Christian demographics. Sixty percent of all the people in the world currently live in Asia, while only 40 percent live in the rest of the world combined (see figs. 6.12 and 6.13). Given global rates of population growth, Asia will almost certainly continue to account for more than half of the world's population for the rest of the twenty-first century. The lingering question is whether Christianity can become as indigenously Asian as it has become African and Latin American.

There is reason to believe this can happen. In the last century, Christianity has put down deeper roots in Asian culture than any time since the tenth century. The churches are full, the number of Christians is growing, and Asian Christians (especially in East Asia) often feel as if they are just as Asian as their other-religious and nonreligious neighbors. But in some countries, Christianity seems to be hitting an invisible ceiling. This is the case, for example, in South Korea. Christians made up less than 1 percent of the population in 1900, rose to 18 percent by 1970, and are about 30 percent of the population today. That growth curve is currently flattening for a variety of reasons, including Christianity's sinking public image due to Christian involvement in political corruption. A dramatic event, such as reunification with the North, could change the dynamics, but at present it seems as if South Korean Christianity may be settling into permanent minority status. The ultimate test case for Christianity's success in Asia will

Figure 6.12
World Population by Continent
(percentage of total)

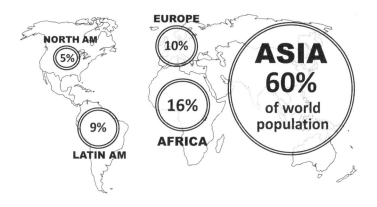

Figure 6.13
Christian Percentage of Population by Continent

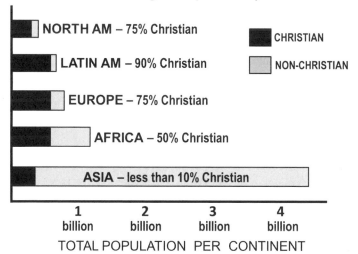

be China. Chinese Christianity is currently experiencing the same kind of amazing growth that South Korea enjoyed during the last century. Christians accounted for less than 1 percent of the Chinese population in 1970, and they are now rapidly approaching 10 percent. Continued expansion seems likely, but further growth will surely increase tensions with the government. No one knows if this will lead to tighter religious restrictions or outright persecution.

Asian Theology and the Ideal of Harmony

Asian Christians are only now beginning to find their own distinctive theological voices. In the words of the Malaysian Methodist theologian Hwa Yung, many Asian Christians remain "bananas" (yellow on the outside, but white on the inside). They need to become more like "mangoes" that are yellow all the way through.[11] His particular concern is that too many Asian theologians have latched onto what he sees as a liberal Western religious pluralism, and he would like them to accentuate the uniqueness of Christianity more forcefully. Whatever their attitude or approach, Asian theologians are becoming more articulate, and their views are beginning to leaven Christian theological reflection worldwide.[12]

Asian theology is rooted in a culture very different from the West. Sociologists and anthropologists have noted that Westerners are taught to see objects and individuals as complete in and of themselves, while Asians are taught to see the world through the lens of relationships. For Westerners, each object or individual has its own identity and significance. For Asians, nothing makes sense all by itself; reality is defined by the connections that exist among things, people included. Western ways of knowing emphasize differences; Eastern ways of knowing emphasize relationships and harmony. The classic Asian symbol of harmony is the yin-yang (see fig. 6.14), which illustrates how opposite or contrary forces, when viewed in relation to each other, form a larger whole. Asians recognize many dualities in the world (light and dark, high and low, hot and cold, life and death, male and female), but rather than seeing them as opposites, which is the tendency in the West, Asians see dualities as harmoniously linked pairs that constantly, endlessly interact without ever reaching a fixed or final resolution.

Figure 6.14
Yin-Yang Symbol

Asia's emphasis on dynamic harmony reflects a different social structure and framework for etiquette than found in the West. In the West, people are expected to declare their convictions boldly and to stand up for themselves. Confrontation is valued. In Asia, much more emphasis is placed on deference to others. This difference is illustrated in the way people greet each other. The West's standard greeting is the handshake, which originated as a way to

---

11. Hwa Yung, *Mangoes or Bananas? The Quest for an Authentic Asian Christian Theology* (Oxford: Regnum, 1997), 240.

12. See Simon Chan, *Grassroots Asian Theology: Thinking the Faith from the Ground Up* (Downers Grove, IL: InterVarsity, 2014).

show that a person held no sword and the meeting was not an attack. The standard Asian greeting is the bow, which is intended to signal reverence or respect for the other. As for family relations, Asia has a long cultural expectation of filial piety. It is mandatory to respect parents and, by extension, all elderly individuals. Thoughtless or immoral behavior by a young person brings shame to the whole family. This is in stark contrast to the West, where the goal of childrearing is to help children become independent, and some degree of adolescent rebellion is expected and even encouraged.

There are strengths and limitations associated with the values of every culture, and this applies to the Asian notion of harmony just as it applies to Western individualism. While Western culture is more brash and brusque than Asian culture, Western cultures also generally assume that everyone is in some sense equal, and personal accomplishment is valued. Most Asians believe society is hierarchical and that those lower on the social scale should show respect and deference to those who are above them. In Asia, people do not presume to be (or to be able to become) something they are not. This stance can encourage a kind of fatalism, a refusal to try something new because it is doomed to fail or be crushed. This attitude is captured in an oft-quoted Japanese proverb: "The nail that sticks out will be hammered down."

Christian theology in Asia is frequently described as a "triple dialogue," an effort to balance (or harmonize) Christian convictions with civic loyalty, with respect for members of other religions, and with concern for the poor. Theology in dialogue with civic loyalty leads Christians to identify positively with their own cultures and nations, affirming what is good rather than searching for failures and shortcomings. Theology in dialogue with other faiths nudges Asian Christians to be respectful of the beliefs and values of their non-Christian neighbors, especially (but not only) when they overlap with Christian beliefs and practices. And theology undertaken in dialogue with the poor leads Asian Christians to speak of *han*, a Korean word describing the pain and resentment felt by those who suffer unjustly.

Civic Loyalty

Most Christians in Asia are eager to affirm their loyalty to their nations and to the cultures in which they live. In actions, if not in words, they say to their neighbors, "We are one of you. We are loyal fellow citizens. We belong here." On one level, such assurances might be the norm for members of minority populations around the world. Their loyalty is questioned by the majority, so it needs to be explicitly and frequently reaffirmed. Christians in Asia have often been viewed as outsiders who follow a foreign religion that was arrogantly imposed by Western powers during the colonial era of the nineteenth and early twentieth centuries, and many Asian Christians still feel compelled to deny their foreignness and declare their patriotism. These declarations are not merely tactics for survival. Most Asian Christians believe that showing respect for one's nation and fellow citizens is part of Christian moral teaching.

Examples of civic loyalty within the Asian Christian community abound, even in places such as the tempestuous Middle East. Thus, when the Palestinian Liberation Organization (PLO), an institution focused on Palestinian solidarity, was first formed in 1964, Christians joined with their Muslim neighbors to create a united Palestinian front, protesting what they perceived as their unjust treatment at the hands of the Israeli government and Jewish settler groups. During the early years of the PLO, the genuine camaraderie between Muslims and Christians, including many Palestinians who were conservative evangelical Christians, was incomprehensible to some Christians in the United States who vigorously disagreed with the politics of the PLO. Even today, when tensions between Muslim and Christian Palestinians have been strained by the radically Islamist turn of Palestinian politics, most Palestinian Christians continue to see themselves as thoroughly Palestinian and share their Muslim compatriots' opposition to Israeli rule.

Christian commitments to civic loyalty and social harmony are even more evident in East Asia. Christianity in Korea is an example. Korea was brutally occupied by Japan from 1910 until 1945. Christians were only a tiny portion of the Korean population, but they took a lead role in resisting Japanese rule. In 1919, when the "March 1 Movement," the main Korean resistance group, issued a declaration of independence from Japanese rule, almost half the signatories (fifteen out of thirty-three) were Christians. Korean Christians have retained a strong sense of solidarity with their non-Christian neighbors ever since, and they have, like all Koreans, been extremely troubled by the North-South division of the Korean peninsula that followed the Korean War in the early 1950s. Many South Korean churches operate retreat centers in the mountains near the division line where congregants can gather to pray for reunification. On a recent trip to one of these Korean retreat centers, a Western visitor was shocked to see "dozens of people fervently praying, kneeling, standing, weeping, in between boulders, behind rocks, all over the hillside and ravine." He expected to hear that some terrible tragedy had just taken place, but he realized that the outpouring of impassioned grief was a routine instance of Korean Christians praying "for the reunification of the two Koreas."[13]

13. Sai R. Park, *The Good Doctor: Bringing Healing to the Hopeless* (Colorado Springs: Biblica, 2010), 62–63.

Social harmony as embraced by Asian Christians does not always have a national focus. Especially among minority people living in Southeast Asia, such as the Karen people of Myanmar and Thailand, loyalty is often more tribal than it is national. These groups include significant numbers of Christians whose newfound Christian faith has merged with their much older ethnic identities to create a doubly strong sense of difference from their mostly non-Christian neighbors. From one perspective, this sense of difference seems "unharmonious," but most of these Christians do not consider themselves to be genuine citizens of the nations where they live. For them, harmony and loyalty are about relationships with their own people and not with the central government, which they often see as an occupying enemy force.

The issue of harmony and civic loyalty has been especially problematic in China because the transition from colonial domination to postcolonial rule was so drastic and dramatic. Technically, China was never colonized by the West, but the so-called Opium Wars of the mid-nineteenth century forced the country to accept both the opium trade and Christian missionaries. It is no surprise that this tragic confluence of God and greed caused many Chinese to see Christianity as a foreign (or even an evil) religion that was imposed on China. In the postcolonial era, many Chinese accordingly thought that getting rid of Western domination necessarily involved getting rid of Christianity. The place of Christianity in postcolonial China was further complicated by an internal power struggle between the communist forces of Mao Zedong (who was an atheist) and the pro-capitalist and pro-Western supporters of Chiang Kai-shek (who was a Christian). When Mao and his communist allies emerged victorious on October 1, 1949, they created a new People's Republic of China (PRC) based on atheistic communist principles. Chinese Christians suddenly found themselves in double jeopardy, being seen as potentially both pro-Western and anti-communist.

In response to the formation of the PRC, some Christian leaders attempted to harmonize their faith with communist values, while others took a hard line against cooperation with the state. Fights between proponents of the two approaches were often nasty and bitter. One person who wanted to harmonize Christianity and Chinese communism was Ding Guangxun, known as K. H. Ting in the West. Ting was educated at St. John's University, an Anglican school in Shanghai, and then briefly worked for the Chinese YMCA. He left China briefly to study in the West (1946–1951), but returned to become the principal of Nanjing Union Theological Seminary. Ting became a leader in the Protestant Three-Self Patriotic Movement (the state-sanctioned Protestant organization) and later chaired the China Christian Council (the national association of all state-approved "above ground" Protestant churches). Ting helped reconnect the Chinese churches with the global Christian community, establishing strong ties with both the World Council of Churches and the evangelically oriented Fuller Theological Seminary in Pasadena, California. Ting died in November 2012 at the age of ninety-seven.[14]

Ting was quick to praise the positive accomplishments of the new communist government. He noted that Christians had worked for years to end opium smoking and prostitution with little to show for their efforts, but the PRC's socialist government had put an end to those practices within a few months after coming to power. Ting said Christians needed to acknowledge this accomplishment and leave their negative stereotypes of China's new communist rulers behind. He also believed that Chinese Christians needed to reframe their basic approach to evangelism and missions. In the past, he said, Christians had often "capitalized on human depravity and lack of virtue as the entering point for preaching about sin and on Christ as Savior."[15] In the new China, Christians had to explain the gospel in terms that affirmed the goodness of humankind rather than merely denouncing human weaknesses and sin.

The task of reimagining the gospel in more positive terms kept Ting occupied for the rest of his life and deeply influenced his view of God. Ting wrote that most Christians had "been trained to think of God largely in terms of superior power which can either crush us or make us powerful." He argued that this "bulldozer God" was not the God revealed by Jesus. The God revealed by Jesus was a God who lures people into relationship, a God who affirms the good things people do rather than simply scolding people for their failures, and a God who loves everyone whether they are Christians or not. Ting mused, "It seems to me that to confess Christ is Godlike is not half so important as to affirm that God is Christlike and that Christlike love is the way God runs the cosmos."[16] This Jesus-centered vision of God and the gospel was good news that could be embraced by Chinese socialists without requiring them to give up their socialism. It was also a theology that allowed Chinese Christians to relate more positively to their non-Christian, and even their atheistic, neighbors (see textbox, Asian Theology: K. H. Ting).

Not all Chinese Christians agree with Ting's theological position, and some have viewed him as a collaborator with communist wickedness. The Chinese Christian dissident Wang Ming-Dao, for example, vigorously rejected Ting's approach, embracing an alternative model that stressed spiritual purity and

---

14. For more on Ting's life and work, see Philip L. Wickeri, *Reconstructing Christianity in China: K. H. Ting and the Chinese Church* (Maryknoll, NY: Orbis, 2007).

15. K. H. Ting, *Love Never Ends* (Nanjing: Yilin, 2000), 411.

16. Ibid., 435–36.

Asian Theology: K. H. Ting

Christians and Atheists

K. H. Ting (1915–2012), a Chinese Protestant church leader and theologian, was one of the most powerful Christians in late twentieth-century China. Ting served as head of the state-sanctioned China Christian Council during the 1980s and 1990s, and he was the principal of Nanjing Union Theological Seminary for more than forty years. This reading calls Chinese Christians to adopt a positive rather than negative stance toward society and to cooperate even with perceived enemies.

The question has been raised as to whether we Christians can be "fellow travelers" with these atheists [i.e., Chinese communists]. My answer is affirmative. All through history, Christians have been fellow-travelling with non-Christians and atheists of all sorts in all sorts of undertaking. Why make an exception now? . . . I would like to say to the revolutionary: "Carry on your valuable work but gain a fuller sense of its meaning and importance by relating it to the ongoing creative, redemptive and sanctifying movement in the universe under what we call God, so that all your undertakings . . . get an even deeper grounding. Religious faith will not dampen your revolutionary spirit, but will purify it, make it more sublime, more acceptable to God." In other words, we do have an evangelistic task here. But that is only half the picture. The other half is the purifying effect the revolutionary could bring to our church in all its oldness, its institutionalism and its immobility. I visualize a day when the two halves will meet and merge. . . .

The revolutionary atheists are not necessarily the enemies of authentic Christianity. In our churches too often contrasts are overdrawn, false simplifications are made of complex problems. The Christian community has become prey to arrogance in its relationship with those it should be seeking to understand. We might ask: Is the church not cutting itself off from valuable allies against idolatry? . . . An atheism that denies false gods who dehumanize people and give their blessing to bondage and injustice—is that not a good partner for a united front for the church on its pilgrimage? . . . Is it really good for us Christians to assume a posture of cynicism, and not one of friendship and goodwill?*

---

* K. H. Ting, *Love Never Ends* (Nanjing: Yilin, 2000), 40–41.

the dangers of being "unequally yoked" with nonbelievers. Wang's Christianity was just as postcolonial and non-Western as Ting's—Wang wanted Chinese Christians to fully control their own churches—but he believed the gospel demanded a countercultural stance, especially when the government was as controlling as China's. As long as the Chinese government continues to disrespect or persecute Christians, many Chinese Christians will continue to agree with Wang. However, his countercultural stance is not the typical Asian

Christian stance. Most Asian Christians seek ways to remain solidly loyal to Christ while simultaneously expressing solidarity with their non-Christian neighbors and loyalty to their non-Christian governments.

Interfaith Etiquette

Interreligious dialogue is still something that is exceptional for many Christians in the West, and entering into such dialogues frequently pushes Western Christians outside their traditional comfort zones. In the West, where Christians are in the majority, Christians typically control their encounters with religious others, choosing when and how to interact with members of non-Christian faiths. Interfaith conversations in the West tend to be relatively formal; people gather specifically to talk about religious differences, and they often do so in highly philosophical or theological terms.

This is not how interfaith relations work in Asia. In Asia, Christians are themselves "the other," and Christians converse every day with the members of other religions who also happen to be their friends, neighbors, fellow family members, or acquaintances. These interactions are nothing like the formal dialogues that take place in the West. They are unscripted encounters that take place in the course of daily life. What is forefront in these conversations is neither evangelism nor philosophical debate. What matters is being a good neighbor or friend or family member or acquaintance. What matters is modeling the gospel in action.

Thomas Menamparampil, the Catholic archbishop of Guwahati in northeastern India, explains, "If we are carriers of a message that invites the whole of humanity to be one, it ought to make us aware of the need for being open to all people," and that includes a "sincere appreciation for what is good" in the religions other people affirm.[17] Archbishop Menamparampil's comments made a good deal of sense to his fellow bishops, who have wrestled with interfaith relations for years. In the 1980s, the Asian Catholic bishops concluded that the contemporary era is fundamentally different from the past and requires a new and more proactive relationship to people of other faiths. They embraced religious pluralism as a "significant and positive" part of God's plan for the salvation of the world and described other religions as "complementary perceptions of the ineffable divine mystery." The bishops even went so far as to suggest that "no particular religion can raise the claim of being the norm for all others." "We religious believers are co-pilgrims," they declared, so the

---

17. Thomas Menamparampil, "A Presence That Challenges and Strengthens," address to the Federation of Asian Bishops' Conference (2009), 4, www.fabc.org/plenary%20assembly /A%20Presence%20that%20Challenges%20and%20Strengthens.pdf.

future of Christianity in Asia means establishing "continuous, humble, and loving dialogue" with people of all faiths.[18]

Respect for the insights and practices of other religions seemed like common sense to Asian bishops who had lived in the swirl of Asian religious diversity for their entire lives. In their view, they were simply stating the obvious. There is goodness and wisdom in all religious traditions, and Christians can acknowledge that reality without compromising their own allegiance to the way of God revealed by Jesus of Nazareth. For some non-Asian Catholics, however, the language of the Asian bishops was troubling. Cardinal Joseph Ratzinger, who later became Pope Benedict XVI, was especially concerned, and he penned the document *Dominus Iesus* in 2000 to set the record straight. He acknowledged that other religions might have some role to play "in God's salvific plan," but he reaffirmed that the "unicity, universality, and absoluteness" of the Christian message could not be questioned.[19] Some Asian Catholics felt chastened by *Dominus Iesus*, but many more felt the cardinal had simply missed the point. For them, interfaith relations are not about drawing theological lines in the sand regarding subjects that might never come up in normal conversation. They are about living harmoniously alongside non-Christian neighbors and respecting the positive insights about God and the world that can be found in Asian cultures and religions.

Many Protestant and Pentecostal Christians in Asia agree with their Catholic counterparts that living harmoniously with people of other faiths is an important part of Christian discipleship. The Indian evangelical theologian Atul Aghamkar, for example, explains that "often it is not the precepts of the Christian faith that are offensive to the people of India, it is the way Christians present them in their life and practice." Aghamkar tries to be humble and gracious in his own work and ministry. He rarely uses the word *Christian* when speaking to Hindus, because the term has become so politicized in recent years and because it still evokes a host of negative stereotypes associated with Western missionaries. So Aghamkar says simply, "I am a follower of Jesus Christ," a self-description that many Hindus can accept as perfectly valid. Rather than pushing for conversions, he strives to change how Christians are perceived, and he tells his fellow evangelicals that

18. Quoted in Jonathan Yun-Ka Tan, "A New Way of Being Church in Asia: The Federation of Asian Bishops' Conferences (FABC) at the Service of Life in Pluralistic Asia," *Missiology: An International Review* 33, no. 1 (2006).

19. Joseph Cardinal Ratzinger, *Dominus Iesus: On the Unicity and Universality of Jesus Christ and the Church* (Rome: Office of the Congregation for the Doctrine of the Faith, 2000), 14–15. www.vatican.va/roman_curia/congregations/cfaith/documents/rc_con_cfaith_doc_20 000806_dominus-iesus_en.html.

Hindus are more likely to listen to them talk about Jesus if the conversation is nonconfrontational.[20]

Aghamkar's aversion to confrontation is consistent with the way most Asians think about religion. Most Asians view religions as ancient repositories of cultural wisdom, resources from which they can draw assistance, insight, and inspiration as needed. The primary question in Asia is not which religion is true but which religion—or cultural tradition, since religion and culture are so difficult to tease apart—might offer helpful guidance in particular situations. The Western notion of belonging to one and only one religion does not resonate with many Asians, and some Asian Christians have adopted this inclusive approach, describing Christianity as only one source of insight that informs their lives. Other Asian Christians, however, who are no less concerned about living harmoniously with their non-Christian neighbors, reject this perspective because it seems to diminish Christianity's claim of uniqueness.

The issue of religious pluralism and inclusivity has enormous implications for how Asian Christians understand the process of conversion. While some Asian Christians would insist that becoming a Christian requires a clean break both with the past and with all other religious traditions, others now suggest that a person can ease into Christianity a little bit at a time. Jesus-influenced but not traditionally Christian movements have sprung up across Asia. In India, the Yesu Bhakta movement attracts people who worship Jesus in private but who refuse to dissociate from their Hindu families and fellow villagers— something a formal, public conversion would require—and who continue to participate in local, communal Hindu rituals. In several predominantly Muslim countries, messianic Muslims and members of Muslim-Christian "insider movements" act externally just like everyone else, including attending Friday prayers and fasting during Ramadan, but internally they view themselves as followers of Jesus. In China, growing numbers of intellectuals who revere the life and teachings of Jesus refuse to name themselves as Christian. Asian Christians are divided on how to respond to such developments, but all Asian Christians agree that more discussion is needed about what it means to be a faithful follower of Christ in the religiously pluralistic context of Asia today (see textbox, Asian Theology: Kosuke Koyama).

Disharmony and the Experience of Han

Because harmony is so strongly valued in most Asian societies, disharmony plays a major role in conceptualizing how present realities fall short of

---

20. Atul Aghamkar, "Hindu-Christian Dialogue in India," *Evangelical Inter-Faith Dialogue* 2, no. 2 (2011): 4, 15.

hoped-for ideals. Many Asian Christians share this sentiment and they have introduced the concept of *han* into their theology as a way of acknowledging the significance of social disharmony. *Han* is a Korean word that refers to the experience of being harmed by the actions of others, not just once but repeatedly. *Han* can be experienced by an individual (such as an abused wife) or by groups of people who are repeatedly mistreated by society, as Koreans were during the Japanese occupation. Those who suffer the effects of *han* are dehumanized. This is social disharmony at its worst, and it affects body

Asian Theology: Kosuke Koyama

The Mixing of Faiths

Kosuke Koyama (1929–2009) was one of Asia's most well-known twentieth-century theologians. A Japanese Protestant, he taught at several theological schools in Southeast Asia and also at Union Theological Seminary in New York. Koyama authored six books on Asian theology. This excerpt from his influential first book, *Water Buffalo Theology* (first printed in 1974), describes Koyama's struggle to understand the relationship between Christianity and other Asian religions.

> In Thailand I was often asked whether the Hindu Upanishads, the Buddhist Tripitaka, or the Confucian Analects could replace the Old Testament. The argument was: if the Old Testament is preparation for the New Testament, can the Upanishads be for Asians a preparation for the New Testament? My response was the Upanishads cannot replace the Old Testament, but the study of the Upanishads will profit our understanding of the Old and New Testaments. Why can it not replace the Old Testament? There is, as it were, a blood relationship between the Old Testament and the New Testament which is not there between the Upanishads and the New Testament. . . .
>
> Then I took a second look at the Upanishads. If I preach the gospel in a culture steeped in Upanishadic spirituality, the question as to whether the Upanishads can replace the Old Testament becomes immaterial since they will read both the Old and New Testaments from the Upanishadic outlook anyway. In all religious discourses, I concluded, replacement is an artificial concept. . . .
>
> [I am], however, concerned about religious syncretism. Religious syncretism is ambiguous, being at times artificial and at other times natural. Religions artificially mixed will be deprived of genuine spiritual power. In fact, religious realities are resistant to such quick and superficial mixing, but at the same time religions influence each other in the longer time scale. . . . All religious teachings are composites of many traditions. There is no pure Buddhism or Christianity. It is not apart from but by means of the sometimes confusing voices of plurality within Christianity that the gospel displays power. And it is there we are to hear the gospel message.*

* Kosuke Koyama, *Water Buffalo Theology*, 25th anniversary ed. (Maryknoll, NY: Orbis, 1999), xii–xiii.

as well as soul. The Korean theologian Chung Hyun Kyung was one of the first to incorporate the concept of *han* into Christian theology (see textbox, Asian Theology: Chung Hyun Kyung). Her thinking was deeply influenced by the story of her own mother, a poor single woman forced to have a baby for a childless wealthy couple and permanently unhinged by grief after her infant daughter was taken away. Chung's writings focus mainly on *han* as it has been experienced by women, but other Asian Christians have begun to use the term more broadly.

A key question that has emerged in recent years is how the notion of *han* might expand the ways in which Christians in Asia (and elsewhere too) describe what is wrong with the world. In Western Christianity, the gospel is often explained in terms of individual sinners and the need to confess sins and seek forgiveness. Asians accept this Western articulation of the gospel as a necessary part of the good news as it was preached by Jesus, but they wonder if *sin*, understood in this way, is comprehensive enough to deal with all that is wrong with the world. Because they see reality relationally, as yin and yang, many Asian Christians wonder if the traditional Western understanding of sin renders the victims of sin all but invisible. To remedy that weakness, some Asian theologians are now suggesting that "sin and *han* must be treated together, if we are to grasp a more comprehensive picture of the problems of the world than that delineated by the doctrine of sin alone."[21]

The term *han* is not used in India, but a concept very much like *han* is pervasive within the Indian Dalit Christian community. Dalits are those at the very bottom of the Indian social hierarchy. In fact, Dalits are so low on the social scale that they have no caste identity at all. In the language of Indian law, they have "unscheduled" status; in common parlance, they used to be called "untouchables." *Dalit*, however, is how most Dalits describe themselves, a Sanskrit term that means "crushed" or "broken." This term certainly reflects the typical Dalit experience. Dalits are often treated with disdain or worse in Indian society as a whole, and even in the churches—where Dalits make up close to three quarters of the membership—they experience the effects of significant prejudice from Christians with higher social standing.

The experience of being a Dalit—and especially of being a Dalit Christian because they are often treated worse than Dalits who are Hindu—can be embittering. Even though they don't use the term, what they are experiencing is a form of *han*. One Dalit Christian explains his own experience of radical social disharmony by saying: "We don't need anybody to die for us. We all

21. Andrew Sung Park, *The Wounded Heart of God: The Asian Concept of Han and the Christian Doctrine of Sin* (Minneapolis: Augsburg, 1993), 10.

Asian Theology: Chung Hyun Kyung

Han

Chung Hyun Kyung is a Korean theologian who is currently a professor of ecumenical studies at Union Theological Seminary in New York. Since 1991, when she gave a controversial speech at the World Council of Churches meeting in Canberra, Australia, Chung has been criticized for what her detractors see as pantheistic and religiously syncretistic views. This selection comes from her first book, published before her speech at Canberra. It explains how *han* provides a larger vocabulary for describing the ways in which sin and evil can deform human lives.

Oppression makes the oppressed experience separation of self. The oppressed woman experiences a most severe split within herself. The sense of who she wants to be as a human being and her reality of [oppression] are radically different and opposite, and this situation produces shame, guilt, and self-hate. Continuous, prolonged shame, guilt, and self-hate then lead Asian women to the pseudo-safety of non-feeling. Numbing oneself for survival is the most tragic stage for the oppressed because the individual loses the power to resist. Through the process of numbing, individuals become separated from themselves, each other, and the God of life. . . .

They call [this experience] han. . . . This feeling arises from a sense of impasse. Often Korean people, especially the poor and women, have not had any access to public channels through which they can challenge the injustices done to them. They have long been silenced by physical and psychological intimidation, and actual bodily violence by the oppressor. When there is no place where they can express their true selves, their true feelings, the oppression becomes "stuck" inside. This unexpressed anger and resentment stemming from social powerlessness forms a "lump" in their spirit. This lump often leads to a lump in the body, by which I mean the oppressed often disintegrate bodily as well as psychologically.*

---

* Chung Hyun Kyung, *Struggle to Be the Sun Again: Introducing Asian Women's Theology* (Maryknoll, NY: Orbis, 1990), 41–43.

die every day. How does the death of Christ substitute for our killings every day? It doesn't. It does not relate to us. But solidarity does. Solidarity [with Christ] is salvation for us."[22] The Dalit theologian James Massey further elaborates this *han*-informed theological perspective: "Western Christian theology is based on the classical Greek dualism between this-world and the other-world, between matter and spirit. In contrast, Dalit theology is soundly rooted in the this-worldly experiences of suffering of the Dalits, and rather

22. Monodeep Daniel, quoted in Elze Sietzema-Riemer, *Christian Dalits: A Research on Christian Dalits in India* (Utrecht, Netherlands: Mission Department ICCO and Kerk in Actie, 2009), 19.

than promising the Dalits a place in heaven, it inspires them to struggle for transforming this world to bring justice for the Dalits."[23] Massey and some other Asian Christians believe that *han*-informed theology must necessarily become political. For them, the righteous harmonizing of society based on biblical principles of justice is the only salvation that matters. Most Dalits, many of whom are Pentecostal, would not agree; they would be suspicious of any theology that became too exclusively political. But almost all Dalits would agree that sin has significant social and political dimensions.

For Asian Christians, it is not just individual acts of sin that matter but also the consequences of those sins for others. Because sin harms others, any proper repentance for sin has to include some effort to repair that harm. In the biblical story of Jesus and the tax collector Zacchaeus (Luke 19:1–10), Zacchaeus is forgiven, then immediately announces he will pay back everyone he has wronged. In fact, he says he will pay them four times more than the loss they suffered. Repentance in this story involves reparation, trying to make right what was made wrong by sinful actions. Zacchaeus sought a just restoration of social harmony. This is a desire and an outcome that most Asian Christians would see intuitively as right, a necessary part of what it means to live and act as a faithful follower of Jesus.

Summary

More than anywhere else in the world, the history of Christianity in Asia has been a series of ups and downs, of expansions and contractions. The gospel was originally announced to the world in Asia where Jesus lived, but Christians have only rarely constituted a majority of the population in any Asian country. For the most part, Asian Christians have been permanent minorities in the cultures in which they have lived. As a result, Asian Christians have learned how to live amicably with people of other faiths. Nonetheless, persecution of Christians has been and still is common. Christianity was obliterated from much of Asia during the 1300s and 1400s, and since then it has generally been considered a foreign religion. However, Christians all over Asia are rediscovering the Asian-ness of their faith, and they are trying to convince their non-Christian neighbors that the gospel truly can be Asian. At present, only about 10 percent of the Asian population is Christian, but since Asia accounts for 60 percent of the world's people, even a small increase

23. "Dalit Liberation Theology: Interview with James Massey," *Christian Persecution India Articles* (blog), February 25, 2005, http://cpiarticles.blogspot.com/2005/02/dalit-liberation -theology-interview.html.

in the Asian Christian proportion will have a significant effect on the global profile of the Christian movement.

The notion of *harmony* forms the center of Asian culture, and increasingly it also defines the heart of Asian Christianity. Christians in the West often pay more attention to differences than to similarities, emphasizing differences among Christians and also differences between Christianity and other religions. Western ethics often focus on drawing lines and taking a stand. Asian Christians, by contrast, are more prone to see relationships and connections. In ordinary life, this blends ethics and etiquette. Being right is not only about standing on principles; it is also about showing appropriate respect to others. Many Asian Christians say that preaching the gospel does not require the denunciation of other religions, and the good news should be proclaimed positively. But Asian Christians know that everything is not right with the world and that things are especially bad for those at the bottom of society. The notion of *han* gives Asian Christians new language for describing the fallenness of the world and also for understanding how God's saving and healing power can transform individual lives and whole societies.

7

North America

IN 1993, THE US CONGRESS passed the Religious Freedom Restoration Act (RFRA). Nearly every religious organization in the nation, conservatives and liberals alike, supported the legislation. The vote was unanimous in the House of Representatives, and it was ninety-seven to three in the Senate, a level of agreement across the political spectrum that is almost unimaginable in today's politically contentious environment. The RFRA was enacted in response to a dispute over indigenous religious practices. Two members of the Native American Church who worked as counselors at a drug rehabilitation clinic in Oregon were fired after testing positive for mescaline in a routine drug screening. The workers admitted to having ingested *peyote* (which contains mescaline) as part of a religious ritual, but they contended that being fired was an unconstitutional abridgement of their religious rights. The case eventually was considered by the US Supreme Court, which ruled that the drug-free requirement for employment at a rehabilitation facility was reasonable and had not been implemented for the purpose of inhibiting anyone's religious liberty. Many Americans, not just Native Americans, saw this ruling as evidence that the government was eroding the edges of religious freedom in the United States, and the RFRA was enacted to protect religious liberties.

Two decades later, in 2014, the RFRA was back in the headlines. This time, the RFRA served as the basis for a lawsuit brought by the family-owned company Hobby Lobby against the Affordable Care Act (popularly known as Obamacare). Once again, the litigation went all the way to the Supreme

Court. The company argued that providing mandated contraceptive health care for female employees, including some drugs the company claimed might induce early-stage abortion, would require the owners of the company to act against their own deeply held religious conviction that abortion is always wrong. The Supreme Court, in a five-to-four decision, ruled in Hobby Lobby's favor, declaring that the RFRA applied not only to individuals but also to family-owned companies like Hobby Lobby. The court's decision was controversial and heavily criticized, and it was scathingly denounced by the four dissenting justices. But while the politics of the decision were polarizing, the basic principle of individual religious freedom was never challenged. In America, religious freedom is not merely protected by the laws of the land, it is a deeply held national conviction.

In this chapter, the words *America* and *American* will be used to refer to the United States of America and its citizens. *North America* will be used to describe the United States and Canada. As a geographically defined continent, North America includes Mexico along with these two countries, but on the basis of culture, Mexico is instead included in the chapter on Latin America. As with all the previous regional chapters, space limitations preclude providing equal coverage of all countries. Because the United States has a population nearly nine times larger than Canada—more people live in the state of California alone than in all of Canada—and because it has a correspondingly greater global influence, the United States will be the focus of most of this chapter, even though Canada has a fascinating religious history that is very different from its neighbor to the south.[1]

America's commitment to religious freedom has produced a freewheeling market of religion in the United States that is globally unique. In America, anyone can start a new religious movement, and if enough people join, that movement will succeed. This differs radically from Europe, where historically only one religion (or, more specifically, one Christian tradition) was allowed to operate freely in any given nation, and where even today state churches or religious quasi monopolies still exist. This is also different from Latin America, where Catholicism remains numerically dominant, even though choice has become part of the religious environment. In North America, by contrast, it is firmly established that matters of faith are purely personal choices. Churches

---

1. For more information on Christianity in Canada, see Phyllis D. Airhart, *A Church with the Soul of a Nation: Making and Remaking the United Church of Canada* (Montreal: McGill-Queens University Press, 2014); Reginald W. Bibby, *Restless Gods: The Renaissance of Religion in Canada* (Toronto: Stoddart, 2002); Terence J. Fay, *A History of Canadian Catholics: Gallicanism, Romanism, and Canadianism* (Montreal: McGill-Queens University Press, 2002); and Mark Noll, *What Happened to Christian Canada?* (Vancouver: Regent College Publishing, 2007).

vie for members in much the same way that businesses vie for customers and clients, and individual believers assess the available options in much the same way that they decide which movie to watch or which car to buy. Even people who live in towns with dozens of churches sometimes attend churches miles away because none of the local options appeal to them.

In many ways, North American Christianity used to be more globally exceptional than it is today. A hundred years ago, no other place operated like America. No place had the same frantic spiritual energy or the same degree of Christian diversity. Today, Christianity around the globe is looking more and more like America. This is largely a byproduct of globalization. Every day, more options related to more products, including religious products, become available to more people around the world. And America has been very effective at exporting its culture and its varieties of Christianity elsewhere. American blue jeans, American food, American music, and American movies are available around the globe, and so is American-style free-market Christianity.

The History of North American Christianity

The history of Christianity in America falls naturally into four time periods. The colonial era lasted from the early 1600s to the late 1700s, during which time religious freedom and Christian diversity became the norm in the region. The nineteenth century was an era of creativity and struggle. Its early decades were characterized by an explosion of new religious attitudes and views; the middle years were dominated by the American Civil War, and the last third of the century was spent trying to return to normal. The early twentieth century pushed America into a new world as the First World War was followed by the Roaring Twenties, the Great Depression, and then World War II. Later in the twentieth century, starting in the 1960s, American faith and life were reconfigured once again, transforming the country from a Protestant nation into one of the most religiously diverse societies on earth.

The Colonial Period

The colonization of North America, as seen through the eyes of Europeans, was not so much a matter of conquest as it was a process of settlement. Jamestown, Virginia, the first permanent European settlement in North America, started in 1607 with just over one hundred people. Small, permanent French settlements were established in the Acadia region of Canada about this same time, and Plymouth Colony was founded in Massachusetts in 1620. The intention of these early settlers, almost all of them Christian, was to build new lives for themselves outside the confines of European culture and custom. They were looking for freedom and for a new start in life.

Native Americans had a very different experience. For them, European colonization was an invasion with devastating consequences for their traditional ways of life and for their very existence. New infections introduced by Europeans, against which Native Americans had no immunity, ravaged indigenous communities. Settlers reported back to Europe that the region's indigenous population was dying so quickly there was no one left to bury the dead. Disturbingly, some settlers interpreted this cataclysm as a divine miracle and thanked God for emptying the land so they could repopulate it.[2]

In contrast to the state-controlled colonization that took place in Latin America, much of the colonization of North America was privately organized and funded. Settlements operated independently of one another, and four different nations were involved (see fig. 7.1). A thinly populated hunter-trapper model dominated in the French-settled lands that would later become Canada and also in the northern regions claimed by Russia, which later became Alaska. An equally thin, primarily military presence defined the Spanish territory that became Florida. The English-dominated colonies that later coalesced into the United States were more heavily populated. People in these Atlantic settlements did not make their way to the colonies in order to fish, hunt, trap, or set up military outposts; they came to build a new society.

Figure 7.1
Zones of Colonization in North America, c. 1750

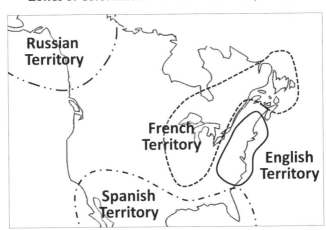

2. See Edward Johnson, *The Wonderworking Providence of Sion's Savior in New England* (London, 1654).

Within the English zone of colonization, three subregions quickly emerged, each with its own distinctive religious profile (see fig. 7.2). In New England, most of the early settlers were Puritans of one stripe or another. Puritans dissented from the state-enforced policies and practices of the Church of England and promoted a more strictly Reformed, Calvinist vision of Protestant faith. In England, Puritans were often harassed for their views, and their dream was to create a "new" England in North America where they could worship God as they pleased. These Puritan settlers were not committed to religious freedom as a general principle; they were interested only in their own religious freedom. They were *pure-itans*, and in order to maintain their communal purity, they banished, or sometimes even executed, individuals who brought divergent religious views into the region. The most infamous incident was the hanging of the Quaker preacher Mary Dyer on the Boston Common in 1660. The great exception to this pattern of religious uniformity was the colony of Rhode Island, which actively championed religious freedom for everyone. Other New Englanders disapproved, but they also found Rhode Island to be useful, identifying it as the "latrine" of the region, a place to which they could flush religious deviants.

Figure 7.2
Thirteen Colonies and Three Zones of British Settlement

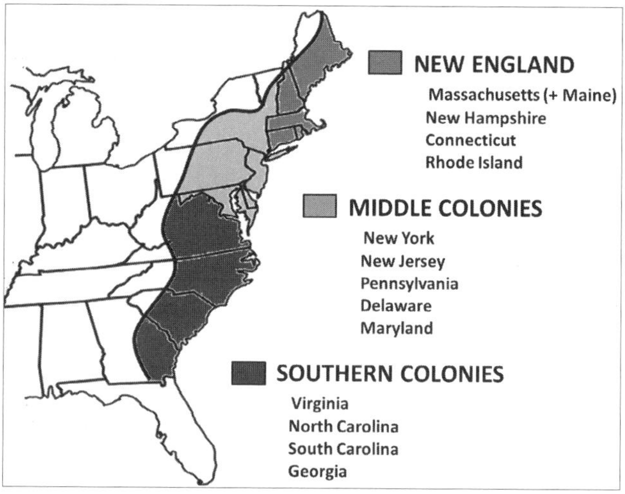

In the Southern Colonies, most early settlers were members of the Church of England (Anglicans). These early settler families soon became the landed aristocracy of the region, and Anglicanism became the religion of the elite.

Southern Anglicanism was later influenced by the ideas of the Enlightenment, and some Southern Anglicans became Deists; but this did not substantially alter the religio-social structure of the region. Most Deists, like most Anglicans, believed in the hierarchical ordering of society. Not surprisingly, Anglicanism had little appeal to lower-class whites or to the slaves brought to the region from Africa. Members of these two groups were attracted instead to forms of Christianity that emphasized equality and that dissociated faith from the social hierarchy. Poor white Southerners could organize their own separate churches in public, but slaves who were Christians typically had to gather in secret. They would meet in the woods at night, where they could not be heard by their masters and overseers, and in that setting they developed their own Christian faith and "invisible" church to help them survive the harshness of Southern servitude. This lower-class, egalitarian style of Christianity, whether it was black or white, tended to be Baptist or proto-Pentecostal in orientation; Baptist and Pentecostal churches still predominate in the South today.

In the Middle Colonies, religion was less controlled and more diverse than in either New England or the South. These colonies were started later than those in the North or South, and they had a harder time recruiting settlers. Eager to welcome whoever would come, they sometimes actively solicited settlers who would not have been accepted elsewhere. This was certainly the case in Maryland, which was created to be a safe haven for Roman Catholics, and it was also true of Pennsylvania, founded by the Quaker William Penn, who believed firmly in religious freedom for everyone. New Jersey and New York were begun as business ventures, and anyone who could contribute something to the local economy was welcomed regardless of his or her religious faith. The de facto religious diversity that emerged in the Middle Colonies was a precursor of what America as a whole would later become.

The religious attitudes of Americans today have been shaped by the experiences of settlers in all three regions. New England provided a sense of God's special providence in governing and guiding the United States. The South added both the Enlightenment perspective that God and God's ways could be discerned by all rational human beings and the Baptist attraction to religious independence. The Middle Colonies contributed practical wisdom about how to live with (or simply ignore) religious differences. But these three regional emphases may never have fused—and a *United* States might not have emerged—had there not been another colonial religious development that connected the three regions together: the series of revivals known collectively as the Great Awakening.

George Whitefield (1714–1770) was the main leader of this Awakening. Born in England, he was an energetic preacher and America's first great entertainer.

It was said that he could bring a crowd to tears merely by pronouncing the word *Mesopotamia*, and the contents of his sermons were fiery. He thundered about God's judgment and punishment in hell, and then he whispered of Christ's love and the hope of heaven. He challenged people to get serious with God, to repent, and to follow Christ fervently. He implored people to be "born again," not merely to assent to the gospel with their heads but to welcome Christ into their hearts. Some fastidious local preachers thought Whitefield's theatrics were over the top, but most of America loved him. Whitefield visited America seven times, preaching in colonial venues from Georgia to Maine. This was the first inter-colony experience that included all of British America, and it helped to spawn a new corporate colonial sense of identity. That new identity included a shared conviction that real religion was personal. It also added fuel to the growing sense of American-British differences that paved the way to independence.

When the American Revolution took place in the late 1700s, this new sense of personal religion played a significant role in uniting the colonies against Great Britain. Rumors began circulating that England wanted to impose an Anglican bishop on the region who would try to force everyone into a single religious mold. American colonists were already opposed to British rule for other reasons, but the fear of imposed religious uniformity added fuel to the fire. Religious diversity was already a well-established reality, and Americans had recently discovered the importance of personal religious experience. Long before religious freedom became the law of the land, it was clear that, if the Revolution was successful, freedom would define the spiritual ethos of the nation.

The Nineteenth Century

In the newly formed independent United States, religious freedom became a fact of life for white Protestants. Catholics remained suspect almost everywhere they lived, slaves had little freedom of any kind, and Native Americans had to cope with having their whole way of life undercut by government policies. But the underlying principle was that church and state should be separate. Slowly this ideal filtered down from the theoretical level to the practical, and it expanded from Protestantism to include all religions. This disestablishment of religion (the separation of church and state) gave rise to what has been called "freedom's ferment,"[3] a tremendous bubbling up of religious innovation during the early years of the American republic. A host of new churches such as the Churches of Christ and the African Methodist Episcopal Church

---

3. Alice Felt Tyler, *Freedom's Ferment: Phases of American Social History to 1860* (Minneapolis: University of Minnesota Press, 1944).

were created, along with many other less traditionally Christian movements and organizations, such as the Shakers, Seventh-Day Adventists, the Oneida Community, the Church of Jesus Christ of Latter-Day Saints (Mormons), and Transcendentalism. Never before had people of faith—understood broadly to include all of humanity's search for spiritual truth, meaning, and purpose—been afforded such leeway to follow whatever path they chose.

The legal separation of church and state did not mean that faith (understood broadly) and public life were disengaged. The Revolution had been powered by a blend of patriotism and faith, and that mixture of political concerns and spiritual convictions continued to infuse public ideas and ideals in the new nation. In the minds of most citizens, the nation itself possessed a kind of sacredness. American Protestants were convinced that the United States was a "righteous empire" that had a special role to play in God's plan for human history.[4] The Presbyterian preacher Lyman Beecher (1775–1863) explained that the grand purpose of the United States was to "show the world by one great successful experiment of what man is capable."[5] The Millennium was dawning, and the new nation's light of liberty would shine forth until the whole world was eventually free. Beecher and many others believed the nation's "manifest destiny" was to occupy the North American continent from shore to shore. More and more land was taken away from Native Americans as white settlers moved farther and farther west (see fig. 7.3).

As the Unites States grew in size, relations became ever more antagonistic between white settlers and Native Americans. There were some attempts to peacefully evangelize the indigenous populations, but this was never a high Protestant priority. Many of the missionaries sent to work with Native Americans had paternalistic attitudes, and they sought to discredit indigenous ways of life and replace them with white European practices and institutions. Children were often taken away from their parents and sent to boarding schools where they could be reeducated into white ways of thinking and living. This missionary policy, often aided by the government, continued well into the twentieth century (see fig. 7.4).[6] But even when Native people fully embraced the practices of white American culture, this did not protect them from abuse. The history of the Cherokee Nation illustrates the point. They had converted

---

4. See Martin E. Marty, *Righteous Empire: The Protestant Experience in America* (New York: Doubleday, 1971).

5. Quoted in Tyler, *Freedom's Ferment*, 1.

6. See David Wallace Adams, *Education for Extinction: American Indians and the Boarding School Experience, 1875–1928* (Lawrence: University Press of Kansas, 1995); and Margaret Connell Szasz, *Education and the American Indian: The Road to Self-Determination Since 1928*, 3rd ed. (Albuquerque: University of New Mexico Press, 1999).

Figure 7.3
The United States in 1800 and 1850

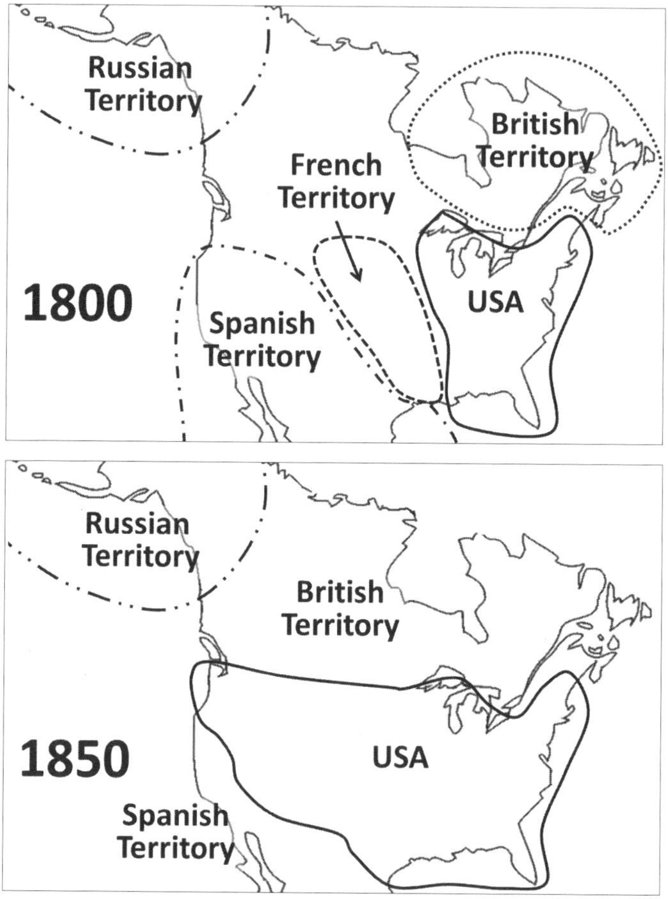

to Christianity and were living in clapboard homes and farming their lands just like their white neighbors when they were forcibly removed from their homelands in Georgia and the Carolinas and marched to Oklahoma along the "Trail of Tears" during the 1830s.

The Southern practice of slavery was another stain on religious freedom. Many of the most ardent spokespersons for freedom and American independence had been slaveholders. Thomas Jefferson, the principal author of the Declaration of Independence, owned slaves, even though he said that he considered the slave system to be a hideous blot on the nation's moral character. Although he freed his slaves in his will, he was unwilling to forego the comforts enabled by slave ownership while he was living. The American Revolution drove home the irony

Figure 7.4. Pupils at Indian boarding school in Carlisle, Pennsylvania (c. 1900)

of slavery in a nation supposedly committed to freedom. In the decades following independence, more American Christians, especially in the North where slavery was less common, began to see slavery as a moral wrong that had to be removed if the nation's special relationship with God was to be maintained. But while many white American Christians were troubled by slavery, they did not see abolition as a viable Christian option because they did not think the Bible unambiguously condemned it. Black Christians, including Frederick Douglass and Harriet Tubman, read the Bible quite differently. Rather than concentrating on a specific passage of Scripture, they focused on the larger gospel mandate of loving God and neighbor, and they asked how Christ's gospel of love could possibly be reconciled with "the corrupt, slaveholding, women-whipping, cradle-plundering, partial, and hypocritical Christianity of this land?"[7]

The logic of the abolitionist argument eventually won the day. By the mid-1800s, many Northern white Christians had come to agree that the deep moral principles embedded in the Bible, sometimes in contrast to its surface meaning, required the ending of slavery. When they voiced those sentiments in their nationally based denominations, the result was division. Southern, slave-holding Baptists split off from their northern anti-slavery compatriots to form their own separate denomination, as did Southern Methodists and Southern Presbyterians. Abolition divided the body of Christ before it divided the nation in civil war.

The American Civil War was long and bloody, and it provoked reflection on all sides. Abolitionists thought their cause was righteous, which justified (and

7. Frederick Douglass, appendix to *The Narrative of the Life of Frederick Douglass* (Boston, 1845).

maybe even required) all the pain and suffering of war. President Abraham
Lincoln was more conflicted in his views, but he had no doubt that slavery
was evil. Because of that, he wondered out loud in his second inaugural
address whether the war would "continue until all the wealth piled by the
bondsman's two hundred and fifty years of unrequited toil shall be sunk,
and until every drop of blood drawn with the lash shall be paid by another
drawn with the sword." Lincoln, and many other American Christians, saw
the war as God's punishment for the sin of slavery.

After the war ended, the late nineteenth century was a time of recovery. In
the more industrialized North, family cohesion became a central concern, and
Christian motherhood was idealized. Gender roles hardened as the workplace
came to be defined by masculinity and competitiveness, while the home was
envisioned as a place of femininity and nurture. Mothers were seen as the
guardians of the home and as the spiritual anchors of their families, responsible for instilling Christian values in their offspring. It was also their role to
preserve the home as a place of respite, crafting a private sphere where gentle-
ness and holiness could flourish and where both fathers and children could
be protected from the evils of the world. Sermons emphasized these themes,
and even salvation itself was conceptualized as coming home to God by way
of returning to the values of mothers.

In the South, a different self-consciousness emerged in the wake of defeat.
Southerners developed the myth of the Lost Cause, interpreting the Civil
War as a Northern attack on the Southern way of life, an attack that in their
minds had little to do with slavery. For many whites, upholding Southern
culture became a religious cause itself, the best way to show the North that
the South would someday rise again. The South blended faith together with
family, farming, local loyalties, and a strong sense of white racial superiority.
Gender roles solidified in the South too, as a new culture of chivalry took hold,
mimicking the knightly culture of medieval Europe, complete with military
manliness and a heightened sense of female purity. Southern whites also felt a
need to keep freed slaves in their place at the bottom of the social order, and
the Ku Klux Klan eventually became the primary enforcement mechanism.
The Klan blended the Lost Cause with Christianity and racism to create a
climate so perverse that lynching black men could seem like a legitimate way
to protect the white Christian social order of the post–Civil War South.

The Early Twentieth Century

Both Northern and Southern ways of life were changed in the twentieth
century as the horse-and-buggy era gave way to industrialism. Henry Ford

started selling cars in 1901, and the Wright brothers piloted the first successful propeller-driven airplane in 1903. Cities replaced gas lighting with electricity, and the first radio station went on air in 1916. Science and technology were becoming the driving forces behind modern life. American Christians were divided on how to respond. Polarized opinions about how, or if, new scientific theories could be reconciled with older Christian beliefs eventually gave rise to the modernist-fundamentalist controversy.

Modernists thought the study of science and history could be a great boon to Christian faith. They believed the theory of evolution, for example, corrected Christianity's outdated and overly anthropomorphic understanding of God. Modernists also hoped that studying the Bible in light of science and history would rein in what they saw as the many strange interpretations of the Bible that flourished in popular American culture. Modernists wanted to remove superstition from faith and to reground Christianity in morality and reason. They also wanted Christianity to become more publicly oriented rather than being focused primarily on family and personal matters.

Like their modernist opponents, fundamentalists also wanted a more "muscular Christianity," but their goal was to flex their spiritual muscles in opposition to what they saw as the corrosive and negative effects of modern thought and science. Evolution was, for them, not a step forward in human understanding of the world but a denial of God's power and control over the universe. Fundamentalists thought the modernist denial of a historic Adam and Eve undercut basic Christian beliefs about sin and salvation, and they saw the scientific study of the Bible as nothing more than a new and fancy way of rejecting the authority of God's inerrant and inspired Word. *Fundamentalists* got their name from a list of Christian beliefs and doctrines they considered fundamental or foundational to Christianity. These fundamental beliefs included the deity of Christ, the virgin birth, the substitutionary atonement, the bodily resurrection of Christ, and the inerrancy of the Bible.

The Scopes trial of 1925 was a decisive skirmish in the battle between modernists and fundamentalists. The case itself was about whether the state of Tennessee could ban the teaching of evolution in public schools. The court ruled in favor of the state, and John Scopes, the high school teacher who had taught evolution, was ordered to pay a $100 fine. But in the court of public opinion, it was fundamentalism that lost. The journalist H. L. Mencken covered the "monkey trial," as he called it, regaling the country with his descriptions of the "yokels" and "Neanderthals" who were arguing against evolution.[8]

8. "Journalist H. L. Mencken's Account of the Scopes Trial," *Baltimore Evening Sun*, 1925, Digital History, www.digitalhistory.uh.edu/disp_textbook.cfm?smtID=3&psid=1077.

After the fiasco of the Scopes trial, the fundamentalist movement went largely underground. Fundamentalists held on to their views, however, and many other Americans shared at least some of their concerns. A key issue had to do with the character of God, and especially with the traditional Christian notion of a personal God, something scholars seemed to deny. Edward Scribner Ames, for example, said that the word *God* did not refer to a personal deity at all but was merely a personification of the "order of nature."[9] Even if they were not fundamentalists, most American Christians believed God was personal and intimately interested in their individual lives. Reuben A. Torrey, a well-known fundamentalist, put those sentiments into words when he proclaimed: "God is a living God [who] hears, sees, knows, feels, wills, acts, is a person. . . . God has a present, personal interest and an active hand in human affairs. He makes a path for His people and leads them. He delivers, saves, and punishes."[10] It was this active, intimate, and personal sense of God's presence in their lives that sustained fundamentalists in the decades following the Scopes trial and that kept the movement alive.

The modernist-fundamentalist controversy dominated public discussions of religion in the early twentieth century, but Christians were also involved in a wide variety of other movements and causes. The fervor that had been evident in the abolitionist movement was redirected toward a range of other social problems: the Social Gospel movement took on urban poverty; the women's suffrage movement campaigned for women's voting rights, achieving success in 1920; and the temperance movement hoped to end alcohol abuse across America. The Constitution of the United States was amended in 1920 to prohibit the legal sale of alcoholic beverages, though the amendment was repealed in 1933 after it became evident that Prohibition spurred the rise of organized crime much more than it curbed alcohol abuse. The repeal of Prohibition dampened Christian zeal to improve society because it showed that simple solutions to complex issues did not always work.

The 1929 stock market crash ended this era of Christian social action. During the Great Depression of the 1930s, Christian outreach became focused almost entirely on responding to immediate human needs—food, shelter, and clothing—rather than on formulating grand plans to improve society as a whole. Christian theology changed as well, as the optimism of the past was replaced by renewed awareness of sin and human fallibility and by a new realism about what politics could and could not achieve. Reinhold Niebuhr's

9. Edward Scribner Ames, *Religion* (New York: Henry Holt, 1929), 177.
10. Reuben A. Torrey, *What the Bible Teaches* (1896; repr., New Kensington, PA: Whitaker House, 1996), 26, 27.

Moral Man and Immoral Society (1932) stoutly rejected the idea that society could ever be perfected and is often cited as a key turning point in this theological transformation.

The Later Twentieth Century

World War II pulled America out of the Depression and gave the nation a new sense of global calling. Emerging from the war as one of only two remaining superpowers, America saw itself as the protector of Western culture, an attitude greatly enhanced by the Marshall Plan that helped rebuild Europe. In its face-off with the communists of the Soviet Union, the other world superpower, America also came to think if itself as the world's great bulwark against atheism and evil. In 1954, Congress voted to add the words "under God" to the Pledge of Allegiance ("one nation *under God*"), and two years later Congress changed the official motto of the country from "*e pluribus unum*" (meaning "from many one") to "in God we trust." America remained overwhelmingly Protestant at this time, but the public rhetoric of faith was simultaneously becoming more inclusive and less religiously particularistic. Television stations ran commercials encouraging people to go to church, but they always added "to the church of your choice."

The election of President John F. Kennedy in 1960 brought Catholicism into the American religious mainstream. The Catholic Church had been the largest single denomination in the country since the 1850s. But Catholics were viewed prejudicially by the Protestant majority, and the overwhelmingly Protestant character of the culture often made Catholics feel marginalized. As an antidote, American Catholics created a whole parallel system of education for Catholic children where they would be protected from Protestant mockery and indoctrination. Catholics also felt peripheral to mainstream American culture, because they frequently lived in ethnic neighborhoods surrounded by fellow Catholics. In the melting-pot culture of postwar America, all of this changed. Catholics, along with Jews, were blended into American public life, and Americans began to describe the nation as "Judeo-Christian" rather than as Protestant or Christian.

"Mainline" Protestantism dominated the American religious scene in the postwar years. The word *mainline* was borrowed from the Philadelphia railroad whose central route or "main line" ran westward through the area's wealthiest suburbs. The term "mainline Protestantism" referred to a select group of older, well-established denominations whose churches were in prime downtown and suburban locations and whose members formed the leadership core of the local community: the American Baptists, Disciples of Christ, Episcopalians,

Evangelical Lutherans, the Reformed Church in America, the United Church of Christ, Methodists, and United Presbyterians. Mainline Protestantism was polite, white, respected, and community-oriented—a perfect fit for a time when millions of Americans were trying to return to normalcy after the war. Church attendance rates in the 1950s were the highest in American history, and membership in civic and social service organizations, such as Kiwanis and the Rotary, also soared. Returning military personnel wanted to "fit in," and they wanted others to fit in too. Being "normal" was a highly valued social ideal during this time.

In the 1960s, the "baby boom" children of the World War II generation came of age, and as they became adults they reacted negatively against the overly polite ways of their parents. They were looking for something that was more authentic and genuine than the compliant and predictable routines of suburban life. Where their parents saw normalcy, the boomer generation saw racial prejudice, hypocrisy, mindless patriotism, repressed desire, and religious formalism. American society was too "uptight" for these young adults, and they protested by "dropping out" of society in droves. They grew their hair long, put on faded blue jeans and tie-dyed shirts, listened to rock and roll, smoked marijuana, and began questioning many of the principles that their parents thought were the bedrock of the American way of life. Trust in the government and community organizations plummeted and so did confidence in the churches, especially the mainline Protestant churches that had positioned themselves at the center of postwar American life. Four interrelated public concerns marked the flashpoints of the time: civil rights, the "war on poverty" (which led to Medicare, Medicaid, and the modern welfare system), opposition to the war in Vietnam, and women's liberation. How the nation's churches responded to these concerns has shaped American religious life ever since.

The civil rights movement was generated largely from within the Christian community. Under the leadership of Martin Luther King Jr. and the Southern Christian Leadership Conference, black Christians insistently but nonviolently told the nation it was time to end racial segregation (see fig. 7.5). In the South, civil rights activists were harassed and sometimes beaten or even murdered. Many Northern white Christians were also concerned about what they perceived as the aggressiveness of the movement. When a group of Northern ministers wrote an editorial in the *New York Times* suggesting that King and his colleagues were expecting too much change much too quickly, he responded in his now famous "Letter from Birmingham Jail." King said that "justice too long delayed is justice denied," and he added: "I guess it is easy for those who have never felt the stinging darts of segregation to say 'wait.' But when you have seen vicious mobs lynch your mothers and fathers at will

Figure 7.5. Martin Luther King Jr. at the March on Washington (1963)

and drown your sisters and brothers at whim; when you have seen hate-filled policemen curse, kick, brutalize, and even kill your black brothers and sisters with impunity . . . then you will understand why we find it difficult to wait."[11] King's words hit home, and many white Christians began to understand that making people wait for justice was no longer acceptable.

The civil rights movement was a clear and unambiguous call to action. Almost everyone agreed that institutionalized racism was wrong, and there were obvious goals to be accomplished, such as desegregating schools and changing voting regulations. In the decades since then, the passion for moral change has remained high, even as the moral terrain of the United States has become more complex and contested. One result has been the emergence of a now long-running "culture war" between social and religious progressives on one side and conservatives on the other. Social and religious progressives tend to lean politically Democratic, while social and religious conservatives generally lean politically Republican. Abortion has been a critical focus

11. Martin Luther King Jr., *A Testament of Hope: The Essential Writings and Speeches of Martin Luther King Jr.* (New York: HarperCollins, 1986), 292–93.

of concern, but differing attitudes about gender, sexuality, and family have added fuel to the fire. Over time, other issues (including gun rights, the tax code, and immigration policies) have been blended into this bipolar split that now characterizes American faith and politics.

The impact on Christianity has been significant. After four decades of culture warring, many American Christians now describe themselves in terms of ethics and public policies as much as or more than they define themselves in terms of doctrine or theology. A second by-product is the formation of religious alliances that would have been unthinkable half a century ago. Thus, conservative Protestants have sometimes discovered that their closest moral and political allies are similarly conservative Catholics, Jews, and Mormons—people most conservative Protestants of the mid-century would have had nothing to do with—and not other Protestants. Liberal and progressive Protestants have similarly bonded with liberal Catholics and Jews and also with totally secular individuals who happen to share their political values.

Denominational loyalties had already been in decline before the culture war began, but they have eroded much faster during the last four decades. While Catholics still know they are Catholics, and most Protestants know they are Protestants, specific denominational identities have been largely set aside. Rather than calling themselves Lutheran or Baptist or Presbyterian, American Protestants are much more likely to say they are "just Christians." In fact, the word *Christian* has begun to function as a synonym for *Protestant*. This is so much the case that even some Catholics now describe themselves as "Catholic, not Christian" to distinguish themselves from Protestantism. Rather than linking themselves to denominations, increasing numbers of American Protestants identify themselves religiously by their connections with individual congregations. In fact, congregation-centered, non-denominational Protestantism is one of the fastest-growing sectors of Christianity in the nation. This is especially true of megachurches with sufficient resources to go it alone, but many smaller congregation have taken this path as well. The nondenominational sector of Protestantism now accounts for 7 percent of the total American population.[12] The nondenominational movement has become so strong that even congregations with continuing denominational ties often downplay those connections, because denominational affiliation has become more of a detriment than an asset in attracting new members. Christianity in America has always been diverse and offered a wide range of choices. In

12. Robert D. Putnam and David E. Campbell, *American Grace: How Religion Divides and Unites Us* (New York: Simon and Schuster, 2010), 103.

the past, those choices were often defined denominationally; today they are likely to focus on congregational connections.

Contemporary North American Christianity

Christianity in contemporary America is becoming more fluid and diverse every day. Nearly every variety of Christianity in the world can now be found in the nation. No other country has more immigrants, or is more multicultural, or has more missionaries around the globe constantly reporting on everything that is happening elsewhere. The complexity of the current scene is a natural outgrowth of the region's long history of religious freedom and of the marketplace of faith created by that freedom.

Three elements of contemporary religion in America will be explored in the following sections: first, the recent history of Protestantism, including its recent loss of majority status and its changing composition; second, the role of faith in public life, not only contributing to the culture war but also participating in civic life and community service more constructively; and third, the newly pluriform character of religion in general within twenty-first-century American culture.

Protestant Decline and Transformation

The United States has never had an official religion, but unofficially America was a Protestant nation until well into the twentieth century. In 1900, Protestants accounted for 80 percent of the population, and they still claimed more than 60 percent of the population in 1970. After 1970, the trajectory of American Protestantism began a steep, downward trend (see fig. 7.6). Precise calculations are impossible because most religious recordkeeping in America indiscriminately combines Protestants with Pentecostals, but it now seems clear that sometime in the late 1990s Protestantism lost its majority status in America. Traditional Protestants now account for only about 35 percent of the American population. If Pentecostals are added to the mix, as many American religious researchers continue to do, the total number is still less than half the population.

While Protestantism as a whole was declining throughout the twentieth century, one Protestant subgroup experienced a significant growth spurt from 1960 to the mid-1990s. That subgroup was evangelicalism. The American evangelical movement emerged from fundamentalism in the late 1940s, positioning itself as a more moderate and socially adept style of conservative Christian faith. Starting off slowly, the movement caught fire in the late 1960s. Led by people

Figure 7.6
**Pentecostals, Catholics, and Traditional
Protestants in the United States**
(as percentage of the total American population)

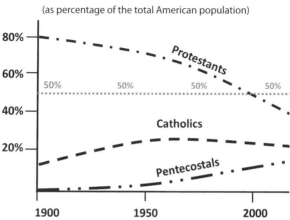

such as the evangelist Billy Graham, evangelicals offered Americans a solid place to stand in the midst of turbulent social change and gave them a new spiritual pathway for connecting with God. As mainstream culture was becoming more secular, and to some observers more morally confused, evangelicalism provided Americans with a combative version of Christianity that many found appealing. In 1970, mainline Protestantism accounted for perhaps 15 percent of the American population, and evangelicalism was slightly smaller. Today mainline Protestants make up only 7 percent of the population while evangelicals claim 25 to 35 percent. The decline of mainline Protestantism has been so dramatic that some scholars now jokingly refer to the movement as "sideline" or "oldline" Protestantism rather than as mainline.[13]

Evangelicalism is the largest and most influential religious movement in America today, but its precise size is hard to measure. Because it is a movement rather than a collection of denominations (as is the case with mainline Protestantism), evangelicalism's size has to be estimated on the basis of survey data. Pollsters typically ask one or two questions to determine whether or not a respondent should be categorized as an evangelical. The first is "Have you been born again?" The second is "Do you believe the Bible is the Word of God?" If these two questions (or sometimes just the first) are answered affirmatively, that person is considered an evangelical. They also sometimes

13. See Pew Research Center, Religion and Public Life Project, "U.S. Religious Landscape Survey" (Washington, DC: Pew Research Forum, 2008), 5; and Gary Langer, "Poll: Most Americans Say They're Christian," ABC.com, July 18, 2014, http://abcnews.go.com/US/story?id=90356.

ask people if they consider themselves to be evangelicals, but this is tricky because the social composition of the movement has changed considerably during the last seven decades. In the 1950s and 1960s, almost all self-declared evangelicals would have been doctrinally conservative Protestants who were suspicious of Pentecostals and thought Catholics were heretics. Today evangelicalism includes almost all of the nation's Pentecostals and it also includes some Catholics who have either embraced evangelicalism's personal piety or who have become allies in the culture war (see fig. 7.7). References to "evangelical Catholics" are now commonplace, but that pairing of words would have been inconceivable three or four decades ago.

Figure 7.7
**Composition of the Evangelical Movement:
1950s and Today**

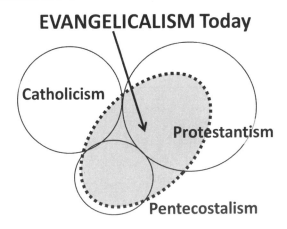

EVANGELICALISM in the 1950s

Catholicism
Protestantism
Pentecostalism

EVANGELICALISM Today

Catholicism
Protestantism
Pentecostalism

The relationship between evangelicalism and Pentecostalism has always been complex. A handful of Pentecostals were involved in the beginning of the movement in the 1950s, but Pentecostals were often excluded from evangelical gatherings because Protestant evangelicals worried that Pentecostals were too experientially oriented to be trusted. However, the two movements always shared much in common, and with time evangelicals became much more comfortable with Pentecostals. In numerical terms this proved beneficial to the evangelical movement as a whole. In the last fifty years, almost all of the growth of the evangelical movement has been generated by Pentecostals (see fig. 7.8).

In 1950, perhaps 5 percent of the American population was Pentecostal, and almost all of these individuals were members of denominations formally defined as Pentecostal, such as the Assemblies of God and the Church of God in Christ. In the 1960s and 1970s, the charismatic movement introduced millions of non-Pentecostal Christians to Pentecostal-like experiences. More recently, from the 1980s to the present, a "third wave" neocharismatic movement has produced a wide variety of "renewalist" congregations, denominations, and quasi-denominations, ranging from Calvary Chapel and the International House of Prayer movement to the Rhema Fellowship.

Figure 7.8
Evangelicalism, Pentecostalism, and Mainline Protestantism
(as percent of the total American population)

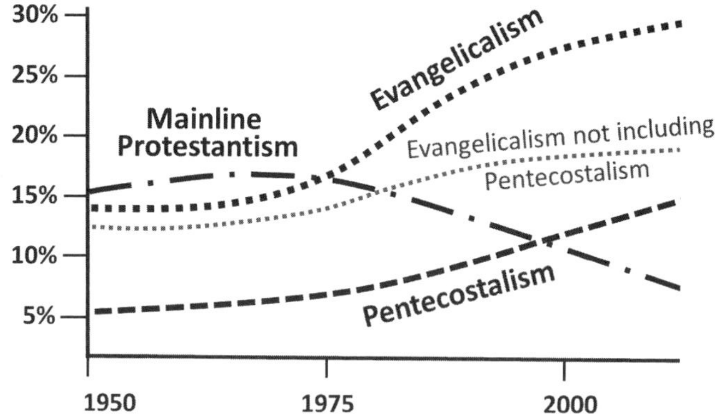

In addition to boosting evangelical numbers, Pentecostalism has also had a leavening effect on the evangelical movement and on American Christianity as a whole. This Pentecostal influence is evident in the styles of worship now used by many non-Pentecostal churches, such as singing praise songs with hands lifted in the air. It is manifest in services of healing prayer that are now common in many churches, including those of mainline Protestantism. And it is reflected in the increasing emphasis placed on experience instead of theology in almost all American churches. Estimating the size and significance of Pentecostalism within American Christianity requires distinguishing between Pentecostalism proper and the larger penumbra of Pentecostal influence. Roughly 15 percent of the American population is now clearly Pentecostal, but the worship practices of as many as a third of all Americans have been significantly (albeit often unconsciously) influenced by the movement.

Church and Community Service

The American culture war has molded public perceptions of Christianity since at least the 1980s, when evangelicals began voting en masse for the Republican Party and for conservative causes in general. The connection between evangelical faith and politics has become so prevalent that younger Americans sometimes equate being a Christian with being a Republican, a pairing they can find unsavory.[14] Younger evangelicals would generally prefer the movement to be less politically conservative. For example, more than 60 percent of younger evangelicals now support same-sex marriage, compared to only 27 percent of evangelicals as a whole.[15]

Many Americans are troubled by the perception that Christianity has been divided along political lines and by the lack of respect that exists between Christians holding different political perspectives. But as dominant as this perception has become, a quick look beneath the surface rhetoric of American religion reveals that most American Christians are not pugnacious culture warriors. Instead, they are religious do-gooders in the best sense of that term, people who are ready to come to the aid of anyone needing help. A recent sociological study confirmed that "regular churchgoers are more than twice as likely to volunteer to help the needy, compared to demographically matched Americans who rarely, if ever, attend church."[16] There are many generous non-churchgoers who contribute mightily to their communities, but churchgoers are significantly more likely than their less religiously active neighbors to be altruistic, empathic, generous with their time and money, and involved in community service.

14. Putnam and Campbell, *American Grace*, 401.
15. Zeke J. Miller, "Why Republicans Are Saying 'I Do' to Gay Marriage," *Time*, March 21, 2013, http://swampland.time.com/2013/03/21/why-republicans-are-saying-i-do-to-gay-marriage/; and Robert P. Jones, Daniel Cox, and Juhem Navarro-Rivera, *A Shifting Landscape: A Decade of Change in American Attitudes about Same-Sex Marriage* (Washington, DC: Public Religion Research Institute, 2014), 11.
16. Putnam and Campbell, *American Grace*, 446.

These statistical findings align with on-the-ground observations. Inquire about who runs the local soup kitchen or the homeless shelter or the tutoring program or the community clean-up drive, and more often than not the program will be staffed by regular church attenders. The same holds true for emergency response teams, since church-related response groups often arrive at disaster scenes even before the Red Cross or government agencies. When sixty-two tornadoes tore through northeastern Alabama one spring night in 2011, for example, the Southern Baptist response team was there before dawn, clearing the roads with their chainsaws so other aid workers could get through and so they could bring in their own Southern Baptist mobile kitchens to make breakfast for those who had lost their homes. Involvement in active service to the broader community is a trait shared across denominational lines, political persuasions, and religious traditions. For most religiously active American Christians, putting faith into action in service to others is much more important than fighting any culture war, a finding that is welcome to those who are weary of political conflict.

Pluriform Religion

In the last two decades, North American society has become religiously *pluriform.* "Pluriform religion" describes a social landscape that is both religiously diverse (there are more different kinds of religions around than there were before) and spiritually fuzzy (meaning that the line distinguishing traditional "organized religion" from other more personal and less institutional forms of spirituality is less distinct). In 1970, more than 90 percent of American citizens were Christian; today only three-quarters identify themselves as Christian. While Christian numbers have been declining, the number of Americans belonging to other religions has grown, rising from 4 percent to 6 percent in the last fifty years. There has also been significant change in the composition of this category. In 1970, almost all Americans in the "other religion" category were Jews. Today, the American Jewish, Muslim, Buddhist, and Hindu populations are all relatively equal in numbers (see fig. 7.9). This new religious diversity is especially visible in the nation's major urban areas.

The most striking change in the American religious profile over the last fifty years has come in the "nonreligious" category, with almost all of this change taking place during the last twenty years. In 1970, only 2–3 percent of the American population said they had no religious faith. By 2000, the percentage had risen to perhaps 7–8 percent. Today, a full 20 percent of Americans say they are religiously unaffiliated, and for Americans under the age of thirty the proportion is over 30 percent. This incredibly rapid move away from

Figure 7.9
The Changing American Religious Profile, 1970 and 2015

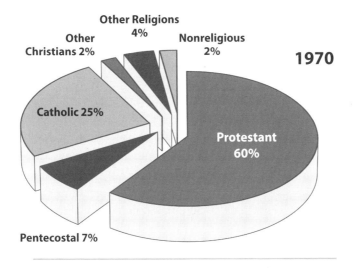

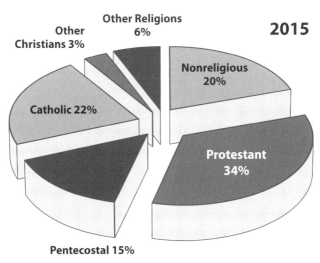

religious affiliation is unprecedented in American history, and some degree of skepticism may be in order. It is likely that many individuals in the nonreligious group have not significantly changed their religious (or nonreligious) beliefs at all, but have simply decided to label themselves in a different way. Only about one-quarter of those who describe themselves as nonreligious are convinced atheists or agnostics. The rest say they are nonreligious because they are "nothing in particular."[17] The bottom line is that about 15 percent of all Americans and about 20–25 percent of younger Americans simply do not know what to call themselves religiously. These individuals are not members of any specific religious group or organization; but many have spiritual hopes and inclinations, and some would identify themselves as followers of Jesus. What is clear is that traditional organized Christianity is not meeting their personal spiritual needs. Many Americans now prefer to use the term *spirituality* to describe their faith commitments rather than the word *religion*. *Religion* in this usage refers to the teachings and normative practices of an organized religious group, and these are often viewed negatively. Religious dogmas and rules are seen as being imposed on individuals from outside, encouraging passivity and potential inauthenticity in matters of faith. *Spirituality*, by contrast, is perceived as arising naturally from a person's inner being, which allows spirituality to be interpreted as something authentic and "real." Each person's spirituality is unique to that individual and, presumably, spirituality cannot possibly be captured and passed along by an institution such as a church. The vocabulary of spirituality versus religion has influenced all North Americans, but it is especially prominent among younger people. Almost everyone under the age of thirty now prefers to be called *spiritual* rather than *religious*.

One outcome of America's newly diverse and spiritually fuzzy landscape is that many Americans, especially younger Americans, have begun describing their religious identities in hyphenated terms such as Buddhist-Christian or Hindu-Jew or some other combination of beliefs and practices drawn from two or more religious traditions. Another outcome is that many secular individuals also now talk openly about their own nonreligious spirituality, and centers for atheistic spirituality have sprung up in some cities.

The terrain of North American faith is being resculpted, and it raises profound questions for churches. How might churches need to change their organizational structures? What roles might churches reasonably expect to play in the lives of individuals? Is the notion of church membership itself becoming obsolete? What roles should rules, doctrine, and spiritual discipline play in the life of faith? Churches are being stretched in new directions, and civil society is being challenged as well. The great majority of community service is now done by the most loyal and dedicated members of Christian congregations—"organized religion" at its best—but who will volunteer to do this work in a "spiritual but not religious" era when people do not attend

17. *"Nones" on the Rise: One in Five Adults Have No Religious Affiliation* (Washington, DC: Pew Research Center, 2012), 42.

religious services? Christians have always claimed their faith is more than mere religion. Jesus himself criticized many of the religious organizations and practices of his day, encouraging his followers to be more personal and authentic in their ways of loving God and neighbor. Seen in that light, not all current changes need to be viewed negatively. Recent trends, however, are clearly calling church as usual into question. Whatever forms North American Christianity may take in the future, they will have to be responsive to the region's new pluriform religious culture.

North American Theology and Freedom

Freedom is part of the social and religious bedrock of America. Schoolchildren are taught to celebrate their freedom of religion, and adults know they can follow any religion they please or none at all. Religiously motivated actions deemed harmful to others are illegal, but freedom of belief and the right to express one's religious (or nonreligious or even antireligious) views is otherwise unlimited. This emphasis on freedom has had a powerful shaping influence on American Christian faith and practice, and it has resulted in the deep American conviction that the only faith worth having is a faith that is freely chosen.

When America's freedom-oriented understanding of faith was first developed in the eighteenth century, it was unprecedented, and to some degree it still is. The idea of religious freedom is now widely embraced around the world, but the consistent practice of religious freedom is far from being the global norm. In Asia, most nations continue to assume that faith must be restrained to some degree by state control and regulation. In Africa and Latin America, religious freedom is not always the reality on the ground. Even in Europe, which prides itself on being more tolerant than any other place on earth, religious freedom continues to be circumscribed in some nations at least some of the time. As extraordinary as the American ideal of religious freedom was when it was first developed, it still remains exceptional today.

This section will describe three particular theological implications of America's emphasis on religious freedom. The first is the idea of "soul liberty," the right of individuals, or more strongly the *responsibility* of individuals, to decide for themselves what to believe and how to live. The second focus is on how belief in religious freedom has affected the way Americans perceive God and Christ, pushing them away from conceptions of God as judge and toward a perception of Jesus as friend. Finally, this chapter examines the social ideal of the nation as a "beloved community," a vision that combines freedom with concern for others.

Soul Liberty

The term "soul liberty" was first coined by Roger Williams (1603–1683), the Baptist minister who founded the colony of Rhode Island. The Puritans of Massachusetts Bay had exiled Williams as a heretic, and he wanted his new settlement to be a place where people could freely follow the dictates of their own consciences. Williams was constantly looking for better and more authentic ways to practice his own Christian faith, and later in life he described himself as a "seeker." His fundamental conviction was that personal religious beliefs should never be coerced or constrained in any way.[18] Modern-day Baptists are more conventional in their beliefs than Williams, but they still affirm the importance of soul liberty or "soul competency," as it is called by Southern Baptists in their position statement on religious freedom: "We affirm soul competency, the accountability of each person before God. Your family cannot save you. Neither can your church. It comes down to you and God."

Roger Williams and the early Baptists were the first to articulate the principle of soul liberty, but the Quaker William Penn, proprietor of the colony of Pennsylvania, eventually became its most ardent defender (see textbox, North American Theology: William Penn). Penn's words continue to resonate with American Christians who believe that religion must be totally voluntary and free if it is to be genuine. Genuine faith expresses what a person believes is true in the deepest recesses of his or her heart, and any external pressures to change what a person believes is an inappropriate intrusion that can be spiritually harmful. True faith is always a matter between God and the person alone. This vision of faith is highly compatible with American Protestantism but less so with American Catholicism. Because the binding authority of the Church is a key Catholic doctrine, American Catholics sometimes feel torn between their American attraction to spiritual freedom and their desire to be loyally Catholic.

While coercion is disallowed in America's vision of religious freedom, persuasion is not. In fact, many American Christians think it is their responsibility to share their faith with others precisely because religion is a matter of free and personal choice. People deserve to be informed about options so they can make intelligent decisions for themselves. Decisions about faith are not merely matters of the mind, however, and American Christians have often used persuasive techniques that include an emotional component. The nineteenth-century revivalist Charles Finney, for example, conducted all-night services

---

18. See Roger Williams, "A Plea for Religious Liberty," in *The Bloudy Tenent of Persecution* (1644).

North American Theology: William Penn

Liberty of Conscience

William Penn (1644–1718) was an English Quaker who founded the colony of Pennsylvania in 1681. Penn visited the colony briefly in 1682 and then returned to Pennsylvania in 1699, hoping to settle permanently in the region. He was forced back to England by a family crisis, however, and he eventually died in Berkshire. Penn envisioned his "holy experiment" in Pennsylvania as a model for a truly Christian commonwealth, a place where no one would be coerced in matters of religion and where all people were free to follow their own differing paths of faith.

> By Liberty of Conscience, we understand not only a mere Liberty of the Mind, in believing or disbelieving this or that principle or doctrine; but the exercise of ourselves in a visible way of worship, upon our believing it to be indispensably required at our hands, that if we neglect it for fear or favor of any mortal man, we sin, and incur divine wrath. . . .
>
> [W]e say, that Imposition, Restraint, and Persecution, for matters relating to conscience, directly invade the divine prerogative, and divest the Almighty of a due, proper to none besides himself. . . .
>
> [Coercion in matters of faith] enthrones Man as king over conscience, the alone just claim and privilege of his Creator, whose thoughts are not as men's thoughts, but has reserved to himself that empire from all the Caesars on earth. For if men, in reference to souls and bodies, things appertaining to this and the other world, shall be subject to their fellow-creatures, what follows, but that Caesar (however he got it) has all, God's share and his own too? And being Lord of both, both are Caesar's, and not God's . . . [and] it defeats God's work of Grace, and the invisible operation of his eternal Spirit, which can alone beget faith, and is only to be obeyed. . . . God shall judge all by Jesus Christ; and that no man is so accountable to his fellow-creatures, as to be imposed upon, restrained, or persecuted for any matter of conscience whatever.*

*"The Great Case of Liberty of Conscience," from *Select Works of William Penn* (1771), www .churchstatelaw.com/historicalmaterials/8_2_3.asp.

(which he called "protracted meetings") where people who were exhausted by the anguish of religious decision making were directed to seats in the front of the room so the spotlight of visibility would help nudge them emotionally to turn their lives over to God. In the twentieth century, Billy Graham held evangelistic meetings he called "crusades" in huge sports stadiums, where he asked people seeking conversion to come forward to meet with trained counselors who could help "lead them to Christ." Those counselors were instructed beforehand to start walking forward as soon as Graham made his appeal, priming the pump and making it easier for potential converts to join the forward flow.

As committed as Americans are to religious liberty, they are not mindless in championing this ideal. While defending the right of individuals and groups to engage in energetic, forceful religious persuasion, they believe that some forms of proselytizing can be coercive. When evangelism turns into spiritual intimidation or religio-psychological bullying, Americans typically label the offending organizations *cults*, a term meant to signal that these groups are not genuinely religious and therefore do not deserve the respect and protection given to legitimately religious organizations and associations.

While almost everyone in America recognizes the importance of this distinction, there is disagreement about precisely where the line between religious freedom and cult coercion lies. One of the most controversial events in this regard was the United States government's standoff with the Branch Davidian community in Waco, Texas, in the spring of 1993. Many Americans regarded the Branch Davidian movement (an offshoot of the Seventh-Day Adventist Church) as a cult, and there was widespread concern that women and children might be being kept in the compound against their will. Allegations of child abuse were also raised alongside concerns about the number of guns owned by David Koresh, the leader of the group. The stalemate lasted fifty-one days and ended when government forces stormed the compound. A large fire broke out, and seventy-six community members were killed, including fifteen children under the age of ten. The nation was shocked by the violence of the government raid, and Americans in general have become more cautious about labeling any divergent religious group a cult.

From the very beginning of the nation, Americans have had strong feelings about religious freedom, and they have exported their views around the world. American missionaries have been the primary exporters, but recently the US government has become involved. In 1998, the State Department's Office of International Religious Freedom was created and charged with "promoting religious freedom as a core objective of U.S. foreign policy." The Office has four specific mandates: to promote freedom of religion and conscience as a fundamental human right; to help emerging democracies establish policies of religious freedom; to assist religious and human rights nongovernmental organizations in promoting religious freedom; and to identify and denounce regimes that trample on religious rights. Nations can insert concerns like these into their foreign policies only when there is overwhelming support from citizens, and this is certainly the case with religious freedom in America. Few other values are held as deeply or shared more broadly across the population as a whole.

Jesus as Friend

Colonial America's vision of God was vividly expressed in the Puritan pastor and theologian Jonathan Edwards's famous sermon titled "Sinners in the Hands of an Angry God." Edwards reminded his audience that "there is no want of power in God to cast wicked men into hell at any moment." His imagery was intense—God "holds you over the pit of hell, much as one holds a spider or some loathsome insect over the fire"—and he warned that all humans "deserve to be cast into hell." God is angry, and "the wrath of the infinite God" is very much to be dreaded. The God of Jonathan Edwards was not a God who coddled sinners; his was a God who elicited respect, reverence, and appropriate fear.

Edwards was one of the most respected churchmen of his era, but many contemporary Americans are repelled by his vision of God. Today God is much more frequently portrayed as a friend who has no desire whatsoever to send people to hell. If some people do end up in hell, it is because they chose hell for themselves. The route from Edwards's stark, monarchical vision of God to the gentle and convivial God of today began with the Puritans themselves. Though they were spiritual stoics, prepared to praise God forever regardless of their own foreordained eternal destination either to heaven or hell, their spirituality was filled with anxiety. New England Puritans wanted to know if they were one of "the Elect," so they examined their lives constantly, looking for signs of grace, seeking evidence of God's presence in their lives, hoping to find some living connection with God buried deep within their hearts.

This longing for God eventually found a powerful outlet in the Great Awakening of the 1730s and 1740s. People all across New England, and the other colonies as well, felt the power of God descend on their lives, sometimes causing them to cry out loud, shake with fits, or even bark like dogs. These awakened Americans continued to believe in predestination—the idea that salvation is entirely a work of God that involves no human effort—but they felt God in ways that assured them they were on the way to heaven and to eternal life with God; and that made them happy.

The colonial Great Awakening was followed by other revivals during the nineteenth and twentieth centuries and, regardless of their theological views about predestination, most Americans began to act as if they had some role in obtaining their own salvation, even if that role was limited to simply "accepting" Jesus as their Savior. A portrait of Christ by the artist Warner Sallman (1892–1968) became extraordinarily popular. The painting, a visual rendering of Revelation 3:20, depicts a gentle Jesus knocking politely at a door that has no doorknob and can be opened only from the inside (see fig. 7.10). The

Figure 7.10. "Christ at Heart's Door" by Warner Sallman

painting's message is straightforward. Christ does not force himself on anyone. He knocks gently, hoping for an invitation to come in, wanting to become both savior and friend. This is the Jesus most Americans affirm today, a Jesus who knows that personal choice is part of salvation and who wants to be a friend.

Many of the people who helped transform the image of Jesus from judge to friend were traditional Christians, but the American notion that religion is necessarily grounded in a direct, personal, voluntary, and unmediated relationship with God also has other sources. The Transcendentalist thinker Ralph Waldo Emerson (1803–1882) affirmed the importance of a personal and unmediated relationship with God in his famous essay "Self-Reliance," suggesting that "the relations of the soul to the divine spirit are so pure that it is profane to seek to interpose helps."[19] "Helps" are anything that undermines

19. Ralph Waldo Emerson, *Essays: First Series* (Chicago: W. B. Conkey, 1900), 66.

direct communication between the individual and God, and American Christians have always wanted to eliminate any obstacles to personal fellowship with God. Americans yearn for an encounter with God that feels like time spent with an old friend who accepts and loves them just the way they are.

This approachable, relational style of connecting with God is reflected in almost all popular Christian literature published in America today. In evangelical circles, it has long been standard practice to say that Christianity is not a religion at all but a relationship with Christ. This distinction has intensified in recent years as the perceived differences between spirituality and religion have grown wider. God is a friend, God loves everyone, and God wants everyone to live a rich and fulfilling life. For many progressive Christians, this vision of God has pushed the church to be welcoming and affirming of everyone, including those from sexual-minority populations. Conservative Christians have a different definition of appropriate inclusivity, but almost all American Christians, regardless of where they fall on the liberal-conservative spectrum, agree that the newer, relational vision of God is a more accurate portrayal of the divine character than the harsher, judgmental vision of God that was common in the past—and churches have become friendlier as a result.

While some American Christians continue to view God as a judge, the idea that Jesus, the Son of God, is a friend is pervasive.[20] Jesus knocks at hearts' doors, Jesus loves little children, Jesus refuses to judge the woman caught in adultery, and Jesus befriends sinners such as the tax collector Zacchaeus. Their attitudes about Jesus frequently merge into how people view God the Father. Americans often use the words *Jesus* and *God* interchangeably. This interchangeability is evident in the language of the bestselling devotional reader *Jesus Calling*, written by Sarah Young (see textbox, North American Theology: Sarah Young). In her writing, "sweet Jesus" and the "Creator of the universe" merge into one, and God's overflowing love warms and comforts everyone.

Beloved Community

America's theological emphasis on freedom has sometimes encouraged an individualistic understanding of Christian faith and life, but faith has always been understood to have a communal dimension as well. When the Puritans disembarked from their ship to launch the Massachusetts Bay Colony in 1630, Governor John Winthrop quoted from Jesus's Sermon on the Mount and famously described the new colony as a "city set on a hill," reminding

---

20. See Paul Froese and Christopher Bader, *America's Four Gods: What We Say about God—and What That Says about Us* (New York: Oxford University Press, 2010).

North American Theology: Sarah Young

Sweet Jesus

Sarah Young is an American Presbyterian laywoman with a graduate degree in counseling. She became a Christian while studying at Francis Schaeffer's L'Abri Fellowship in Switzerland, and later she and her husband served as missionaries in Japan. *Jesus Calling* (2004), one of the bestselling religious books in American history, records her "listenings," messages she received while sitting quietly in God's presence. This excerpt from the book's introduction describes the genesis of the book and her relational vision of God.

One night I found myself leaving the warmth of our cozy chalet to walk alone in the snowy mountains. I went into a deeply wooded area, feeling vulnerable and awed by cold, moonlit beauty. The air was crisp and dry, piercing to inhale. Suddenly I felt as if a warm mist enveloped me. I became aware of a lovely Presence, and my involuntary response was to whisper, "Sweet Jesus." This utterance was totally uncharacteristic of me, and I was shocked to hear myself speaking so tenderly to Jesus. As I pondered this brief communication, I realized it was the response of a converted heart; at that moment I knew I belonged to Him. This was far more than the intellectual answers for which I'd been searching. This was a relationship with the Creator of the universe. . . .

I wanted to hear what God had to say to me personally on a given day. I decided to listen to God with pen in hand, writing down whatever I believed he was saying. . . . Soon, messages began to flow more freely. . . . I have continued to receive personal messages from God as I meditate on Him. The more difficult my life circumstances, the more I need these encouraging directives from my Creator. Sitting quietly in God's Presence is just as important as the writings I glean from these meditation times. In fact, some days I simply sit with Him for a while and write nothing. During these times of focusing on God, I may experience "fullness of joy" in His Presence (Ps. 16:11 NKJV), or I may simply enjoy His gentle company and receive His Peace.*

* Sarah Young, *Jesus Calling: Enjoying Peace in His Presence* (Nashville: Thomas Nelson, 2004), vii, xii–xiii.

them "without dissimulation, we must love one another with a pure heart fervently. We must bear one another's burdens. We must not look only on our own things, but also on the things of our brethren."[21] Christians in America frequently remind themselves that the freedom to pursue personal dreams functions best when it is coupled with concern and respect for others.

More than three centuries later, the Reverend Dr. Martin Luther King Jr. invigorated the civil rights movement and all of America with the same message. King sought political change, wanting the laws of the land to be rewritten

21. John Winthrop, "A Model of Christian Charity" (1630).

so that black Americans could enjoy all the same freedoms as white citizens. His commitment to freedom was unwavering and absolute: "There is nothing in all the world greater than freedom."[22] But for King, as with Winthrop, freedom was not merely freedom from constraint; it was also freedom to love, care for, and respect others. King frequently said, "No one is free until we all are free." As a citizen of the United States, King was calling the nation back to its own founding ideals, back to the Constitution and even further back, to Winthrop's vision of loving others without dissimulation. As a Baptist minister, King was calling Christians back to the words of Jesus and to the gospel mandate of loving others in the same way they loved themselves. His hope was to inspire the American people to freely recommit themselves to caring for one another. King used the term "the beloved community" to describe this fellowship of freely given love and compassion (see textbox, North American Theology: Martin Luther King Jr.).

Americans have at times been spectacular failures at living up to their own ideals of freedom and community, as evidenced not only by the tragedy of slavery but also the abominable treatment of Native Americans. Contemporary Americans are learning from this blemished history, and some are discovering new insights from indigenous Christian communities. The Native American theologian Randy Woodley says the core values of the Indian way of life are strikingly similar to the principles of *shalom* as articulated in the Bible. Rather than focusing on competition, *shalom* encourages cooperation. Rather than emphasizing the immediate freedom to act, *shalom* fosters reflection on longer-term consequences. And rather than seeking personal triumph, *shalom* cultivates a communal understanding of success that includes all the members of the society or tribe. Woodley says that both indigenous American traditions and biblical *shalom* "have justice, restoration, and continuous right living as their goal."[23] Theologians such as Woodley, who challenge the negative consequences of America's individualistic freedom, point churches toward a fuller sense of Christian freedom, one that is more aware of others.

America's vision of religious freedom, like everything else in America, is multivocal and complex. It includes people such as Roger Williams and William Penn, who stressed the importance of individual freedom, and it also includes those who have helped and are still trying to help American Christians develop a richer, more communal understanding of the responsibilities that come with freedom. There is some tension between these two ideals. Finding

22. Martin Luther King Jr., *I Have a Dream: Writings and Speeches That Changed the World* (San Francisco: HarperSanFrancisco, 1992), 27.

23. Randy S. Woodley, *Shalom and the Community of Creation: An Indigenous Vision* (Grand Rapids: Eerdmans, 2012), xv.

North American Theology: Martin Luther King Jr.

"The Beloved Community"

Martin Luther King Jr. (1929–1968) was a Baptist minister and leader of the civil rights movement. His efforts helped change American society, and his speeches and writings inspired advocates of freedom around the world. Dr. King, as he is affectionately known, was awarded the Nobel Peace Prize in 1964. King was a realistic optimist who said that the long arc of the universe bent toward justice. He was also a staunch defender of nonviolence as the best method and perhaps the only genuinely Christian way of changing society, themes highlighted in this excerpt.

> We have before us the glorious opportunity to inject a new dimension of love into the veins of our civilization. There is still a voice crying out in terms that echo across the generations, saying: "Love your enemies, bless them that curse you, pray for them that despitefully use you, that you may be the children of your Father which is in Heaven."
>
> This love might well be the salvation of our civilization. This is why I am so impressed with our motto for the week, "Freedom and Justice through Love." Not through violence; not through hate; no not even through boycotts; but through love. It is true that as we struggle for freedom in America we will have to boycott at times. But we must remember as we boycott that a boycott is not an end within itself; it is merely a means to awaken a sense of shame within the oppressor and challenge his false sense of superiority. But the end is reconciliation; the end is redemption; the end is the creation of the beloved community. . . .
>
> Now the fact that this new age is emerging reveals something basic about the universe. It tells us something about the core and heartbeat of the cosmos. It reminds us that the universe is on the side of justice. It says to those who struggle for justice, "You do not struggle alone, but God struggles with you."*

*Martin Luther King Jr., *I Have a Dream: Writings and Speeches That Changed the World* (San Francisco: HarperSanFrancisco, 1992), 21–23, 27.

an appropriate balance between individualism and the need for healthy communities is a perennial challenge for American Christians, and it continues to prompt creative theological reflection.

Summary

North America is a land of immigrants who arrived to start their lives anew and to build a society where all people could live according to their own religious beliefs and principles. Freedom has accordingly always been a central concern for American Christians, and many view freedom as part of the core message of the gospel. This emphasis on freedom has sometimes led Americans to run roughshod over people who got in their way, but it has also resulted in an amazingly robust Christian community. Nowhere else in the world has there been more Christian theological and institutional creativity, expressed in an enormous variety of denominations and a vast array of parachurch organizations that address a wide diversity of needs and causes.

Freedom is increasingly becoming a major concern for Christians all around the world. In global perspective, *freedom* frequently focuses on religious freedom in the most basic sense of the term: freedom to practice one's faith without restraint or persecution. But freedom also means the freedom to think for oneself and to define the parameters of one's own Christian faith and practice. As freedom becomes a more visible aspect of Christianity worldwide, American Christianity's long struggle to balance freedom from restraint with community responsibilities may serve as both a warning and model about how freedom and Christian faith can interact.

Conclusion

THIS BOOK HAS EXPLORED the global diversity of contemporary Christianity, diversity that combines the long-standing pluralism provided by church traditions (Catholicism, Orthodoxy, Protestantism, and Pentecostalism) with the more recent pluralism resulting from regional cultures and geographic perspectives. Christianity is now expressed in joyful diversity by cultures from every region of the world. The Great Commission of Jesus, the call to "go and make disciples of all the nations, baptizing them in the name of the Father and the Son and the Holy Spirit" (Matt. 28:19), is being lived out across the globe in a raucous and jubilant celebration of the gospel's transformative influence on earth. The evangelization of the whole world—making sure that everyone hears the gospel—is being realized as the message of Jesus circles the globe and attracts followers from every nation.

Christianity is now the most globally diverse and globally dispersed religion in human history. No other faith has ever had more followers in more places around the world; no other religion has ever been charged with greater global responsibilities. Nations are committed to their own survival and their own best interests, but Christianity is a global movement that is united by a commandment to love and serve all the people of the world. If Christians chose to work together, their corporate actions could impact global peace and justice to a far greater degree than any other religious or political organization.

However, the Christian movement is now so big and so diverse that some observers suggest it is impossible to speak meaningfully about *Christianity* in the singular. Because the beliefs and practices of Christians around the world are so varied and at times contentious, some analysts now suggest that the word *Christianities* in the plural is the better description of the movement.

The plural noun may reflect empirical realities, but it does not describe the ideal: a community of mutual love and compassion in which all the followers of Jesus participate.

Growing numbers of Christians around the world today are embracing this ideal. While affirming their own cultural and theological perspectives, they are simultaneously reaching out to others, trying to articulate a new vision of Christian unity within diversity. The late Pope John Paul II, the most widely traveled pope in history who visited 129 countries during his years in office, developed his own vision of Christian unity amid diversity more than twenty years ago. His book *Crossing the Threshold of Hope* emphasizes that the gospel can be expressed in many different ways through many different cultural and theological traditions. Rather than identifying these differences among Christians as problems to be overcome, he argued that cultivating "a plurality of ways of thinking and acting [and] of cultures and civilizations" might be a necessary step toward discovering the genuine, complex unity that Christ hoped his followers would someday embody on earth.[1]

An academic argument by the well-known sociologist Howard S. Becker makes a similar point. Talking about human life in general (not specifically about Christianity), Becker says that "when sociologists look at other cultures, they hope to see something different from what they see at home." But differences between cultures are rarely absolute; cultures are not totally discontinuous. Becker says that comparative sociologists typically try "to use what they see elsewhere to enlarge their understanding of events and organizations at home. Sometimes, more ambitiously, they [even] hope to learn something about all countries, about countries in general."[2]

Becker's sociological description of cultural interaction can apply to the development of globally minded Christians. They eagerly learn about the ways Christians think and live elsewhere, discovering how the gospel is embodied around the world today. Then they try to understand how patterns observed elsewhere can inform the way they live as Christians in their own communities, and they strive to decipher what the overlapping similarities and differences among Christians worldwide can tell them about the gospel in general.

This kind of global comparative study of Christianity can be messy and sometimes confusing. While the ideas and actions of Christians around the world often do overlap, they do so only to some degree and often in complex ways. This has implications for theology. In the past, most theologians (and

1. John Paul II, *Crossing the Threshold of Hope* (New York: Knopf, 1995), 147, 153.
2. Howard S. Becker, *What about Mozart? What about Murder? Reasoning from Cases* (Chicago: University of Chicago Press, 2014), 5.

especially those in the West) have relied on the seemingly clear and concise categories of philosophy to structure their work. Christian theology was assumed to be as logical and consistent as philosophy at its analytic best. But this approach may not make sense in a global age. The differences that exist among Christians worldwide do not fit neatly into any one particular set of logical categories. Instead they blend with and bend around one another in fascinating ways, merging and diverging in patterns that are more flexible and fluid than they are either logical or precise. Because of this, theological thinking in the present global age may need to become more sociological or anthropological, and more poetic and artistic, than it has been in the past.

Christian theology—along with Christianity in general—is rapidly and unavoidably becoming a cross-cultural endeavor. Talking across cultures, whether by theologians, ministers, or laypersons, is different from typical conversation within a given culture. Speakers from the same culture can assume a great deal of common vocabulary, which allows them to describe events or objects in great detail. The day's weather, for example, is not just hot or cold; it is hot and muggy and hazy and miserable, or it is frigid, bitter, and bitingly cold. But speakers with limited knowledge of the other's language will use only simple words—hot or cold—perhaps augmented by gestures such as waving one's hand in front of one's face to indicate it is really hot or by shrugging tightly in a fake shiver to indicate it is really cold. Cross-cultural conversations are simplified and demonstrative, and, for that very reason, they sometimes help people see the world in news ways. The creativity required to make oneself understood and to understand the other can itself be enlightening.

Christians seeking to communicate with other Christians around the world may find that they similarly need to simplify their questions and to gesture or demonstrate (rather than verbally articulate) some of their answers. The reward for doing so can be enormous. When speaking monoculturally (within one's own culture to other members of that same culture), it can be tempting to simply repeat verbal formulas of faith as they have come to be expressed in that particular culture. Engaging in cross-cultural conversations about faith requires deep, genuine listening along with concentrated, creative thinking.

A quick review of themes from chapters in this book highlights some of the questions being raised by Christians around the world today. In Africa, for example, Christians give God many different descriptive names. This African practice raises a simple but profound question for all Christians: Who is God? The Western Christian formulation of the Trinity is one way of answering that question, but it is not an exhaustive answer, and it says little about God's character. The fact that African Christians typically see God as related to all of creation—including Christians, non-Christians, and the whole of the natural world—makes this question even more interesting. Who is God for Christians? Who is God for others? Who is God for the natural world? Describing God with words and metaphors drawn from many different cultures can be a fruitful starting point for global Christian conversation.

A Christian looking at the global situation today is also likely to ask another straightforward question: What is wrong with the world? The gospel is predicated on the assumption that the world as it presently exists is not how God ideally wants it to be. God speaks the gospel—the good news—into the world in order to nudge the world and individual human lives toward the ideal. When and how have things gone so wrong? Western Christians have typically used the word *sin* to describe the less-than-ideal state of the present world, and sometimes the notion of being *fallen* is used. Western Christians often locate the center of the problem in individual wrongdoing, with the solution presumed to be a matter of personal forgiveness. Asian Christians use the term *han* to describe at least part of the not-rightness of the world, a way of thinking that emphasizes the social character of the world's fallenness and that addresses the needs of people who have been wounded and deformed by the sins of others.

Christians in Latin America raise a slightly different question: What does the good news of the gospel offer? Latin American Christians often use the word *liberation* to answer this question. Christians from other regions of the world use different terms. Orthodox Christians from Russia and Eastern Europe, for example, might say *deification* is the best answer. Christians in the West have typically used words such as *salvation* or *sanctification* or *redemption*. What has prompted different groups of Christians to develop different metaphors and analogies for describing the impact of the gospel on the world and individual lives? What can be learned from these divergent, but not at all antithetical, ways of understanding the goal of the gospel?

A fourth question could be asked about the character traits that define Christian maturity. Sometimes the ideal Christian life is described in terms of *purity*; sometimes it is described in terms of *spiritual power*; sometimes it is described in terms of *holiness*. All of these characteristics tend to emphasize individual attributes. Asian Christians might add the notion of *harmony* to this list, a concept that is much more social in connotation. For Asian Christians, the mark of Christian maturity is knowing how to live harmoniously with other people and the natural world.

Christianity has always been communal. Everyone who is a Christian today learned about Jesus through someone else. But Christianity is simultaneously deeply personal. It is about an individual's personal relationship with God and with others. There is no one "best" or "right" way of being a Christian that applies to everyone. Global conversations about Christian faith and life are enriching the pool of resources that Christians everywhere have for reflecting on both of these dimensions of gospel living. Christians worldwide are reaching out to connect with one another in ways that would never have happened in earlier centuries.[3]

While this pluralistic approach to faith is in some sense new, it is also simultaneously ancient. The Bible itself tells about people who followed Jesus in very different ways. It records the stories of individuals such as Mary, who believed God's message immediately, along with stories of people such as Thomas, whose first impulse was to doubt. It tells of people such as James, who favored rules and regulations, and of people such as Paul, who was more willing to go with the flow of the Holy Spirit's leading. The diverse stories of characters in the Bible have been appropriated by generation after generation of Christians living in diverse communities around the globe. Some people come to Christ via dramatic conversion experiences, while others back their way incrementally into faith. Some Christians feel God in their lives every day, and some live on faith alone, with little or no emotional confirmation from God—including very devout Christians such as Mother Teresa.[4]

Each Christian living around the globe today has unique gifts and weaknesses, and each deals with unique trials, tribulations, joys, and successes. The same can be said of cultures and theological traditions. Each culture and theological tradition has its own strengths and its own weaknesses. How could this not be true given that every culture is composed of human beings and

---

3. See, for example, David A. Badillo, *Latinos and the New Immigrant Church* (Baltimore: Johns Hopkins University Press, 2006); Mark R. Gornik, *Word Made Global: Stories of African Christianity in New York City* (Grand Rapids: Eerdmans, 2011); Wesley Granberg-Michaelson, *From Times Square to Timbuktu: The Post-Christian West Meets the Non-Western Church* (Grand Rapids: Eerdmans, 2013); Jehu Hanciles, *Beyond Christendom: Globalization, African Migration and the Transformation of the West* (Maryknoll, NY: Orbis, 2009); and Russell Jeung, *Faithful Generations: Race and New Asian American Churches* (Piscataway, NJ: Rutgers University Press, 2005). In terms of understanding the more formal ways in which Christians from different places and traditions are now talking to one another, see Jeffrey Gros, Ann Riggs, and Eamon McManus, *Introduction to Ecumenism* (Mahwah, NJ: Paulist Press, 1998); Pantelis Kalaitzidis, Dietrich Werner, and Thomas E. Fitzgerald, eds., *Orthodox Handbook on Ecumenism: Resources for Theological Education* (Oxford: Regnum, 2014); Michael Kinnamon, *Can a Renewal Movement Be Renewed?: Questions for the Future of Ecumenism* (Grand Rapids: Eerdmans, 2014); Steven R. Marmon, *Ecumenism Means You, Too: Ordinary Christians and the Quest for Christian Unity* (Eugene, OR: Wipf and Stock, 2010); and Wolfgang Vondey, *Pentecostalism and Christian Unity: Ecumenical Documents and Critical Assessments* (Eugene, OR: Pickwick, 2010).

4. See Mother Teresa and Brian Kolodiejchuk (editor), *Mother Teresa: Come Be My Light; The Private Writings of the Saint of Calcutta* (New York: Doubleday, 2007).

that every theological tradition must rely on human language to articulate its values and beliefs? This is precisely why understanding the global dynamics of contemporary Christianity is so important. It is at the intersections where different individuals and cultures and traditions meet that Christians may have the best opportunity to learn from one another.

Acknowledgments

A PROJECT SUCH AS THIS can be completed only if many people and organizations are willing to help, and I have, over the course of writing this book, accumulated a huge debt of gratitude to many different individuals and institutions.

As always, I am grateful to my students and colleagues at Messiah College for creating an educational environment that encourages the kind of commingling of academic inquiry and spiritual interest that is evident in this book. Messiah College has been a productive and congenial setting for my teaching and scholarship for more than thirty years, and I am thankful to the institution for granting a sabbatical leave so I could work on this project.

This book is immensely better than it otherwise would have been because of the support of the Louisville Institute. The institute provided a research grant in 2013 that allowed me to travel the country and converse with scholars about how best to organize and structure this book. Their insightful and creative suggestions guided decisions about what to include in this volume and how to frame the presentation of material. During these conversations, I was reminded over and over again of how incredibly diverse the global Christian movement is and how varied the interpretations of that movement have become. Without the criticism and advice of others, made possible by the Louisville grant, this book would be much less balanced in its content and perspective. It would also be a much less helpful starting point for individuals seeking to understand others and locate themselves in the welter of Christian movements and sub-movements that can now be found around the globe.

Much of this book was written during the spring of 2014, when I was a distinguished visiting scholar at Pepperdine University in California. I am deeply indebted to Pepperdine University for this opportunity. Pepperdine is a wonderful place to think and write. The campus culture is lively, the library staff is immensely helpful in securing needed resources, and the university as a whole, from top to bottom, is unendingly hospitable and kind.

I am thankful to Dana Robert, director of the Center for Global Christianity and Mission at Boston University, and to Todd Johnson, director of the Center for the Study of Global Christianity at Gordon-Conwell Theological Seminary (which oversees the World Christian Database), for inviting me to participate in a World Christianity Forum they organized in the fall of 2013. The main purpose of the meeting was to bring together the directors of university-based centers for the study of world Christianity from around the world for conversation about coordinating their research efforts and defining the emerging academic field of world Christianity studies (or, alternatively, global Christian studies, since the name of the field is still contested). Several scholars of global Christianity also attended, and having access to all of these people in one place at one time was a tremendous boon for thinking through the design and outline of this book. An added word of thanks is extended to Todd Johnson and the World Christian Database (WCD). Unless otherwise indicated, all the Christian population numbers in this book are based on the WCD—how could anyone write anything about global Christianity without this resource?—and I am especially grateful to Todd for his careful explanation of WCD estimates regarding the number of renewalist Christians around the world.

Many individuals provided helpful input and feedback related to various portions of the book, and I am truly grateful for each interaction. I apologize in advance for failing to include the names of everyone. Among those who offered useful advice in conceptualizing particular chapters of the book or in structuring the book as a whole are Scott Appleby (University of Notre Dame), Ted Campbell (Perkins School of Theology), Joel Carpenter (Calvin College), Jehu Hanciles (Candler School of Theology), Verity Jones (Christian Theological Seminary), William Lawrence (Perkins School of Theology), Gustav Niebuhr (Syracuse University), Dan Philpott (University of Notre Dame), Bridget Satchwell (First Presbyterian Church of Berkeley), Ron Sommerville (Christian Theological Seminary), Anne Thayer (Lancaster Theological Seminary), and Randy Woodley (George Fox Evangelical Seminary). Several individuals read part of the manuscript and offered insightful criticism and advice, precisely the kind of feedback every author hopes to receive, including Bill Dyrness (Fuller Theological Seminary), Charles Farhadian (Westmont College), Michael Kinnamon (Seattle University), and Scott Sunquist (Fuller Theological Seminary). Finally, four people graciously agreed to read the whole manuscript, and all four of them provided detailed and essential commentary about how to improve it: Cathy Barsotti and Rob Johnston from Fuller Theological Seminary; Bill Burrows, former editor at Orbis Books and current research professor of missiology at New York Theological Seminary; and Kathryn Jacobsen, professor of global health at George Mason University.

Bob Hosack, Jeremy Wells, Paula Gibson, Bryan Dyer, Lisa Ann Cockrel, and the rest of the team at Baker Academic have been not only highly professional but also supportive and kind. They have made producing this book a pleasure.

In all that I do, this project included, one person makes everything better, smoother, and more fun: my wife, colleague, frequent coauthor, and friend Rhonda Hustedt Jacobsen. This book would never have happened without her. She is both the joy of my life and the best editor I can imagine. Despite Rhonda's best efforts, and despite all the wonderful help and advice I received from everyone else, this book still has flaws. All of those remaining flaws can be attributed wholly and solely to me.

Bibliography and Further Reading

Adeney, Miriam. *Kingdom without Borders: The Untold Story of Global Christianity*. Downers Grove, IL: InterVarsity, 2009.

Alexander, Paul. *Signs and Wonders: Why Pentecostalism Is the World's Fastest Growing Faith*. San Francisco: Jossey-Bass, 2009.

Alfeyev, Hilarion. *Orthodox Christianity*. Vol. I, *The History and Canonical Structure of the Orthodox Church*. Yonkers: St. Vladimir's Seminary Press, 2011.

Allen, John L., Jr. *The Future Church: How Ten Trends Are Revolutionizing the Catholic Church*. New York: Doubleday, 2009.

———. *The Global War on Christians: Dispatches from the Front Lines of Anti-Christian Persecution*. New York: Image, 2013.

Anderson, Allan. *An Introduction to Pentecostalism*. 2nd ed. New York: Cambridge University Press, 2014.

———. *To the Ends of the Earth: Pentecostalism and the Transformation of World Christianity*. New York: Oxford University Press, 2013.

Anderson, Allan, and Edmond Tang, eds. *Asian and Pentecostal: The Charismatic Face of Christianity in Asia*. 2nd ed. Eugene, OR: Wipf and Stock, 2011.

Ateek, Naim Stifan. *A Palestinian Cry for Reconciliation*. Maryknoll, NY: Orbis, 2009.

Atkins, Nicholas, and Frank Tallett. *Priests, Prelates and People: A History of European Catholics since 1750*. New York: Oxford University Press, 2003.

Badillo, David A. *Latinos and the New Immigrant Church*. Baltimore: Johns Hopkins University Press, 2006.

Barrett, David B. *Schism and Renewal in Africa: An Analysis of Six Thousand Contemporary Religious Movements*. Nairobi: Oxford University Press, 1968.

Barrett, David B., George T. Kurian, and Todd M. Johnson. *World Christian Encyclopedia*. 2nd ed. New York: Oxford University Press, 2001.

Bauman, Chad. *Pentecostals, Proselytization, and Anti-Christian Violence in Contemporary India*. New York: Oxford University Press, 2015.

Baur, John. *2000 Years of Christianity in Africa*. Nairobi: Pauline Publications Africa, 1994.

Bays, Daniel. *A New History of Christianity in China*. Oxford: Wiley-Blackwell, 2012.

Bediako, Kwame. *Christianity in Africa: The Renewal of a Non-Western Religion*. Maryknoll, NY: Orbis Books, 1996.

Bergunder, Michael. *The South Indian Pentecostal Movement in the Twentieth Century*. Grand Rapids: Eerdmans, 2008.

Binns, John. *An Introduction to the Christian Orthodox Churches*. New York: Cambridge University Press, 2002.

Brenneman, Robert. *Homies and Hermanos: God and Gangs in Central America*. New York: Oxford University Press, 2012.

Brown, Callum G. *Religion and Society in Twentieth-Century Britain*. New York: Pearson, 2006.

Brown, Candy Gunther. *Global Pentecostal and Charismatic Healing*. New York: Oxford University Press, 2011.

Brown, Peter. *The Rise of Western Christendom: Triumph and Diversity, A.D. 200–1000*. Oxford: Wiley-Blackwell, 2013.

Bujo, Bénèzet. *African Theology in Its Social Context*. Nairobi: Pauline, 1992.

Burgess, Tanely M., and Eduard M. Van Der Maas, eds. *International Dictionary of Pentecostal and Charismatic Movements*. Rev. ed. Grand Rapids: Zondervan, 2002.

Byrnes, Timothy A., and Peter J. Katzenstein, eds. *Religion in an Expanding Europe*. New York: Cambridge University Press, 2006.

Case, Jay Riley. *An Unpredictable Gospel: American Evangelicals and World Christianity, 1812–1920*. New York: Oxford University Press, 2012.

Chan, Simon. *Grassroots Asian Theology: Thinking the Faith from the Ground Up*. Downers Grove, IL: IVP Academic, 2014.

Charbonnier, Jean-Pierre. *Christians in China, A.D. 600 to 2000*. San Francisco: Ignatius Press, 2000.

Chaves, Mark. *American Religion: Contemporary Trends*. Princeton: Princeton University Press, 2011.

Chestnut, R. Andrew. *Competitive Spirits: Latin America's New Religious Economy*. New York: Oxford University Press, 2003.

Clapsis, Emmanuel, ed. *The Orthodox Churches in a Pluralistic World: An Ecumenical Conversation*. Geneva: WCC Publications. 2004.

Cleary, Edward L. *How Latin America Saved the Soul of the Catholic Church*. Mahwah, NJ: Paulist Press, 2010.

———. *The Rise of Charismatic Catholicism in Latin America*. Gainesville: University Press of Florida, 2011.

Cleary, Edward L., and Timothy J. Steigenga, eds. *Resurgent Voices in Latin America: Indigenous People, Political Mobilization, and Religious Change*. Piscataway, NJ: Rutgers University Press, 2004.

Cox, Harvey. *Fire from Heaven: The Rise of Pentecostalism and the Reshaping of Religion in the Twenty-First Century*. New York: Addison-Wesley, 1995.

Cruz, Joel M. *The Histories of the Latin American Church: A Handbook*. Minneapolis: Fortress, 2014.

Daughrity, Dyron. *The Changing World of Christianity: The Global History of a Borderless Religion*. New York: Peter Lang, 2010.

Davie, Grace. *Europe the Exceptional Case: Parameters of Faith in the Modern World*. London: Darton, Longman, and Todd, 2002.

Davies, Noel, and Martin Conway. *World Christianity in the 20th Century*. London: SCM, 2008.

Donovan, Vincent J. *Christianity Rediscovered*. 25th anniversary edition. Maryknoll, NY: Orbis, 2002.

Dyrness, William, Veli-Matti Kärkkäinen, Juan F. Martinez, and Simon Chan, eds. *Global Dictionary of Theology: A Resource for the Worldwide Church*. Downers Grove, IL: IVP Academic, 2008.

Eck, Diana. *A New Religious America: How a "Christian Country" Has Become the World's Most Religiously Diverse Nation*. San Francisco: HarperOne, 2001.

Elizondo, Virgilio. *Guadalupe: Mother of the New Creation*. Maryknoll, NY: Orbis, 1997.

England, John C. *The Hidden History of Christianity in Asia*. Delhi: ISPCK, 2002.

Escobar, Samuel. *Changing Tides: Latin America and World Mission Today*. Maryknoll, NY: Orbis, 2002.

Evers, Georg. *The Churches in Asia*. Delhi: ISPCK, 2005.

Farhadian, Charles E., ed. *Introducing World Christianity*. Oxford: Wiley-Blackwell, 2012.

Fernando, Leonardo, and G. Gispert-Sauch, *Christianity in India: Two Thousand Years of Faith*. Delhi: Penguin Books India, 2004.

Fletcher, Richard. *The Barbarian Conversion: From Paganism to Christianity*. Berkeley: University of California Press, 1997.

Fox, Thomas C. *Pentecost in Asia: A New Way of Being Church*. Maryknoll, NY: Orbis, 2002.

Francis, Mark R. *Local Worship, Global Church: Popular Religion and the Liturgy*. Collegeville, MN: Liturgical Press, 2014.

Freston, Paul. *Evangelicals and Politics in Asia, Africa, and Latin America*. Rev. ed. New York: Cambridge University Press, 2004.

Froese, Paul, and Christopher Bader. *America's Four Gods: What We Say about God—and What That Says about Us*. New York: Oxford University Press, 2010.

Frykenberg, Robert Eric. *Christianity in India: From Beginnings to the Present*. New York: Oxford University Press, 2008.

Gallagher, Robert L., and Paul Hertig. *Landmark Essays in Missions and World Christianity*. Maryknoll, NY: Orbis, 2009.

Garrard, John, and Carol Garrard. *Russian Orthodoxy Resurgent: Faith and Power in the New Russia*. Princeton: Princeton University Press, 2008.

Gbowee, Leymah. *Mighty Be Our Powers: How Sisterhood, Prayer, and Sex Changed a Nation at War*. New York: Beast, 2011.

Gebara, Ivone. *Out of the Depths: Women's Experience of Evil and Salvation*. Minneapolis: Fortress, 2002.

Gifford, Paul. *African Christianity: Its Public Role*. Bloomington: Indiana University Press, 1998.

Gonzáles, Ondina E., and Justo L. Gonzáles. *Christianity in Latin America: A History*. New York: Cambridge University Press, 2008.

Gornik, Mark R. *Word Made Global: Stories of African Christianity in New York City*. Grand Rapids: Eerdmans, 2011.

Granberg-Michaelson, Wesley. *From Times Square to Timbuktu: The Post-Christian West Meets the Non-Western Church*. Grand Rapids: Eerdmans, 2013.

Greeley, Andrew M. *The Catholic Imagination*. Berkeley: University of California Press, 2000.

———. *Religion in Europe at the End of the Second Millennium: A Sociological Profile*. New Brunswick: Transaction, 2003.

Gregory, Brad S. *The Unintended Reformation: How a Religious Revolution Secularized Society*. Cambridge, MA: Harvard University Press, 2012.

Griffith, Sidney H. *The Church in the Shadow of the Mosque: Christians and Muslims in the World of Islam*. Princeton: Princeton University Press, 2008.

Grimm, Brian J., and Roger Finke. *The Price of Freedom Denied: Religious Persecution and Conflict in the Twenty-First Century*. New York: Cambridge University Press, 2011.

Griswold, Eliza. *The Tenth Parallel: Dispatches from the Fault Line between Christianity and Islam*. New York: Farrar, Straus and Giroux, 2010.

Gros, Jeffrey, Ann Riggs, and Eamon McManus. *Introduction to Ecumenism*. Mahwah, NJ: Paulist Press, 1998.

Hanciles, Jehu J. *Beyond Christendom: Globalization, African Migration, and the Transformation of the West*. Maryknoll, NY: Orbis, 2008.

Hartch, Todd. *The Rebirth of Latin American Christianity*. New York: Oxford University Press, 2014.

Hastings, Adrian. *African Catholicism: Essays in Discovery*. Philadelphia: Trinity Press International, 1989.

———. *The Church in Africa 1450–1950*. New York: Oxford University Press, 1994.

Hawn, C. Michael. *Gather into One: Praying and Singing Globally*. Grand Rapids: Eerdmans, 2003.

Hollenweger, Walter J. *Pentecostalism: Origins and Developments Worldwide*. Grand Rapids: Baker Academic, 2005.

Hunt, Robert A., ed. *The Gospel among the Nations: A Documentary History of Inculturation*. Maryknoll, NY: Orbis, 2014.

Hunter, Harold, and Neil Ormerod. *The Many Faces of Global Pentecostalism*. Cleveland, TN: CPT Press, 2013.

Hutchinson, Mark, and John Wolffe. *A Short History of Global Evangelicalism*. New York: Cambridge University Press, 2012.

Irvin, Dale T., and Scott W. Sunquist. *History of the World Christian Movement*. Vol. I, *Earliest Christianity to 1453*. Maryknoll, NY: Orbis, 2001.

———. *History of the World Christian Movement*. Vol. II, *Modern Christianity from 1454–1800*. Maryknoll, NY: Orbis, 2012.

Isichei, Elizabeth. *A History of Christianity in Africa: From Antiquity to the Present*. Grand Rapids: Eerdmans, 1995.

Jacobsen, Douglas. *Thinking in the Spirit: Theologies of the Early Pentecostal Movement*. Bloomington: Indiana University Press, 2003.

———. *The World's Christians: Who They Are, Where They Are, and How They Got There*. Oxford: Wiley-Blackwell, 2011.

Jenkins, Philip. *God's Continent: Christianity, Islam, and Europe's Religious Crisis*. New York: Oxford University Press, 2007.

———. *The Next Christendom: The Coming of Global Christianity*. New York: Oxford University Press, 2007.

Jeung, Russell. *Faithful Generations: Race and New Asian American Churches*. Piscataway, NJ: Rutgers University Press, 2005.

John Paul II (Pope). *Crossing the Threshold of Hope*. New York: Knopf, 1995.

Johnson, Todd, and Kenneth Ross, eds. *Atlas of Global Christianity*. Edinburgh: Edinburgh University Press, 2009.

Johnson, Todd M., and Cindy M. Wu. *Our Global Families: Christians Embracing Common Identity in a Changing World*. Grand Rapids: Baker Academic, 2015.

Juergensmeyer, Mark. *The Oxford Handbook of Global Religions*. New York: Oxford University Press, 2006.

Kalu, Ogbu, ed. *African Christianity: An African Story*. Trenton, NJ: Africa World Press, 2007.

———. *African Pentecostalism: An Introduction*. New York: Oxford University Press, 2008.

Kanagy, Conrad L. Tilahun Beyene, and Richard Showalter. *Winds of the Spirit: A Profile of Anabaptist Churches in the Global South*. Harrisonburg, VA: Herald, 2012.

Katongole, Emmanuel. *The Sacrifice of Africa: A Political Theology for Africa.* Grand Rapids: Eerdmans, 2010.

Kaye, Bruce. *An Introduction to World Anglicanism.* New York: Cambridge University Press, 2008.

Kim, Sebastian C. H., ed. *Christian Theology in Asia.* New York: Cambridge University Press, 2008.

———. *In Search of Identity: Debates on Religious Conversion in India.* New Dehli: Oxford University Press, 2003.

Kim, Sebastian, and Kirsteen Kim. *Christianity as a World Religion.* New York: Continuum, 2008.

Kinnamon, Michael. *Can a Renewal Movement Be Renewed? Questions for the Future of Ecumenism.* Grand Rapids: Eerdmans, 2014.

Koschorke, Laus, Frieder Ludwig, and Mariano Delgado, eds. *A History of Christianity in Asia, Africa, and Latin America, 1450–1990: A Documentary Sourcebook.* Grand Rapids: Eerdmans, 2007.

Koyama, Kosuke. *Water Buffalo Theology.* 25th anniversary edition. Maryknoll, NY: Orbis, 1999.

Kyung, Chung Hyun. *Struggle to Be the Sun Again: Introducing Asian Women's Theology.* Maryknoll, NY: Orbis, 1990.

Leustean, Lucian N., ed. *Eastern Christianity and Politics in the Twenty-First Century.* London: Routledge, 2014.

———. *Eastern Christianity and the Cold War, 1945–91.* London: Routledge, 2010.

Lewis, Donald M., and Richard V. Pierard. *Global Evangelicalism: Theology, History and Culture in Regional Perspective.* Downers Grove, IL: IVP Academic, 2014.

Linden, Ian. *Global Catholicism: Diversity and Change since Vatican II.* New York: Columbia University Press, 2009.

Luhrmann, T. M. *When God Talks Back: Understanding the American Evangelical Relationship with God.* New York: Alfred A. Knopf, 2012.

Lynch, John. *New Worlds: A Religious History of Latin America.* New Haven: Yale University Press, 2012.

MacCulloch, Diarmaid. *Christianity: The First Three Thousand Years.* New York: Viking, 2009.

———. *The Reformation.* New York: Penguin, 2005.

Madeley, John T. S., and Zsolt Enyedi, eds. *Church and State in Contemporary Europe: The Chimera of Neutrality.* Portland: Frank Cass, 2003.

Magesa, Laurenti. *What Is Not Sacred? African Spirituality.* Maryknoll, NY: Orbis, 2013.

Mandryk, Jason. *Operation World: The Definitive Prayer Guide to Every Nation.* 7th ed. Colorado Springs: Biblica, 2010.

Marmon, Steven R. *Ecumenism Means You, Too: Ordinary Christians and the Quest for Christian Unity.* Eugene, OR: Wipf and Stock, 2010.

Matovina, Timothy. *Latino Catholicism: Transformation in America's Largest Church.* Princeton: Princeton University Press, 2012.

Mbiti, John S. *Concepts of God in Africa.* London: SPCK, 1970.

McGrath, Alister E. *Christianity's Dangerous Idea: The Protestant Revolution—A History from the Sixteenth Century to the Twenty-First.* New York: HarperOne, 2007.

McGuckin, John Anthony. *The Orthodox Church: An Introduction to Its History, Doctrine, and Spiritual Culture.* Oxford: Blackwell, 2008.

Michalski, Krzysztof, ed. *Religion in the New Europe.* New York: Central European University Press, 2006.

Miller, Donald E., and Kimon H. Sargent, eds. *Spirit and Power: The Growth and Global Impact of Pentecostalism.* New York: Oxford University Press, 2013.

Miller, Donald E., and Tetsunao Yamamori. *Global Pentecostalism: The New Face of Christian Social Engagement.* Berkeley: University of California Press, 2007.

Moffett, Samuel Hugh. *A History of Christianity in Asia.* Vol. I, *Beginnings to 1500.* San Francisco: HarperSanFrancisco, 1992.

———. *A History of Christianity in Asia.* Vol. II, *1500–1900.* Maryknoll, NY: Orbis, 2008.

Noll, Mark. *The New Shape of World Christianity: How American Experience Reflects Global Faith.* Downers Grove, IL: IVP Academic, 2009.

Oduyoye, Mercy Amba. *Beads and Strands: Reflections of an African Woman on Christianity in Africa.* Maryknoll, NY: Orbis, 2004.

Orobator, Agbonkhianmeghe E. *Theology Brewed in an African Pot.* Maryknoll, NY: Orbis, 2008.

Ott, Craig, and Harold A. Netland. *Globalizing Theology: Belief and Practice in an Era of World Christianity.* Grand Rapids: Baker Academic, 2006.

Palmer, Martin. *The Jesus Sutras: Rediscovering the Lost Scrolls of Taoist Christianity.* New York: Ballantine, 2001.

Park, Andrew Sung. *The Wounded Heart of God: The Asian Concept of Han and the Christian Doctrine of Sin.* Minneapolis: Augsburg, 1993.

Parratt, John, ed. *An Introduction to Third World Theologies.* New York: Cambridge University Press, 2004.

———, ed. *A Reader in African Christian Theology.* Rev. ed. London: SPCK, 1997.

———. *Reinventing Christianity: African Theology Today.* Grand Rapids: Eerdmans, 1995.

Patil, R. R., and James Dabhi, eds. *Dalit Christians in India.* New Delhi: Manak, 2010.

Penyak, Lee M., and Walter J. Petry. *Religion and Society in Latin America: Interpretive Essay from Conquest to the Present.* Maryknoll, NY: Orbis, 2009.

———. *Religion in Latin America: A Documentary History.* Maryknoll, NY: Orbis, 2006.

Pew Forum on Religion and Public Life. *Faith on the Move: The Religious Affiliation of International Migrants*. Washington, DC: Pew Research Center, 2012.

———. *Global Christianity: A Report on the Size and Distribution of the World's Christian Population*. Washington, DC: Pew Research Center, 2011.

———. *Spirit and Power: A 10-Country Survey of Pentecostals*. Washington, DC: Pew Research Center, 2006.

———. *Tolerance and Tension: Islam and Christianity in Sub-Saharan Africa*. Washington, DC: Pew Research Center, 2010.

———. *U.S. Religious Landscape Survey—Religious Affiliation: Diverse and Dynamic*. Washington, DC: Pew Research Center, 2008.

Phan, Peter, ed. *Christianities in Asia*. Oxford: Wiley-Blackwell, 2011.

Prien, Hans-Jürgen. *Christianity in Latin America*. Boston: Brill, 2013.

Putnam, Robert D., and David E. Campbell. *American Grace: How Religion Divides and Unites Us*. New York: Simon and Schuster, 2010.

Rémond, René. *Religion and Society in Modern Europe*. Oxford: Blackwell, 1999.

Rittner, Carol, John K. Roth, and Wendy Whitworth, eds. *Genocide in Rwanda: Complicity of the Churches*. St. Paul: Paragon House, 2004.

Rittner, Carol, Stephen D. Smith, and Irena Steinfeldt, eds. *The Holocaust and the Christian World: Reflections on the Past, Challenges for the Future*. New York: Continuum, 2000.

Rivera, Luis N. *A Violent Evangelism: The Political and Religious Conquest of the Americas*. Louisville: Westminster John Knox, 1992.

Robert, Dana. *Christian Mission: How Christianity Became a World Religion*. Oxford: Wiley-Blackwell, 2009.

Rosman, Doreen. *The Evolution of the English Churches 1500–2000*. New York: Cambridge University Press, 2003.

Roudometof, Victor. *Globalization and Orthodox Christianity: The Transformations of a Religious Tradition*. New York: Routledge, 2014.

Ryman, Björn. *Nordic Folk Churches: A Contemporary Church History*. Grand Rapids: Eerdmans, 2005.

Sanneh, Lamin. *Disciples of All Nations: Pillars of World Christianity*. New York: Oxford University Press, 2008).

———. *Whose Religion Is Christianity? The Gospel beyond the West*. Grand Rapids: Eerdmans, 2003.

Schreiter, Robert J. *The New Catholicity: Theology between the Global and the Local*. Maryknoll, NY: Orbis: 2005.

Schwaller, John Frederick. *The History of the Catholic Church in Latin America: From Conquest to Revolution and Beyond*. New York: New York University Press, 2011.

Sennott, Charles M. *The Body and the Blood: The Middle East's Vanishing Christians and the Possibility for Peace*. New York: Public Affairs, 2001.

Shaw, Mark. *The Kingdom of God in Africa: A Short History of African Christianity*. Grand Rapids: Baker, 1996.

Sundkler, Bengt, and Christopher Steed. *A History of the Church in Africa*. New York: Cambridge University Press, 2000.

Sunquist, Scott W., David Wu Chu Sing, and John Chew Hiang Chea, eds. *A Dictionary of Asian Christianity*. Grand Rapids: Eerdmans, 2001.

Synan, Vinson. *The Holiness-Pentecostal Tradition: Charismatic Movements in the Twentieth Century*. Grand Rapids: Eerdmans, 1997.

Tamez, Elisa. *Through Her Eyes: Women's Theology from Latin America*. Eugene, OR: Wipf and Stock, 2006.

Taylor, William D., ed. *Global Missiology for the 21st Century: The Iguassu Dialogue*. Grand Rapids: Baker Academic, 2000.

Tennent, Timothy C. *Theology in the Context of World Christianity: How the Global Church Is Influencing How We Think about and Discuss Theology*. Grand Rapids: Zondervan, 2007.

Thornton, John K. *The Kongolese Saint Anthony: Dona Beatriz Kimpa Vita and the Antonian Movement, 1684–1706*. Cambridge: Cambridge University Press, 1998.

Ting, K. H. *God Is Love*. Colorado Springs: Cook Communications, 2004.

Toft, Monica Duffy, Daniel Philpott, and Timothy Samuel Shah. *God's Century: Resurgent Religion and Global Politics*. New York: W.W. Norton, 2011.

Tombs, David. *Latin American Liberation Theology*. Boston: Brill, 2003.

Tutu, Desmond. *No Future without Forgiveness*. New York: Doubleday, 1999.

Vondey, Wolfgang, ed. *Pentecostalism and Christian Unity: Ecumenical Documents and Critical Assessments*. Eugene, OR: Pickwick, 2010.

Walls, Andrew F. *The Cross-Cultural Process in Christian History: Studies in the Transmission and Appropriation of Faith*. Maryknoll, NY: Orbis, 2002.

———. *The Missionary Movement in Christian History: Studies in the Transmission of Faith*. Maryknoll, NY: Orbis, 1996).

Ward, Kevin. *A History of Global Anglicanism*. New York: Cambridge University Press, 2006.

Ware, Timothy. *The Orthodox Church*. London: Penguin, 1997.

Wariboko, Nimi. *The Pentecostal Principle: Ethical Methodology in New Spirit*. Grand Rapids: Eerdmans, 2012.

Webster, John C. B. *The Dalit Christians: A History*. 4th ed. Delhi: ISPCK, 2000.

Wickeri, Philip. *Reconstructing Christianity in China: K. H. Ting and the Chinese Church*. Maryknoll, NY: Orbis, 2007.

Woodley, Randy. *Shalom and the Community of Creation: An Indigenous Vision*. Grand Rapids: Eerdmans, 2012.

Wuthnow, Robert. *Boundless Faith: The Global Outreach of American Churches.* Berkeley: University of California Press, 2009.

Xi, Lian. *Redeemed by Fire: The Rise of Popular Christianity in Modern China.* New Haven: Yale University Press, 2010.

Yang, Fenggang. *Religion in China: Survival and Revival under Communist Rule.* New York: Oxford University Press, 2012.

Yong, Amos. *The Spirit Poured Out on All Flesh: Pentecostalism and the Possibility of Global Theology.* Grand Rapids: Baker Academic, 2005.

Yung, Hwa. *Mangoes or Bananas? The Quest for an Authentic Asian Christian Theology.* Oxford: Regnum, 1997.

Index